Preface

I first met Norman Grubb just after World War II. I had recently graduated from Glasgow University and my first introduction to WEC was hearing him speak. His message was simply, "We don't care how many degrees you've got, if you're not filled with the Spirit, God can't use you." This intrigued me!

Through meetings, counseling sessions, and reading Norman's books, I was ushered into a new spiritual era — one of restfulness in Christ's sufficiency within. What a marvelous change this brought about!

The crisis actually happened during a visit to Rees Howells in South Wales (skillfully engineered by Norman, so that my wife and I would get a good dose of Howells' teaching!). I'll never forget the powerful witness of the Holy Spirit in my heart that *His fullness within* was a settled issue.

Instead of our going to India with WEC, Norman suggested we stay in Britain and help in the development of a new training center that WEC was commencing under the guidance of Fran and Elsie Rowbotham. Through their lives I saw faith, costly discipleship and fellowship in action, and this gave us further excellent training in New Testament living.

Norman's visits to the new center were always eagerly anticipated, and as he shared more and more of his own spiritual pilgrimage and insights we each grew and followed on.

We later joined him in the U.S.A. branch of the mission, fully expecting to start a training center there; but out of the blue, in 1960, a pressing call came from our Australian branch, asking us to take charge of the new WEC school in Tasmania. Now we were on our own! But we proved the principles in which we were well grounded in Glasgow, and between 1960 and 1978 we saw the school develop until today it has a student body of around 80 on a very adequate campus near the city of Launceston, Tasmania.

Having grasped and proved these principles of our union with Christ, the way opened up for me to minister all over Australia and New Zealand. In many Keswick Conventions, teaching missions, youth camps, Bible colleges and so on, I was able to share these deeper insights regarding the life of realized union, and this helped to attract to the college young people who wanted to learn more. Many joined the WEC as a result.

Meanwhile Marie, my wife, had started a women's Bible study in our lounge. It came out of seeking to counsel one needy local woman. She got so much from those sessions that she asked if she could bring a few neighbors! It grew till sixty or so were packed in week by week — again attracted and held by the teaching of the New Testament principles we had learned in the early days from Norman.

This was the start of a Group Bible Study movement that has spread worldwide. Today, thousands in Australia, New Zealand, the United Kingdom, Korea, Holland and elsewhere are using the "Geared for Growth" study materials prepared by Marie and a team of writers.

Of course, we're still learning ourselves, and while we don't slavishly follow every line of Norman's teaching (in fact many letters have passed between us on matters about which we don't see eye to eye!) the fact remains that these early insights into union with Christ, the fullness of the Spirit, intercession and creative faith have proved to be living, vital spiritual principles that have kept us steady when the winds of opposi-

SUMMIT LIVING

These readings are taken from the following books and booklets by Norman Grubb:

After C. T. Studd *
C. T. Studd
Christ in Congo Forests *
Continuous Revival
The Deep Things of God
The Four Pillars of WEC †
God Unlimited
The Key to Everything
The Law of Faith
Leap of Faith
The Liberating Secret
Nothing Is Impossible *
Once Caught, No Escape
Rees Howells, Intercessor
The Spontaneous You
Touching the Invisible
Who Am I?
Yes, I Am

* Out of print.
† Available through WEC International, Box 1707, Fort Washington, PA 19034.
Otherwise, these books are available through the Christian Literature Crusade, Box 1449, Fort Washington, PA 19034.

SUMMIT LIVING

Selected Daily Readings

NORMAN GRUBB

compiled by
Stewart Dinnen

CHRISTIAN LITERATURE CRUSADE
Fort Washington, Pennsylvania 19034

CHRISTIAN LITERATURE CRUSADE
U.S.A.
P. O. Box 1449, Ft. Washington, PA 19034

CANADA
Box 189, Elgin, Ontario KOG 1EO

GREAT BRITAIN
51 The Dean, Alresford, Hants., SO24 9BJ

AUSTRALIA
P. O. Box 91, Pennant Hills, N.S.W. 2120

NEW ZEALAND
591 Dominion Road, Auckland

Unless otherwise indicated, the Scripture quotations used in the headings are from the New International Version. ©The New York International Bible Society, 1978. The Scripture quotations in the readings are from the King James Version.

PRINTED IN THE UNITED STATES OF AMERICA

tion and discouragement have blown in our faces.

The preparation of this book of extracts is a symbol of our indebtedness to a twentieth century missionary statesman, saint, warrior and reformer!

—*Stewart Dinnen*

Foreword

It was a total surprise to me — and, I must say, a great thrill — when Stewart Dinnen told me that he had it in mind to produce a book of daily readings from the books I have written. They cover a period of fifty years — since when I first wrote the life of C. T. Studd. This was followed by *After C. T. Studd*, a history of missionaries in our Worldwide Evangelization Crusade ranks whose lives I thought were a definite inspiration: Alfred Buxton, Fenton Hall, Jack Harrison, Edith Moules. After this I wrote of another whose life in the Spirit had a great influence on me, Rees Howells.

From these I moved on to a number of books in which I greatly desired to share the actual "ways of God" in our own lives, about which I was first deeply concerned when I sought to bring Christ to my African friends in the Congo. I "caught on" to that great urge which Paul had: to be sure that those New Testament churches he had founded should be kept on solid foundations. That is, not merely to experience an introduction into the family of God by the new birth and the blessing of justification by faith, but to realize another truth that had been specifically revealed to him, as described in his letter to the Galatians. I speak concerning God's purpose by which we believers are in an inner union with Him, Spirit to spirit (1 Corinthians 6:17), and are the spontaneous expressors of Himself in the world. For the "old spirit of error" who expressed his false deity nature in our forms is now fixedly replaced by the Spirit of Truth, manifesting Christ "formed in us." This is the reality C. T. Studd used to speak of when he prayed that his brother Africans would be "Jesus Christ running about in black bodies"!

I knew that Stewart had been using these various books as one means of preparing our WEC recruits at the Missionary Training College of which he was Principal in Glasgow, Scotland, and later in Tasmania. Also during the last several years, as he has been occupied with leadership training overseas. Now he has begun a three-year period as International Secretary of WEC, so I have no idea how he has found time for all the research needed to produce these readings.

I must say I am very thankful that the Lord has led him to do this, and I believe they will be the word of the Spirit — "hot shot," as it were — to those who read these daily portions.

My loving greetings to all patient, persistent readers.

Norman Grubb

Table of Contents

"Unless you change and become like little children, you will never enter the kingdom of heaven" — Matthew 18:3.

God forever gives, man forever receives. In the glory of His grace, that is what God never ceased to do. "He giveth, and giveth, and giveth again." Therefore salvation, just as much as creation, is every iota a gift. And man, of whom it is said concerning his creation, What hast thou that thou hast not received?, can never experience the abc of his re-creation in Christ until he is brought back to the act of simple reception. As Jesus said, "Except ye become converted and become as little children, ye cannot enter the kingdom of heaven." Every iota of works, of self-effort, has to disappear. Faith, so far from being works, is really only the flash of recognition of what is: in this case, already redeemed, if we only knew it. I hope I have made this clear, because it is the first infant experience of the lost secret of humanity, a secret we shall never outgrow and never replace, for it is humanity's sole basic capacity.

The Creator gives all by giving Himself, the creature receives all; and the faculty of receiving is so simple, obvious, natural and automatic that it can hardly be called an action at all. It is the first activity of a newborn babe, receiving air, receiving nourishment. It is the continued activity which sustains all life. And that is faith. The repentance side of faith is in essence the breaking down and giving up of a false faith which we have received from Adam, a faith in our own self-righteousness, our own religion, our own philosophy; the receiving of a false self-reliance as a basis of living. Thus it is the negative side of faith, the saying no to an illusory faith.   — *The Deep Things of God*

1

"Every spirit that acknowledges that Jesus Christ has come in the flesh is from God" — 1 John 4:2.

The proud human heart never can and never will [believe], for it leaves man with no shred of self-justification. God alone could do for us what we could never do for ourselves, and God took flesh to do it. No one really believes this, although we may say we do, until the Spirit of God reveals it to us. And the Spirit can only reveal it when He has first given us a glimpse of what we really are in the sight of God, and that also is by revelation.

He uses means — the Bible, preaching, personal witness, the lives of living Christians, sometimes disappointments, loss or sorrow; but the light has to shine, and we respond to it. That very response is a conviction of the Spirit which we cannot escape. We at last realize what we are and admit it. That is what the Bible calls the gift of repentance, the change of mind concerning ourselves, such a change affecting conduct and producing what the Bible calls "works meet for repentance."

This gift of repentance is really the reverse side of that one fundamental response God quickens in us — faith. It is the quickening or re-directing of the one automatic faculty with which the creation is endowed, as well as being the most elementary and utterly simple — the faculty of reception. We have sought to make it clear from the beginning that the Creator-creature relationship is, in the nature of things, of one kind only — that of giving and receiving.

— *The Deep Things of God*

"It is by grace you have been saved, through faith"
— Ephesians 2:8.

At the time of conversion we have become so convinced
of our lost condition, through the impact of the outer law,
that we are willing to take a revolutionary faith-action. We
become aware through the written word — the one material
link in the process — of the offer of forgiveness, a removal
of all that guilt which propels us to a destiny in hell. And
much more, we hear of acceptance by a loving, uncondemn-
ing Father who offers the gift of eternal life, purchased by
the historic event of His Son's public death on our behalf.
And that death, we discover, resulted in a further event
which is "beyond human history," His bodily resurrection
— attested to by numerous of His disciples; and His unconditional offer to be our Savior requires only that we believe
and receive Him as alive from the dead! But that receiving
means transferring our faith to the reality of a Person whom
we can neither feel, see, nor touch, and who in His resurrection is an absurdity to material-world thinking. This is why
it becomes a crisis moment. It is the *absurdity* of faith! Now
is the first time we affirm that we are believing in One who
was not only crucified — a fact verifiable in history — but
who is living, risen from the dead — foolishness to the
world, and impossible of material verification! That is why
it is the greatest moment in our human history.

How does that faith become fact? By an inner spirit-
knowing. None on earth can say *how* we know . . . or if we
really *do* know! But *we know* that we know. Into us has
come an inner awareness, what Paul calls "the Spirit bearing witness."

— *Yes, I Am*

"I know whom I have believed" — 2 Timothy 1:12.

"One thing I know, that, whereas I was blind, now I see." Spirit-reality is never provable to material sense.

This spirit-knowing of the new creation has *two confirming evidences.* One is given the Bible name of "peace." "Being justified by faith, we have peace with God." It is precious indeed, but in its essence it still has a selfish element of satisfying me: I am so glad that I now have peace with God and there is nothing between us. Peace is the first baby-step of assurance given us by God, because as babes we are in a condition in which we have never yet desired anything except for ourselves, so can only be reached by an answer that will satisfy *us.* God's love always reaches out to meet my need at its own level.

But the *true* new-creation reality is neatly packaged inside this gift of peace; for we might not take it were it publicly revealed at the outset. It is the fact of "other-love": that our new relationship is to the living Trinity — Father, Son and Spirit — which is a *Lover-Trinity.* And here is where we are taken unawares. We who have been compulsively *self*-lovers now find we can't help loving the Son who died for us, and the Father who sent Him, and the Spirit who sheds this God-love abroad in our hearts; and this being *other*-love, we equally can't stop wanting to share with others this ultimate reality which is now ours. We become other-lovers. Of course, we do not at first realize that this is not *we* loving (for the human self cannot love in this manner) but that *He* is loving by us.

— *Yes, I Am*

"Anyone born of God does not continue to sin" —
1 John 5:18.

Our real problem has never been the sins we have committed, but the sinner who commits them. It is this infected ego, this deified self in me, of which my sins are only an outward expression. If I lose my temper, if I hate or resent, if I lie or respond to a lust, it is my infected "I" which has done it because it likes to — that is my basic trouble. It is this "I" which has been the hateful false god in the usurped temple of my personality. It is this "I" which all men really worship, unless it has been exchanged for the great I AM. It can be a most respectable "I", for a certain amount of respectability is a pleasant clothing for it and only seats it all the more firmly on its false throne. Love for one's own family, class or nation, morality, religion can all be its clothes. It has its unpleasant side, for it is a slave to its own lusts, passions and ambitions, and shoulders other selves out of its way to obtain them; but on the whole it can progress fairly well, if it can preserve the eleventh commandment, "Thou shalt not be found out"!

Now this is the nerve-center of the trouble which must be eliminated. It must be destroyed — nothing short of that will do. It is not the original self which must be destroyed. That would be absurd; God made that to be His dwelling place, His cooperator, His fellow. It is the spirit of *independence in the self*, the virus in the self, producing a self that lives unto itself and by itself, the self that has turned in on itself. In other words, it is not the self which must be destroyed but the Satanic spirit of egoism in the self.

— *The Deep Things of God*

*"I have been crucified with Christ and I no longer live,
but Christ lives in me"* — Galatians 2:20.

The perfect Scriptural presentation of this relationship, given in complete and masterly outline with almost the stroke of a pen, and yet weaving together all the intricate threads that make the pattern of the new life in Christ, is Galatians 2:20. The first half of that verse will repay unceasing study, until the Spirit illuminates in personal understanding and experience the fundamental and subtle balance of truth in the three operative statements — "I am crucified with Christ": "nevertheless I live": "yet not I, but Christ liveth in me."

The first is clear, in the light of what we have already been seeing of the death of Christ and of ourselves in Him. The "I" which has been crucified with Christ is, of course, the old egocentric self with which we came into the world.

The second — "nevertheless I live" — is the new Paul, our new selves, risen from the dead in Christ, the same self as before so far as our organs and faculties are concerned, but "renewed in the spirit of our minds," "created in righteousness and true holiness," the risen self to which Paul refers when he says, "Reckon ye *yourselves* to be dead indeed unto sin, but alive unto God." This renewed "I" has a pure heart (Acts 15:8; 1 Peter 1:22), a purified soul (1 Peter 1:22), pure mind (2 Peter 3:1), dedicated body (Romans 6:13; 12:1), is the temple of the Holy Ghost.

But then Paul definitely qualifies this second statement by a third: "Yet not I, but Christ liveth in me." Why does he do this? Because the real new "I" is Christ in me.

— *The Deep Things of God*

"God . . . was pleased to reveal his Son in me" —
Galatians 1:15-16.

There can be only one possible purpose in God's grace in salvation — to restore man to his sole and original destiny: "Christ in you, the hope of glory."

We stress this again because the only infallible, inexorable consequence of a sinner receiving salvation is not always made plain by gospel preachers. It is often easy to get the impression that it is certainly necessary to have our sins forgiven, to be delivered from the wrath to come, to receive an assured entrance into heaven; but to submit to the total control of Christ is something which may and should follow, but does not necessarily do so; and even that it is possible to enjoy the former without the latter. Nothing could be more false or absurd. There is no salvation conceivable, possible or actual, other than God's way in infinite grace of destroying the false form of life in which man lives, and replacing it by the true. The false form of life is that which has self in the center. The true form of life is that which has God at its center — Christ living in me.

It is for that reason Paul used the striking expression in Galatians 1:17 to describe his conversion — "when it pleased God . . . to reveal His Son *in* me." The startling fact is that on the road to Damascus it was the exalted Christ who spoke to him from heaven; yet he writes years afterwards that the outcome of God's dealings with him those three eventful days was not an external revelation of an ascended Christ but an internal revelation of the Indwelling Son.

— *The Deep Things of God*

"We proclaim to you the eternal life, which was with the Father and has appeared to us" — 1 John 1:2.

The atoning work of Christ, which makes it possible for a lost sinner to stand in the sight of God as one who had never sinned, is only the gateway to life, not the life itself. The life itself is, and can never be anything but, Jesus Himself, "that eternal life which was with the Father and was manifested unto us," coming into the cleansed vessel, occupying His holy temple, being the life of the branch now attached to the Vine, the life of the member of the body now attached to the Head.

Do we see the point? Salvation is only salvation when it is God — Father, Son and Holy Spirit — returning to live in the personality created for Him, but exiled from Him through the Fall. This is the inner reality of such parables as the prodigal returning to his Father. Therefore salvation is only salvation to any individual believer when the Spirit has given the inner witness of the Indwelling Christ.

It is certainly true that a new-born babe in Christ might not be able to interpret his new living experience in these exact terms; but it *must* be true that he has not merely an external faith in a Christ crucified 2000 years ago, but also, as the inevitable result of the heavenly gift of repentance toward God and faith toward our Lord Jesus Christ, the inner revelation of "Christ in me," *my* Savior, *my* Lord, evidenced by an inner witness that is both incomprehensible to the world and indescribable.

— *The Deep Things of God*

"They are not of the world" — John 17:16.

Though we are Christ's, we share in this divided world. We are part of it. We eat its food, partake in its activities, earn its money, taste of its sorrows and tragedies, endure its temptations. Though one'd with Christ in spirit, we are still one with the world in body.

Therefore, though new men in Christ, we still have a duality of consciousness: we have self-consciousness, world-consciousness, flesh-consciousness as well as Christ living in us. Not that it is wrong to be self or world-conscious; we are in the world (but not of it: John 17:13,16), in the flesh (but not of it: Galatians 5:24), in self (but not of it: Galatians 2:20). A great proportion of our waking hours must necessarily be spent in the affairs of this world, with Christ in the background rather than the foreground of our consciousness. Sin only enters when we are consciously drawn into activities and attitudes which we know to be displeasing to Him.

While we are in this divided world we cannot have solely a Christ-consciousness; we must also have a self-consciousness. Certainly it is the renewed self, which knows how to maintain its abiding place; yet it is also a self-conscious self, responsive to all the stimuli of its environment, therefore as open to temptation fleshward as to Christ-control spiritward. It is still a case of "nevertheless I live," as well as, "yet not I, but Christ liveth in me."

— *The Deep Things of God*

"We . . . who have the firstfruits of the Spirit groan inwardly as we wait . . . for our adoption" — Romans 8:23.

We shall never in this life be free from a sense of self, as well as a realization of the indwelling Christ. We shall never, therefore, be free from temptation in a world that exists to tempt, nor be free from the daily necessity of vigilance and abiding. The chapter of triumphant living, Romans 8, significantly enough is the very chapter which warns against the subtleties of the surrounding flesh, and expresses our groanings amidst our rejoicing — as we long for the final redemption of the body, and are saved, not only by faith, but by hope.

For this reason, then, it is of utmost importance that we understand the exact relationship between the renewed self and the other Glorious Self, Christ Himself who dwells within. It is the hardest lesson we have to learn, and cannot be learned except in the hard way. Nothing but frequent and strong doses of the false activities of self can teach us this lesson. It is peculiarly subtle because it is now not a case of a troublesome *bad* self, but an anxious, frustrated, condemned *good* self; not good in the positive sense of being able to do good things, but good in the negative sense of wanting to do good and no longer wanting to do evil; a purified self, but though pure, still empty: just as a cup may be clean, but what really matters is the fluid it contains.

— *The Deep Things of God*

"Jesus . . . said to Peter, 'Out of my sight, Satan!'"
— Matthew 16:23.

Our nature is one thing, influences upon our nature another. In our unredeemed condition, the influences to which we temporarily responded were upward, we were tempted upward; but such responses did not make us good, because we were owned by the evil (self-loving) spirit. We continued basically to walk that same broad road to destruction.

It is equally so in the redeemed life. We need to get one fact clarified. We must not locate either evil or good fundamentally in us humans. Evil is a person, good is a Person. Evil is that spirit of evil, good the Holy Spirit. That is why when Jesus as a man was called "Good Master," He immediately repudiated the name and said, "Why callest thou Me good? There is none good but one, that is, God." And when Peter on one occasion urged Him to look to His own self-preservation, Jesus said to him, "Get thee behind Me, Satan."

Jesus traced a self-interested statement back through Peter to its source in Satan. He did not mean that Peter was permanently possessed by Satan. He had just told Peter that he had the Spirit of God (Matthew 16:17); but Peter was responding to a temporary influence downward. Just as the good was not in Jesus as the Son of man, nor the evil in Peter, so with us.

Our nature is the nature of the one who indwells us, and we share that nature and live that quality of life.
— *God Unlimited*

"We were by nature objects of wrath" — Ephesians 2:3.

We humans, as we have seen, have always been containers of another, the false god or the True. The nature we have manifested has not been our own; it has been the nature of the one indwelling us. These are the two natures the Bible speaks of. In our unredeemed condition we were "by nature the children of wrath," because we contained "the spirit that now worketh in the children of disobedience." In our redeemed lives, there have been given to us "exceeding great and precious promises, that by these ye might become partakers of the divine nature." We were "slaves of sin," now we have become "slaves of righteousness."

In the old the trend of our lives was downward on the road of self-love. In the new the trend of our lives is upward on the road of self-giving. This is what the Bible means by the old man and new man. The old man was I with the old spirit within me, the new man is the same I with the new Spirit within me. We can never be old man and new man at the same time, for the one becomes the other. "Seeing that ye have put off the old man with his deeds; and have put on the new man" — not put one on top of the other, like an overcoat over a coat, but taking off one to wear the other.
— *God Unlimited*

"I know that nothing good lives in me" — Romans 7:18.

Most mistakenly we often seem to think that God put Adam there to test him, to see whether he would obey or not. Not so. It was because by no other means could he discover his own innate *helplessness*.

It was not as we often erroneously think, that Adam could have done the good deed of rejecting the advances of Satan. If that were so, man could be good by his own unaided effort. But he was placed between those two trees to learn that of himself he can do nothing good, and is not expected to! It was to teach him the basic fact of his creation, that his own human spirit is an empty, helpless vessel so far as living the good life is concerned: "in me, that is in my flesh (my humanity) dwelleth no good thing." He was not created to be good. He was created to be indwelt by the Good One, and the negative command not to eat of the tree, followed by the direct temptation to do so, was not to stir into action some potential capacity in Adam for obedience and goodness nor to demonstrate that he could be good if he would, but to reveal to him the one essential point he had to learn about himself — that he was created helpless so far as being and doing good is concerned — and then that his little human spirit had one marvelous potentiality: it could be the container of the Divine Spirit via the tree of life, and yet not lose its own individuality in being so; but [the fact is] that the two can dwell together, each in the other, in an eternal fruitful bond of union.

— *The Liberating Secret*

"The death he died, he died to sin once for all" —
Romans 6:10.

"Made sin" is almost unthinkable; for sin is Satan's label, just as we might say love is God's.

Where does the spirit of error live? In human bodies, ever since Adam and Eve partook of that forbidden fruit. So when Jesus in His body hung on the cross, "made sin," that body represented all the bodies of humanity, which are all containers of sin. Yes, He *in His body on the cross* was made the representative for all the bodies of the human race having Satan, sin's originator, living within.

Paul can authoritatively state in Romans 6: ". . . in that He died, He died unto sin once" — not, in this context, died *for* our *sins*, but died *unto sin*. (That is why the blood is not mentioned by Paul after Romans chapter 5. From there onward the subject is His *body death*.) Christ's burial was to signify in plainest terms that no spirit remained in it.

So now Paul just as boldly states that we believers, being *buried with Him*, are "dead to sin" — a truth way beyond being only cleansed from sins. *We are no longer containers of sin* (the same thought as being containers of Satan), and we are to state this truth and affirm it as completely as we state and affirm that we are justified from our sins. "The body of sin" is "done away with" (Romans 6:6 NASV), meaning that our bodies are no longer sin's dwelling place. And we are to reckon on this as *fact* (Romans 6:11). To reckon a thing to be so, to count on it as fact, is the first stage of faith that affirms. And "reckoning" will later become "realizing."

— Yes, I Am

"When the woman saw that the fruit of the tree was good for food and pleasing to the eye . . . she took some and ate it" — Genesis 3:6.

There is one historical reality for which we can all be endlessly thankful, and that is that Adam and Eve's disobedience was not of the same quality as Satan's. We have seen how Satan rebelled against God in a total sense from his central self — his spirit. He intended not just to escape God's notice in disobedience, but to replace God Himself and be a god of the opposite quality, of self-centered self. Eve, on the other hand, was deceived and tricked into a self-gratifying action under the stimulation of her soul and body desires, but not from her total inner self, her spirit. She had no intention or desire to cast God out of her life, but merely, as it were, to do something she should not when He was not looking! Hers was sinning from soul and body influences and not from the central self.

So she was within reach of the Father and, though a *captive* of Satan, was not like a *son* of Satan. Indeed, fallen men are called "children" of the devil, but never "sons" — though they may ultimately become that by free choice. And that is why, thank God, all members of the human race not only *are* guilty but, hide it how they may, *know* they are guilty, convinced by that light in their spirits which still lights every man. We all know we should live by brotherly love: most philosophies and political parties have that as their main objective. Thank God that though we don't now know *how* to, we at least know we *ought* to. We love our darkness, but we know there is light.

— *Yes, I Am*

"Walk before me and be blameless" — Genesis 17:1.

It seems that God's Spirit has to take every forward-moving soul through a drastic process of self-exposure. That undiscovered self-principle lurking in the depths, that root of sin, has to be looked in the face. Its presumptuous claim to be a sufficient source of wisdom and ability has to be exposed in its falsity. Its save-yourself attitude has to be recognized and rejected. And such knowledge can only come through failure, through humiliation, through despair. Then, and then only, is the soul ripe for that inner leap of faith: the dying of the old, the rising of the new, the full and final enthronement of its proper Lord.

Abraham took fourteen years after his first great step of obedience and consecration when "he went out, not knowing whither he went." Twice over, in the flight to Egypt and the advice of Sarah concerning Hagar, his subtle old self swept him off his feet; first, in a panicky effort to save his own skin, and second, by preferring the advice of his wife to the plain word of God. By these two excursions into by-path meadow, the hidden existence of his fallen self was exposed to him in its two main centers of entrenchment, through the body and mind. At last he was in a condition of brokenness, in which God could speak to him that word of final deliverance, "Walk before Me and be thou perfect."

— *The Law of Faith*

*"How much more, then, will the blood of Christ . . .
cleanse our consciences!"* — Hebrews 9:14.

The completed revelation of the meaning of the blood,
given us in the New Testament, is found in Hebrews 9. The
life is in the blood, therefore the shedding of the blood
means the pouring out of the life. It is the public evidence of
the completed sacrifice (9:22). Thus whenever the blood of
Christ is mentioned as the ground of our salvation and
cleansing, the meaning is that the shedding of that blood in
public two thousand years ago was conclusive evidence that
He paid the full price for the remission of sins. To make the
evidence unmistakable is the reason why John so stressed
that he saw the blood and water come from His side, and
"bare record, and his record is true: and he knoweth that he
saith true, that ye might believe"; and says again that "there
are three that bear witness on earth, the Spirit, and the
water, and the blood."

The sacrifice once made, completed and witnessed, is
our solid ground and title for having no more consciousness
of sins. This is the cleansing in the blood, and this is what it
means when we say a thing is "under the blood." For this
reason we glory in the blood, and count it supremely precious. Our consciences are freed and cleansed as we see with
the eye of faith that blood shed on Calvary, and its silent
message to us over the years that full atonement was made
by the outpoured life of our Savior. "How much more shall
the blood of Christ . . . cleanse your conscience from dead
works to serve the living God."

— *The Liberating Secret*

"When I want to do good, evil is right there with me" —
Romans 7:21.

The human self never was and never can be independent self. It only imagined it was so in its unregenerate days, not knowing its inner satanic lord and master. But because of this false imagination, we carry over into our redeemed life, into the new man, the instinctive idea that we can be self-active for God now; and we go to it. We *try* to pray, we *try* to love, we *try* to witness, we *try* to keep God's commands, we *try* to study the Bible, and the wheels of our trying run pretty heavily. And as we try, the very opposite to what we aim at gets hold of us and we seem to ourselves more sinful than before we were saved! For we cannot be a vacuum. If it is not Christ in us, then it is Satan; and when we do not abide in Christ according to Romans 8, and foolishly or ignorantly think that we can live the Christian life under our own steam, then in our soul and body (our flesh when apart from the Spirit) there is the uprising of sin (the self-loving spirit), and our helpless response to it.

Satan invades the self that is enticed away from Christ. He does not take over the inner citadel of the human spirit which is in union with God's Spirit; but he sends his soldiers over the walls and diverts attention to himself and claims some temporary footing. Repentance, confession and cleansing in the blood are the weapons which send him flying again.

— *God Unlimited*

The New Creation

"The old has gone, the new has come! All this is from God, who reconciled us to himself through Christ" — 2 Corinthians 5:17-18.

Fulani [an early Congo Christian] has no hands. Sold as a child to be the wife of "a disagreeable old head man, who was ill-kempt, dirty, and not often sober, she was a slave of the older wives" (writes Edith Moules), "but most of all she hated from the bottom of her heart her horrible old husband.

"She ran away. Caught and brought back, she ran away again. This time her husband was really angry. He tied her wrists together very tightly with strong native rope; then he suspended the shrieking child by the ends of that rope to the rafters of an old hut. But this was not all. He beat the little wriggling form with a whip and left her hanging there suspended by the wrists for two whole nights.

"She was taken down at last, and the burst, bleeding and suppurating arms were bound up native fashion, but later one hand sloughed right off to the wrist and the other was shrunken and twisted permanently out of shape. This all happened some years ago and the old husband is now dead. Fulani is happily married and has a dear wee babe of her own. How she manages him with no hand one is left to wonder, but her cheerfulness is amazing and would put many to shame. It has often been said, 'Why bother about the heathen?' But as Fulani goes about, gripping her dear babe with those awful wrists, this poor little woman still speaks to me of benighted souls without the gospel."

— *After C. T. Studd*

"If anyone is in Christ, he is a new creation" —
2 Corinthians 5:17.

Barnepetia was at the nationals' conference — with no
ears. "One day the Medjes came to my village to kill and eat"
(he told Mary Rees, whom he accompanied on her evange-
listic treks). "My mother put me on her back and ran with
me for life. An enemy followed and stuck her in the back
with a spear. Afterwards they cut up my mother into pieces.
I saw them with my own eyes, and I saw my mother's blood
all around. Said one man, 'Take the child away from his
mother's blood,' and he did; he wiped my eyes and nose for
me and he arranged me very nicely. Then he said, 'Take the
meat, I will take the boy. He shall grow up with me and be
my slave.'"

One morning at dawn the poor lad thought he would run
away. But he was captured, thrashed, and put in the stocks.
Then his owner one day was worse for drink and in a frenzy
said, "Because you ran away, I will cut off your ears." "So he
took me from the stocks and cut off my ears and my body
was covered with blood."

Years later, after the earless lad had heard of Jesus
through Miss Roupell, his sorrow was turned into joy, and
his radiant testimony is, "I desire that all the people in the
world shall know Jesus Christ."

— *After C. T. Studd*

"Why did he murder him? Because his own actions were evil and his brother's were righteous" — 1 John 3:12.

None but a righteous God could be God, nothing but righteousness could be the foundation of His throne. The broken law upon which His creation is based must have its penalties, if it is a law. If His eternal nature is to reward the good, He must also inevitably punish the evil. In no other way could He be righteous. No mere forgiveness, then, could be a just forgiveness, unless it was grounded on full satisfaction for the wrongdoing.

What a Redeemer we have, who provided a salvation with no loopholes in it! Man's reasoning might and often does suggest some easier way, which is always, when traced to its roots, a subtle refusal to face the stark reality of lawlessness in a law-based universe. Abel knew it, when he first approached God with a blood sacrifice, the life of another symbolically shed for him. Cain, in the blindness of religious self-righteousness, offered his own good works, so much more pleasant and self-gratifying. But which touched reality? Which had the witness from God? The tragic end tells us, when Cain hated Abel for his glowing testimony to acceptance with God. And why did he hate him? John tells us (1 John 3:12) because Abel struck at the roots of self-righteousness and exposed it as sin, which could only be expiated by God's appointed sacrifice, to which God bears faithful witness in the believer.

— *The Deep Things of God*

"It was not with perishable things . . . that you were redeemed . . . but with the precious blood of Christ" — 1 Peter 1:18-19.

This primary and fundamental aspect of the atonement is always represented in Scripture by the word "blood." "The precious blood of Christ." It is the first and necessary Godward side of the process of redemption. It was the solution, first, as we have said, of God's problem. How could He be just and the justifier of the unjust? *His* wrath must first be propitiated: *His* holiness vindicated: the punishment of *His* broken law inflicted. Nothing in the Bible stands out more prominently than the sacrifice God appointed and declared to be the satisfaction of all those claims. It was His own outpoured life.

No wonder the blood is holy and precious to all believers. No wonder it is the point of attack and derision by those who hate to own themselves as sinners. It represents the uniqueness of that holy sacrifice, the blood He shed alone, the winepress He trod alone. It is His atoning work which none other shares. The cross, the manward aspect of Calvary's redeeming work, we share; the blood, the Godward aspect, is the sacred offering of the Son to the Father. And because He accepts it, we can do so. We need not question that sacrifice, nor its efficacy. He appointed it. He accepted it. He invites, He urges, He commands us to do the same. No sinner pleases the heart of God by remaining a penitent. No, if repentance is sincere, let us not add sin to sin by failing to believe in the blood. If good enough for Him, it is good enough for us. Nothing pleases the Father more than the faith of a sinner in the efficacy of the precious blood.

— *The Deep Things of God*

"Therefore, my brethren, you also have become dead to the law through the body of Christ, that you may be married to another" — Romans 7:4 (NKJV).

[Paul] uses the marriage illustration, just as he had used the owner-slave illustration, to bring home the truth to us that we humans are always under a deity management. So there's no such thing as we humans remaining unmarried, just the same as we couldn't remain free from slavery.

The marvel of God's grace, says Paul, is that at the moment our old marriage was broken by the death of Christ our representative, immediately in His resurrection He became our new Husband in place of Satan. There's no such thing as a time period in which we are a kind of widow! We have immediately changed husbands and entered into our new marriage contract in which "the law of the Spirit of life in Christ Jesus has made us free from the law of sin and death" (8:2).

When I inwardly know this and have the facts in clear focus, I find that my new Husband has me, to my delight, in His total ownership; and I have nothing to do in our family life beyond producing the fruits of our marriage, the fruit of the Spirit. Then the law has disappeared from me, because my new Husband, who is the resurrected Christ, fulfills it by our union life. I thus have become dead to the law in its outer form — the form in which God first sent it, so as to expose me to the reality of my old Satan-husband.

What perfect joy for us who have come this whole way by grace into our new union and know, in its full reality, our marriage to our new Husband!

— Yes, I Am

"They saw a fire of burning coals there with fish on it, and some bread. . . . Jesus said to them, 'Come and have breakfast'" — John 21:9,12.

I believe in a secular Christ. I do not believe in a religious Christ.

I believe one of the whole difficulties of Christianity is we've put Christ in a special building for a special occasion, with special forms of worship, special music, special everything.

Cut the special out; put your hands in your pocket and go in your old blue jeans. Christ is a secular person.

If Christ is your other self, Christ washes dishes.

If Christ is your other self, He spanks the youngsters.

If Christ is your other self, He handles the accounting machine and runs the business.

Christ, therefore, is a very common person.

You're a very common person — I assure you of that. That's why I believe in a common Christ — because He lives in common people!

Obviously, humanity has become separated from God. Before I can live in the kind of familiarity with God that He intends for me, I need to know the basis for that kind of relationship. I need to know my title. Once I am sure of my foundations I can forget them and go ahead. Once I am sure of the road under my feet I can proceed to walk confidently.

— *The Key to Everything*

"The word of God is living and active. . . . It penetrates even to dividing soul and spirit" — Hebrews 4:12.

Your mind (your knowledge) *expresses* itself in reasons. But reasons can vary. They can be influenced by all sorts of things.

Your heart *expresses* itself through the affections, the emotions. That's where you feel. But feelings can vary — quite apart from the set purposes of the heart. We say, "I don't feel like this," or "I feel spiritually cold, or dead or dry," and they are all illusions of the soul.

Neither reason nor emotion is our real life, which is deep inside us.

Now, we live where we love. That's what the Bible calls the heart. That's not the emotions; it's the set of life, the choices, the purposes where one of the two spirits is joined to us — the false spirit of self-love, called the spirit of error, who is in us from birth; or the true Spirit of self-giving, the Spirit of God, called "the Spirit of truth," who replaces the false spirit in us by redemption and rebirth.

We have to learn how to discern between soul and spirit (Hebrews 4:12). We have to refuse in our spirit, our real selves, to be dominated by the reactions of the emotions or the reasons — our souls.

When we have learned to discern and to discipline the reactions of the soul, then through our reasons and our emotions we channel Christ, and are not moved by the reflex action of the world coming back at us.

But how can I do this? you say.

You can do this because "he who is joined to the Lord is one spirit."

— *The Key to Everything*

"May your whole spirit, soul and body be kept blame-less" — 1 Thessalonians 5:23.

A great many of our confusions in life begin because we haven't discerned between soul and spirit. The Bible ana-lyzes the human personality into three parts (for everything is a trinity). It speaks of "your whole spirit and soul and body" in 1 Thessalonians 5:23.

Look at the order: not body, soul and spirit — that's *our* order. God's order is spirit first: "I pray God your whole spirit and soul and body be preserved blameless."

To put it briefly, spirit is the seat of ego; soul is the seat of the emotions and of reason.

Spirit is the ego, the self. God is spirit and He is the first ego, the first self. We are spirits, of whom He is the Father (Hebrews 12:9). He is the Creator of body and soul, but the Father of spirits.

Down in that center — the spirit — is where you know and love. Knowledge and love — mind and heart — are the real self, the real person. That's where you irrevocably live.

How do you know Jesus Christ? I can't tell you. Some-how you've come past the realm of just knowing about this Person called Jesus Christ and He is real to you.

I understand that, you say. *I'm at home with that. The knower just knows!*

That isn't giving a reason, is it? It's something intuitive inside you, and that's your spirit. That's different from reason.

But your soul is more external. It is how you express your spirit.

— *The Key to Everything*

> *"God made him who had no sin to be sin for us"* —
> 2 Corinthians 5:21.

Our first response to the greatness of grace shown in our Lord Jesus Christ was simply to recognize our outer sinfulness, to believe that our guilt and curse had been removed by His shed blood.

But what we did not know then (and were not within reach of understanding) was that this was no *real* salvation if it delivered us merely from the outer penalty of our sins but left us as "vessels of wrath" — still containers of the inner *sin-person*, that old serpent the devil, still reproducing his evil fruit by us. Complete salvation must rid us of producer as well as product, cause as well as effect, sin as well as sins.

This *total salvation* — the totality of Christ's cross-redemption — is the *deeper* discovery which Paul himself didn't see in its full implication until he lived three years in Arabia. That revelation was centered around not the blood but the physical body of Jesus on the cross. And what is the importance of that? It is because *a living body is the dwelling place of the spirit,* and therefore *when a body dies, the spirit is no longer in it.*

"We are convinced," he in effect wrote in 2 Corinthians 5:14-21, "that when the Savior died on our behalf it was a *body* death, and this means if He died for all, then we all died." And what did His body represent before God? Paul tells us in verse 21 that "God made Him who knew no sin to be sin for us." Please note: *sin* is not *sins*. By His shed blood He "bore away our sins," but in His crucified body He "was *made sin.*"

— *Yes, I Am*

"The Lord God called to the man, 'Where are you?'"
— Genesis 3:9.

The effects of [Adam and Eve's] disobedience were the opposite to what the natural guilty world would expect God's reaction to be. We would think God would, in anger and wrath, turn His back on the two. But it was precisely the other way around. It was Adam who hid from God, not God from Adam. Here was God "walking in the garden in the cool of the day" and looking for Adam. But where was Adam? Hidden in the bushes. Nor was God displaying some wrathful retaliation, but only questioning Adam . . . to bring the reality of the disobedience home to him. For when He came face to face with the three; the serpent and Adam and Eve, there was not a word of condemnation or wrath against the two, but only His full curse on Satan. To Adam and Eve everything God said was to clarify to them the "beneficial" consequence which they, thankfully, could not escape — a way of life which always has sorrow at its roots. God said in effect, "Eve, you will have sorrow one way; Adam, you will have sorrow another way." That was all.

And of course, the point of the sorrow would be that the whole human race through all its centuries of history would always be inwardly miserable, always knowing they were missing the mark and meaning of life, always seeking a phony happiness which would always escape them . . . and thus, always at the heart of every man, however covered up, is a sense of lostness and a longing for fulfillment. That alone was God's judgment on His disobedient children, a judgment totally for their benefit.

— *Yes, I Am*

"We . . . are being transformed into his likeness with ever-increasing glory, which comes from the Lord, who is the Spirit" — 2 Corinthians 3:18.

In our souls we all differ: you're very quick and I'm slow. One person is cautious, another person is dashing. Variety is in our soul life — that is, in the emotions and the reason. These are the varied expressions of the inner spirit.

Now you may say in your soul life — in your emotions or your reason — "I don't like that person."

We have an affinity with some people and not with others. We're just made like that.

But you have to move back from your soul-affections (your emotions) to the inner spirit-love.

This business of emotions is most important, because dozens of Christians live with their feet dragging with a sense of condemnation and failure because they *feel* away from God, or they *feel* cold, or they *feel* guilty, or they *feel* weak, and so on.

They haven't discerned between the variable emotions of the soul and the unvarying reality of spirit — *where God's Spirit of love is eternally our other self in our spirit.*

How can I be cold when I have that permanent fire within me — Jesus Christ?

Move back from your soul-affections and say, "No, He's here."

How can I feel dry when I have a permanent well of water inside me —Jesus Christ?

— *The Key to Everything*

"He who unites himself with the Lord is one with him in spirit" — 1 Corinthians 6:17.

Your other self is Christ. It is not you, it's Christ.

There are two selves joined in one; and the other self is Christ.

That's why it's indivisible. That's why it's ridiculous to look around or above and try to find Christ.

You don't try to find yourself, do you? Wherever you go, you are there, aren't you?

However you feel about it, you can't escape your self.

And your other self is Christ; you can't escape Him either!

The other verse that goes with that one, which I always think is so marvelous, is perhaps my favorite in the Bible. It is Galatians 2:20, where Paul says, "I am crucified with Christ. . . ."

That's the old Paul out.

Then he says, ". . . nevertheless, I live."

That's the new Paul in Christ: a living, thinking, willing, feeling, battling human. A real person.

But listen: then he corrects himself and adds, "Yet not I, but Christ liveth in me."

He could very easily have said, "Nevertheless I live *and* Christ lives in me" — as if Christ lived near him or close by him.

But you see, he replaced self by Christ.

That's the point.

He said, "Nevertheless, I live — excuse me, the real I isn't I at all; it is Christ."

— *The Key to Everything*

"Moses saw that though the bush was on fire it did not burn up" —Exodus 3:2.

Moses, like every one of us, had to learn that you don't do God's work by self-effort and self-wisdom.

Moses, in his own opinion, had been a very uncommon royal bush, and God doesn't live in uncommon royal bushes. Then Moses saw this sight: God's presence, God's word out of a common bush — and as the divine fire consumes the bush, it refuels it. "The bush was not consumed."

Once you have come to understand that your basic function is a constant recognition of Another, the whole of life is transformed.

It isn't a matter of continually allowing Him to come into your life, because you have received Him. But it is the recognition of Another.

Another is the functioning one.

Another is the Person who inspires the prayers and imparts the faith and thinks the thoughts through our minds and expresses His compassion through our hearts and puts our bodies into action.

Once you've seen that, you see that He is the illimitable One.

Then you relax and say, "This is what life is basically: Another living His life in me."

You've got your key to everything.

Every problem becomes an opportunity.

Every tough spot becomes a chance to enjoy the luxury of seeing Him deliver us out of it. And you welcome such spots.

— The Key to Everything

"The body is a unit . . . and though all its parts are many, they form one body. So it is with Christ"— 1 Corinthians 12:12.

Two in one; one in two. We see the paradox in the vine and the branch illustration because, though the vine and the branch make one, Jesus says that the branch must "abide in the vine." Though the vine is the life and the branch the channel, yet the branch does things. It utilizes the sap and produces leaf and flower and fruit.

But its activity is secondary to its receptivity. This is where we fail. We make activity a substitute for receptivity. It is its outcome.

Paul gave us another illustration: that of head and body. Head and body make one organism, one life.

You can't divide head and body. My name is Norman Grubb. But my head is not Norman and my body Grubb! You can't divide the two.

The Bible tells us the same thing. For instance, 1 Corinthians 12:12 speaks of the body as *being* Christ. It says, "As the body [the body is, of course, the believers joined to Christ] is one and hath many members, so also is Christ." The body is called Christ — not the head.

We are part of a vital organism which is an ascended, glorious, perfect Christ — the eternal Christ.

We are part of Him, yet we remain ourselves.

—The Key to Everything

"A vessel for honor, sanctified, useful to the Master, prepared for every good work" — 2 Timothy 2:21 (NASV).

A finite language cannot completely portray the infinite. So different illustrations are necessary in order to complete the picture of our relation to Him.

Look at the number of times the Bible calls us vessels. "We have this treasure in earthen vessels that the excellency of the power may be of God, and not of us." We are "vessels, sanctified, meet for the Master's use, prepared unto every good work."

Now you see at once the beauty of the illustration: a vessel is a hollow object made to contain something. And God has made us vessels.

Of course, if God makes us vessels, He fills us. God doesn't fool with His creation; if He made anything to be filled, He must see to it that it gets filled.

This is *our* receptivity. The whole function of the vessel is to receive something.

Now get this clear: *the vessel never becomes the liquid, nor the liquid the vessel.* I add this because we humans are so proud that there creeps into us the idea that we can be deified. That is *blasphemy.* There is no such thing as self-deification, except that of Satan, the pseudo-God, and what we share with him. The divine can dwell in the human, but forever the human is the human and the divine the divine. God has said, "I will not give My glory to another."

That is the vital importance of the vessel illustration: we are forever the container; He is that which we contain. That relationship never changes.

— *The Key to Everything*

"Christ is all, and is in all" — Colossians 3:11.

I came to a statement which gathered all together and finished off my investigations by its absoluteness. The verse was Colossians 3:11, where it says of believers in Christ that "Christ is all and in all."

Christ *is* all, not Christ has all.

And if Christ is all, what's left for me? Not much, by my mathematics!

I had thought I was somebody, and had something or could get something. I found God had taken the lot. Christ is all.

Then I got the link. Christ is all *and in all.*

Then I saw for the first time that the only reason for the existence of the entire creation is to contain the Creator! Not to be something, but to contain Someone.

So there dawned a very important truth. We humans naturally regard the human self as important. But we've got the wrong ideas of the reason for the existence of the self.

An immense distortion has come into the very warp and woof of humanity. It's the distortion of the ego — of the self. Though we feel self to be important, all of this showed me that self is extremely unimportant.

There is only one Self in the universe who is really important. I would almost say there is only one Self.

Why? Because there's only one Person in the universe who ever said, "I Am."

We are told that at the end of the history of the universe it is God who will be all in all. God all in all! Then what's left?

— *The Key to Everything*

34

"Christ the power of God and the wisdom of God" —
1 Corinthians 1:24.

Love [is] not a thing I can have. Love is exclusively a
Person. *God* is love. Therefore, there is no other pure,
self-giving love in the universe beyond Him Himself. Love is
exclusively a characteristic of one Person only —and that's
not Norman Grubb.

That was a deflation for me. I had thought I could have
love imparted to me, channeled into me, and I'd be more
loving. But I suddenly found God saying, "You'll never have
one iota of love. I am love, and that's the end of it."

Love is a Person; one Person only loving — and that's
not I, and that's not you. God is love and, therefore, love is
God loving.

That set a new trend of thought going. I began to relate
this to my other need: power. And I suddenly found a verse
in the first chapter of 1 Corinthians where it says that Christ
is the power of God. Not Christ *has* the power, but He *is* the
power.

Once again, I had thought power was something which
was given to me, and I'd be a powerful servant of Jesus
Christ. I suddenly found that power, also, is a Person. And
that person is not I but is exclusively Christ, who is God.

I also suddenly found that eternal life is not something *I*
can ever have – for Jesus did not say, "I *have* the life to give
you," but "I *am* life."

— *The Key to Everything*

"I consider them rubbish, that I may gain Christ" —
Philippians 3:8.

Exactly as the body is dependent on the head and the head governs the body, so we forever remain the dependent member in the union.

And the union is never safe until we know that.

So, until you have a few good knocks on the head and discover your conceited self, you're not safe to know the union. Maybe you've had plenty of knocks. They're the healthiest thing we can have. We've got to be made safe and understanding for this tremendous relationship.

He is the Lord. We are the co-operators. We are receivers.

Basically every one of us has regarded life as something *we* must live, although we are glad to have the help and grace of God to assist us. Even though we are redeemed people, without realizing our error, we rely mainly on our self-activity.

Basically, every one of us has thought, "We're the people; let's get on with the work."

That is the reason for the long periods of training through which we read God took all His servants in Bible times. Look at Moses. Few can equal his consecration. He threw away a throne as "the son of Pharaoh's daughter," with all "the treasures of Egypt" and "pleasures of sin for a season." And he did all this for the mysterious Christ who had not even come — for he "esteemed the reproach of Christ greater riches," the record says.

— *The Key to Everything*

"I am the vine; you are the branches" — John 15:5.

The actual fact of the relationship of the union cannot be safely realized, or lived by, until once and for all it has sunk into and become fixed in our consciousness that He is always the all, and we nothing but the container, the vessel. That is why the vessel relationship is a necessity as a permanency in our consciousness, before the union relationship can safely be to us what it really is.

The analogies of the union given by Jesus and Paul are likening our relationship to Vine and branch, Head and body. In each case they form a unity. When we look at a tree, we do not divide in our minds between trunk and branches, we see one tree — a unity. Equally a head and body form a unity, and we regard them as such. When we see people, we do not see so many heads and bodies: we see just persons — a unity. We do not even speak of a union, which directs the attention to two coming together to make one. We speak of a unity where the two have become one. So it is with the Trinity and us.

Now we come to God's sole purpose in Christ dying and rising, and we with Him: the destruction in death of the old union with "the spirit that worketh in the children of disobedience," and the union in resurrection with "the Spirit that raised up Jesus from the dead" — God Himself: and the union has produced the unity.

— *The Spontaneous You*

> *"Do you not know that your body is a temple of the*
> *Holy Spirit?"* — 1 Corinthians 6:19.

Paul said, "He that is joined to the Lord is one spirit." In that unity He has become the real I; again as Paul wrote, "I live, yet not I, but Christ liveth in me."

In other words Paul did not say that he and Christ lived side by side within him, as if it were "I live *and* Christ lives in me"; but that though he was a living human, as much after conversion as before, yet the real Paul was no longer himself, but another Self in his place: "I live; yet not I, but Christ lives in me." The real Paul was Christ walking about and talking, just as Paul wrote in another place, "Ye are the temples of the living God; as God hath said, I will dwell in them and walk in them."

That is why Jesus had said, "Ye *are* the light of the world," not "You *have* the light." If we have a thing it is not we, but just something we hold in our hands, as it were. But Jesus did not say, "You are darkness, but you have Me who am light." He said, "You *are* light." But how could that be when we are darkness and He is the light? Unity. Because He and we are one; therefore, He says, "You are the light." That is why John wrote, "If we love one another, it is God dwelling in us and His love perfected in us." Our loving is really He loving by us. Again unity.

— *The Spontaneous You*

"Christ in you, the hope of glory" — Colossians 1:27.

The inner choices of the will are given outward expression in the body, as when we choose to sit in a chair, we then sit. So the inner action of the will in this greatest of all affirmations is confirmed by confession of the mouth. Some opportunity is taken to express our faith-in-action to ourselves and to others: I did it with my pen, drawing a picture of a tombstone with my name on it which I could visit to remind me of the end of an old union to a false god. It took a little time longer to have an equal consciousness of the resurrection!

But the all-important consummation of such faith is that what we attach ourselves to by the act of faith attaches itself to us, and makes us know it. Food in the stomach, air in the lungs, the chair we sit on, have all become conscious realities to us.

So now, this highest dimension of faith, not merely in our reconciliation to God, but in His eternal, unchangeable, factual unity with us, equally produces its settled awareness of this supreme fact of human history.

The inner awareness comes in different ways — to me not till two years from my committal of faith, and then by a kind of flooding of inner certainty — that was all.

But the point is that faith has not completed its function until it is consummated by an experienced certainty of the thing appropriated.

— *The Spontaneous You*

"You are light in the Lord" — Ephesians 5:8.

We have to pass through three phases in our attitude towards an understanding of ourselves. We start life by a false attempt at self-appreciation. We try to make out we are all right: "going about to establish our own righteousness," the Bible calls it. That phase finishes when we become honest about ourselves in the sight of God; and our repentance toward God and faith toward our Lord Jesus Christ is an end to our false self-appreciation.

This is often followed by a long period of self-depreciation. As new-born Christians, we are making the discovery that it is not in redeemed self, any more than it was in unredeemed self, to be what we should be. So we are much more conscious of our failings, our inadequate human selves, than we are of Christ in us.

We say that if God does anything with our lives, it is in spite of us (whereas in fact it is because of us), and so forth. This is the phase of temporary self-depreciation.

The third and final phase is rightful self-appreciation. This is when in the unity we have found forever we are only the vessels that contain God; but we are vessels, and more, we are vessels who are really persons; and our humanity is now the self-expression of the Living God. *We* are the light of the world. *We* are the eternal love in action. The center of our inner consciousness has moved over from self-depreciation to God-appreciation and thus to self-appreciation.

— *The Spontaneous You*

"The Spirit himself testifies with our spirit that we are God's children" — Romans 8:16.

Spirits are of different quality from souls or bodies. They function differently. Bodies are separate entities; one is distinct from another, and remains so. So also souls, which are the varied individual forms through which the inner ego expresses itself, each different as everything in nature is different: one quick, another slow; one gentle, another firm; one rational, another intuitive, and so on. But spirits unite. They interpenetrate. One dwells in another. We have seen that in the Trinity, One in the Other, yet each separate Persons. We see it in the Savior on earth, who at one time says, "I and My Father are one"; yet at another, "The words that I speak unto you I speak not of Myself; but the Father that dwelleth in Me, He doeth the works." Both a union and a distinction between Them at the same time. And above all in the marvelous words of Paul in 1 Corinthians 6:17, "He that is joined unto the Lord is one spirit."

I a spirit and the Lord the Spirit, when joined, are one spirit-union. We see the same all through the references in the Bible to the Holy Spirit. He is always spoken of as indwelling. The Old Testament prophets spoke of "the Spirit of Christ which was in them." We are believers, "if so be that the Spirit of God dwells in" us. And the place of union is told us in that same chapter (Romans 8:16), "The Spirit Himself beareth witness with our spirit."

God the Spirit indwells human spirits. The Creator Self indwells the created selves, Spirit in spirit. The I AM of God in the I am of man.

— *The Liberating Secret*

> *"My power is made perfect in weakness"* —
> 2 Corinthians 12:9.

If we are to be the sons we are meant to be, we must know ourselves and how we fit into the picture. The whole purpose of God in our human history is that first we discover ourselves, and then learn the difference between being a wrong self and a right self. Then we can be the sons of God.

Our trouble is that we have lost sight of the basic relationship between God and His universe, including ourselves. The best way I can put it is the interrelation between positive and negative. I have already touched on this a little, but we now need to see it very plainly. A positive and negative are the two sides of the same thing: light and darkness, smooth and rough, love and hate, sweet and bitter, and so all down the line. The one, the positive, is the thing. The other, the negative, is the lack of that thing. Light is no-dark, love is no-hate, smooth is no-rough. And the negative is only observable where the positive is not in operation. Yet the positive is built on the negative. There is no such a thing as the one without the other. Love is only known as love because there could be no-love. Sweet is only known as sweet because there could be no-sweet.

The perfect relationship between the two is that the positive has "swallowed up" the negative, to use the Bible expression we have already quoted — 2 Corinthians 5:4 or 1 Corinthians 15:54; or in the sense of 2 Corinthians 12:9: "My strength is made perfect in weakness."

— Who Am I?

"God has raised us up with Christ and seated us with him" — Ephesians 2:6.

[Satan] will make it always appear to us that there is still this old separation, the fruit of the Fall. God is still away there in heaven, while we are here on earth; whereas the Scripture says that, even with regard to the risen and ascended Christ, we are raised and seated with Him — in Him in the heavenlies, even as He is in us in the earthlies.

Satan knows that if he can keep us in the delusion of separation we are at his mercy, weak in a crisis, wavering in a decision. We feel our weakness, bewail our ignorance, for we see our separate selves and know their limitations and corruptions; and the best which we can attain to is to call on God to send help from without.

If we cast aside the suggestions of Satan, the delusions of our own feelings of separation, the sense of weakness and ignorance; if we boldly possess our possessions in Christ, draw the sword of the Spirit upon the deceiver, declare by God's word that we are one with Christ and with one another, one mystic organism, with one divine life flowing in and through all: then we *are* strong by faith, for His strength is in us; we *are* wise, for His wisdom is ours; we *have* love, joy or any other needed grace of the Spirit, for we are permeated with Him. All we need to do is to go forward in this faith, and we shall find that what is true in the realm of the Spirit becomes manifest, through our faith, in the realm of the senses.

— *Touching the Invisible*

"He is a chosen vessel unto me" — Acts 9:15 (KJV).

We humans are basically containers, and nothing else. I have already referred to our misconception of the function of the human self, and here it is. Through the self-sufficiency we inherited from the Fall, we instinctively regard ourselves as something very much more than containers. "Vessels" the Bible calls us; it was the first description given by the Ascended Christ of the most dynamic Christian of history, the Apostle Paul: "He is a chosen vessel unto Me"; just a vessel, that was all. Were all the dynamism, the wisdom, the revelations, the passionate love, the self-sacrifice then attributes of the vessel, or of Him whom it contained?

Paul himself went on to call us all "earthen vessels." Not even tin cans, but nearer to crack-pots! Humbling, self-emptying, an offense to any man not enlightened to facts by the Spirit of God. But let us get it plain, and without equivocation. If God is the All, and we are merely the means of His Self-manifestation, is it not a fact that we must be just containers? "Christ *is* all and *in* all." "Temple" is another like metaphor, for a temple has no reason for existence except to house its god: "Ye are the temples of the living God; as God hath said, I will dwell in them, and walk in them."

— *God Unlimited*

"A vessel for honor, sanctified, useful to the Master"
—2 Timothy 2:21 (NASV).

Activity is not the function of a vessel, but receptivity. Here we reach right down to the roots. Receptivity is the simplest, most child-like human function. In Bible terms, it is not works, but faith. But what we have to relearn is that receptivity is not *a* function, but *the* function. All other functions are by-products. The whole of life is a parable of this. Is not everything some form of the self-giving of God? And do we not totally live by what we receive — food, air, the floor boards beneath our feet, the clothes on our backs? And in most cases something has died to give us life.

Life is surely based on receptivity, and the Bible word for receptivity is faith. Can anything be simpler? How wonderfully God has made us: to live, spiritually and materially, by exercising a capacity which is as near as possible to doing nothing — just receiving. Not reaching up to drag things down, but things poured upon us in such abundance that we just open our mouths and they are filled; and the gift of gifts we receive is Himself.

"Wait a minute," you may object, "but we do have to act also." Certainly, activity is a product of receptivity, but not a substitute for it.

— God Unlimited

"His body . . . the fullness of him who fills everything in every way" — Ephesians 1:23.

We are body to head. Again that makes one Person, just as it was one Tree. So one that the Bible even speaks of the body (not the head) as Christ (1 Corinthians 12:12). Yet the body is as solely the agent of the head, as branch of vine. The total dependence is maintained. The union is maintained. But in head and body, the activity of the members comes to the fore. A body is made for action. A head is useless without a body, so the body in Ephesians 1:23 is specifically spoken of as the fullness of the head. They are necessary to each other.

So here we come back full circle to active self, but dead, risen and ascended, and thus forever knowing itself as basically containing the Other, motivated by The Other, He living His own life and expressing His own self through ourselves; yet we freely in action, just as if it were we, thinking, willing, working, laughing, talking, living as normal human beings in normal situations, and the world thinking it is just we, except for something unusual they can't identify about us. What? We know: "Your life is hid with Christ in God . . . Christ our life."

— *God Unlimited*

Union With Christ

"Apart from me you can do nothing" — John 15:5.

The Vine and branch truth emphasizes the indissoluble union of Christ and the believer. We are organically one. One tree, one life; yet in that relationship Jesus underlined the fact that we, the branches, are merely channels of the sap from the vine. A branch is more than a channel, because a branch is alive whereas a pipe is not, and a branch does absorb and utilize the sap to produce the fruit. It is not entirely inactive, though entirely dependent. But it was the dependence Jesus was pointing to: "Apart from Me, ye can do nothing."

So that illustration is taking us one [step] further than the vessel. First, we are merely containers. Then, having absorbed and accepted that fact, we are more. We are united to Him whom we contain in a way a vessel can never be united to the liquid in it. We are united because we are living people as He is the Living Person; yet in that union, as branch to vine, we remain as totally dependent as the vessel. Without the sap flowing through us, we can do nothing. Yet it is this time a living dependence, for we are to "abide in the Vine."

— God Unlimited

Union With Christ

"For to me, to live is Christ" — Philippians 1:21.

We redeemed people are paddling in the muddy shallows when we are constantly concerned with what benefits we receive from Him.

The real truth is that He has found us, made us His dwelling place, and lives His own life in us.

What then is a totally committed Christian? He has ceased to be his own —neither people, possessions, nor life is his. All he has is Jesus. And what kind of person is Jesus? Unconditional love. Life's occupation, life's absorption, is expressing the love of Jesus in our world. Nothing one iota less. To me to live is Christ — all things counted refuse that I may win Christ (not by effort but by faith that He is what He is in me); and that means the life He will live out in me will be a participation in His power, His vicarious sufferings, and His death for sinners and enemies.

That is this life — Christ formed in us — no question about uncertainty of consecration or doubts about His permanent indwelling; no pursuit of personal revival, refreshment, renewal; but the clear recognition of this unchanging Other Person of love who has begun to live His eternal life of self-giving love through us. This has become our adventure for eternity, the upspringing well and the outpouring rivers.

— *God Unlimited*

"Don't you know that you yourselves are God's temple?" — 1 Corinthians 3:16.

We are called the temples of the living God, the buildings in which God may be seen; and we are the earthen vessels whose treasure is the Christ within. Temple and vessel don't illustrate the unity, but do make it plain that they are merely negative containers, and we don't look for change or improvement in them.

So then how does all this work out? First, by a recognition, which is a revelation, that the human self by itself can only be motivated by its own self-interests; for its only true place in creation is in its unity with God, as the means by which He manifests Himself in other love through our human selves. Apart from our destined place in the unity, we can only be self-loving selves. Therefore it is useless and a waste of time for us to ask God to make us loving, or patient, or pure, or to free us from human reactions of hate or fear or worry or depression. It is asking an absurdity and an impossibility. The human self can never change. The vessel can never be the living water it contains. The branch cannot be the vine.

When that recognition is a reality to us, then we can start by accepting ourselves in our weakness and all normal human reactions.

— Who Am I?

"God did not give us a spirit of timidity, but a spirit of power, of love, and of self-discipline" — 2 Timothy 1:7.

I know no more illuminating truth for our generation than the "mystery" which Paul said he was commissioned to reveal to the Gentiles — "Christ in you."

All power is mine if He is my life; all guidance is mine if His mind indwells mine; all authority is mine if I share His throne as a king and command deliverances according to His instructions to me (Mark 11:22-24).

I have no excuses for failure. God has not given me the spirit of fear, but of love, power and sanity.

We are set in our day and generation to be overcomers, not to sail through calm seas but to walk on storms, to replace need with supply, to transform aspiration into realization. The language of defeatism, fear, lack and weakness is not to be in our vocabulary. "Let us go up at once and possess it, for we are well able to overcome it. As for these giants, they are bread for us," we say with sturdy Caleb. We are to act as the men of faith of old; we are to visualize our goal in clear outline; we are to take it for granted that we shall reach it, for have we not both the commission and anointing of God? We are to lay our plans, build our organizations, produce our written and verbal pronouncements, pray our prayers, do our work, not as those who will fail and fall by the way, but as those who will finish the work we have been sent to do, as did our Lord and Savior.

— *After C. T. Studd*

"He himself bore our sins . . . so that we might die to sins and live for righteousness" — 1 Peter 2:24.

It is important to note the implications of the word "death" in the Scriptures. Many stumble at this point. They say, "How can I call myself dead to sin, buried with Christ, and so on, when the next moment I am very much alive to the solicitations of sin?" The answer is that death in the Bible is used to pronounce a clean-cut separation from a thing. But at the same time we must also remember that it is death to one thing and resurrection to another. It never means a total blotting out of a personality. Such a thing is an impossibility. Therefore if a person is dead to a certain thing, but also alive to another, he is genuinely cut off from the one and attached to the other; but if he is still in the sphere where both those things are active, it doesn't say that he cannot hear the voice of the other calling him back to the old relationship. He is not necessarily out of calling distance.

The proof of that is twofold. Adam was told he would surely die if he broke God's command in the Garden. He did, and died spiritually. He died out to God and came alive to Satan. Thus we are all by nature "dead in trespasses and sins." But though Adam died towards God, was he out of hearing distance of God? No indeed. God at once set in motion His plans of grace to recall him completely from his false allegiance to Satan. God set to work to reverse that false death and resurrection. This He did in Christ, and now it is reversed in Him, for we have died to sin and live unto God.

— *The Liberating Secret*

"Count yourselves dead to sin but alive to God in Christ Jesus" — Romans 6:11.

All men can see the fact of substitution: that, as the Savior hung on the cross in our place, He paid the penalty for our sins: "He bore our sins in His own body on the tree," and that "He was made sin for us that we might be made the righteousness of God in Him." But the further fact implied in His substitutionary act is that, if He died in my place, in the sight of God it is really I who died there.

That is more difficult to grasp. Look at it this way. In Central Africa, if an African does not pay his annual tax and is arrested, he has to pay for it by several weeks in prison. But being clannish, it is not an uncommon sight to see a man standing before the judge about to receive his sentence, when his brother runs up and puts down the tax money for him. The judge then notes against the prisoner's name in his records that he has paid his tax. Now the point of the illustration is that the judge does not put down the brother's name; he is not interested in the brother. He merely notes against the prisoner's name, which is already on his charge sheet, that he has paid his tax. Now that is identification. We may put it like this. When Jesus died in my stead, it was I who was God's concern. He did not need to die; He had no sins needing atonement. God is interested in *my* having died, for it was *my* penalty He paid.

— *The Liberating Secret*

"Don't you know that all of us who were baptized into Christ Jesus were baptized into his death?" — Romans 6:3.

The cross has to be real before there can be a steady realization of the resurrection. It is a real death in experience, and probably there has to be a period when we are much more conscious of our having died with Him than having risen with Him. By no other means can we be understanding servants of Christ. We must have really tasted of the self-defeating activities of independent self in our redeemed lives, and have really become soured on them. We must have come to some final point of desperation and despair to have learned our lesson with an utter finality that this way of life, of us serving Christ rather than of Him serving Himself in and by us, is a spill-over into our new lives of the great curse of the Fall, the delusion of self-sufficiency.

It has to be a revelation — that the ultimate form of sin is a misuse of self, just as it then can become a personal revelation that the misuse of self is what was removed in the cross and is thus removed in us. And then can come the revelation of Christ, the real new Self in ourselves.

— *God Unlimited*

"I am again in the pains of childbirth until Christ is formed in you" — Galatians 4:19.

Paul commented that he now lived, not by his own flickering faith but by the Believer within him, whose faith never fails and who now exercised His faith through Paul: "the life that I now live in the flesh I live by the faith of the Son of God." This was Paul's testimony to sanctification, not some static experience of a thing called "holiness," but an organic relationship with an indwelling Christ living His own life within him, the most delicate conceivable interaction of grace between the redeemed human personality and the Redeemer within, of which we say more later.

In one other sentence, he revealed the secret resources of his life of service, and it is the same again. The One who worked effectively in Peter in his ministry to Israel, Paul wrote in Galatians 2:8, "the Same was mighty in me toward the Gentiles." Remarkably phrased again. Not making Paul mighty, but being Himself the mighty One in Paul; only this time that gracious and holy Self not merely shining out through Paul's personality, but working His mighty works of salvation in others through Paul. Here was Paul's dynamic of service, his enduement with power from on high. And this threefold experience of inner union with Christ in regeneration, sanctification and service — this profound realization that this alone is eternal life — makes him write in Galatians 4:19 that he travailed in birth, not until the Galatians came to Christ but until He was formed in them, the Son of God in His full stature living His life in them.

—God Unlimited

"He that sanctifieth and they who are sanctified are all of one" —Hebrews 2:11 (KJV).

So this is what a "normal" man is: not himself, but God dwelling and working in him. Ours is not a God afar off, but God within. In light of this Jesus said, "I and My Father are one"; yet within that union They were two — "I and My Father." And the whole point is that this is not a description of Himself as Jesus the Son of God, unique and different from us, but of Jesus as the Son of man, of whom it says in the Epistle to the Hebrews that "He that sanctifieth and they who are sanctified are all of one."

Jesus Himself had prayed that we should all know this same oneness with each other: "I in them, and Thou in Me, that they may be made perfect in one." And John wrote in his letter these categorical statements: "As He is, so are we in this world"; and, "If we love one another, God dwelleth in us, and His love is perfected in us"; and "He that dwelleth in love dwelleth in God, and God in him."

We do remain ourselves — very much ourselves, as we shall be seeing —just as Jesus was so much Himself that the world could never ignore Him as the perfect man, whether they believed in His deity or not. Yet it is *this* upon which we are centering our attention: There was never a moment when He did not know that He and His Father were in an eternal *union*, so that who He was, was the Father being manifested in and through His Son. So our being rebuilt as whole persons must first have *our union* with God through His Son established, and only then do we also freely live in the easy paradox of also being ourselves.

— Yes, I Am

"Through the law I died to the law so that I might live for God" —Galatians 2:19.

The primary purpose of this great chapter is to show us that death to sin (the theme of Romans 6) includes death to law (Romans 7:4). Until I consciously know and enter into the reality of the cutoff from my old husband and my marriage to the new, I am "in between" — in an illusory condition of independence — and thus actually under the control of my old husband.

Paul shares in detail his own agonizing battle with his personal responses to indwelling sin, and his own total failure to win the battles. "O wretched man that I am!" Then comes his blinding flash of revelation that, while he lived in the delusion of being an independent self, indwelling sin falsely claimed to possess him ("I am carnal, sold under sin"). Then comes the glory of the revelation—the One who had cast out the lying usurper has now *replaced* him. So indwelling sin is now replaced by the indwelling Christ!

God's law, which looks like an enemy condemning me, is really my friend, for it is the ultimate and necessary means of revealing to me that *self-relying self is an illusion.*

"Ye are become dead to the law." How? Because law came into existence only to reveal my slave relationship to Satan and sin and to enlighten my mistaken, deluded self. When at last I know that in Christ I am totally cut off from sins, from sin, and from its claims on me — and realize that the indweller is Christ Himself, by the Spirit — then I also know that *my inner Christ is the whole law in spontaneous operation.*

— *Yes, I Am*

> *"Who will rescue me from this body of death? Thanks be to God — through Jesus Christ our Lord!"* — Romans 7:24-25.

It looks as if we have two natures — my redeemed self that wants to do good, and indwelling sin which defies and defeats me — dog eating dog. And thousands of God's people think that's all it can be: a life of struggle, striving, and much failure . . . with self-condemnation.

And that, of course, is the big lie. But the vital point is that I can't see it as a lie until I first have finally, once for all, got out of my system this delusion that I myself can do good or evil. It is because of this delusion that I either accept guilty failure or put on false self-righteousness.

But now came the breakthrough of this whole revelation to Paul — that the human is never anything but the vessel, container, branch, etc., of the indwelling deity. Now he sees it! "The law has nothing to say to *me*. It is not *I* who am covetous; those sinful urges come from an altogether *different* source — not I, but indwelling sin."

The law has really been my friend . . . hanging over me and putting its pressure on me until at last I see my delusion about self-effort living. Until I see that *self-effort is Satan's principle* the power of indwelling sin has me in its control.

So here is the revelation of total importance — or shall we say, the negative side of the total positive revelation. We can compare it to our prior experience in our unsaved days: I could not settle into the positive recognition of Christ as my substitute and sin-bearer until I first knew, in a total negative way, that I was a lost sinner, with my righteousness as filthy rags . . . and I could do nothing about it. Only then could I say, "Oh, I see! *He* took my place." — *Yes, I Am*

*"By dying to what once bound us, we have been released
from the law"* — Romans 7:6.

The point that Paul is now writing about, and bringing
to its climax in Romans 7, is that we've not yet properly
understood our relationship to our two "husbands." The
tangle is caused by the false idea of myself as an independent
person, about which I've been deceived from the Fall. Not
knowing that as a sinner I lived under the total management
of my old husband and solely expressed him and repro-
duced his children, but wrongly thinking I then had an
independent life of my own, I started out living my new life
thinking that now also, as a redeemed human, I have an
ability of my own and so can fulfill the law. And so my
former husband catches me unawares. When I think I ought
to be "doing my own thing" for God (for now, being
redeemed, I delight in the law of God), Satan cunningly
re-exerts his control over me and causes me to fulfill his will.

How can this be? Because "doing my own thing" is
Satan's principle, the very cause of his and Adam's fall. It is
the sin principle. Here then is the value of the continuing law
to my life. I needed to have one final radical exposure of the
"nonsense" of my supposed independence. By this, at last, I
can see I have never been independent, because the self-
relying self was the sin-spirit in me. Until, however, I consciously know and enter into the reality of not only my
cutoff from my old husband, but also my marriage to my
new Husband, I will still be in an illusory condition of
independence, and so actually under the remote control of
my old husband. There is no in-between status.

— Yes, I Am

"Christ is all, and is in all" — Colossians 3:11.

It is a glorious experience when God confirms His presence in us by His gifts of the Spirit, as He did at Pentecost. This is a gracious manifestation of the Spirit as power, and produces such marvelous effects on us that at first we may think we now have all. But in fact, that first impartation of power has to be inwardly expanded . . . through our personal pilgrimage in the delusion of self-effort living in Romans 7, and then through the wide-open gateway into the full freedom of Romans 8. *Then* He is known and established in us as the living Person He is, not merely manifested in power.

Therefore those who have experienced the baptism of the Holy Spirit — with the sign or gift of tongues, or other gifts — have been highly privileged in this great stepping-stone into Christ as all in all. We can then expand that great primary experience into its full reality by moving in by faith into the "Christ is all and in all" of Colossians 3:11. Today I often find that those who have had a charismatic experience more readily respond to the revelation of the total Christ-union-and-replacement reality than do those who are inclined more to the objective relationship with Christ, as apart from us in His risen and ascended position at the right hand of God. Though they know and love the Lord, they're often fearful of and cautious about too close an approach to Paul's mystery, "hidden, but now made manifest to His saints . . . which is Christ in you, the hope of glory." Some even label it as some form as "mysticism," dangerous and fanatical.

— Yes, I Am

"I belong to my lover, and his desire is for me" — Song of Solomon 7:10.

I have to say again and again that this union life is different from a committed, dedicated relationship to Christ in which we still see ourselves as two and thus are occupied in depending on Him and receiving from Him the immediate supplies for life. *Union* is different.

We had, as selves, to go through the process of deceived self, then through self dead to sin and Satan, and thus pass out of self-condemnation into where the central fact now is that He is fully formed in us (Galatians 4:19). But thereby we discover *right self.* The whole purpose of God is that we should be the total persons by whom He can express His total self.

Paul confidently said, "I live by the faith-recognition that He has loved me and given Himself for me." So I then surely can love myself. If I'm good enough for *Him*, then I'm good enough for myself. This is something really new and fresh when it comes to us. At least it was to me. I am to drop those belittling, downgrading statements about myself. If I am an earthen vessel, it doesn't mean earthy in a derogatory sense, but "human"; and He was human, and God was manifested in that humanity.

So I am no longer a wretched man, but a whole (and holy) man. I am to be myself! Unafraid. *Yes, I am*, and like Paul, I can do all things in Christ, as Christ. I am well able (like Caleb). I'm full of power and of judgment and of might (like Micah). I am my Beloved's and His desire is toward me (as His spouse) (Song of Solomon 7:10).

— Yes, I Am

"Therefore, if anyone is in Christ, he is a new creation; the old has gone, the new has come!" — 2 Corinthians 5:17.

There was a friend in Bournemouth — my father had by now moved to a church in Poole, near Bournemouth — who was a retired Royal Artillery major, an original, interesting fellow, named Major Gartside-Tippinge. He had a lovely home and grass tennis court. He was also a very keen Christian and especially keen on getting boys to Christ. His wife was a sister of D. E. Hoste, the General Director of the China Inland Mission. He used to invite my brother Harold and me over to tennis, and then, if he could, catch us after in his drawing-room for a talk about our need of salvation, which we called having a "pi-jaw."

On one such visit my brother escaped somehow, but I was caught in the drawing room. All I remember Tippinge asking me was the pertinent question, Did I belong to Christ?

Somehow I did manage to admit that I could not say He was personal to me. Tippinge got me on my knees, made me pray something, and I got up as I got down and escaped.

But on my way home on a double-decker bus, the implication of what I had said got its teeth into me. I knew the gospel, and that if I could not say Christ was my personal Savior, I was going to hell. And I knew too, through the guilt of my sins, that I deserved to go there. At last this was real to me; so as soon as I reached my small bedroom at the top of the house, I got on my knees and for the first time in my life meant it when I asked, according to the Lord's prayer, for my sins to be forgiven.

— *Nothing Is Impossible*

Testimony — Norman Grubb

"Be transformed by the renewing of your mind" —
Romans 12:2.

The first deep affection I had was for a beautiful girl about four years older than I, daughter of a near neighbor, a coal-merchant and mayor of the town.

A favorite uncle, the Rev. George C. Grubb, who had a great spiritual influence on my life, and whom I loved greatly — full of Irish fun, yet filled with the love of God — was staying with us. He was world-famous in evangelical and Keswick Convention circles. This Uncle George gave me a little booklet. I don't remember its contents except that it was like handing me a red-hot poker. It was suddenly burned into me that I could not have both Christ and the one who was against Christ in the center of my heart.

How I fought this. I remember throwing the booklet on the floor and wishing I had never seen it. This was a far fiercer battle than anything involved in accepting Christ. Why should I not keep both the girl and Christ? Our relationship was a healthy friendship. But the Voice persisted. You cannot have both. If you hold to her, you lose Christ.

It was like a hell, and I was traveling to and fro to Salisbury ordering and buying my subaltern's uniform. What agonizing journeys those were. I tried my father. He was permissive and left me with the impression that I could have both. But that Voice persisted. Finally, I tried my mother, and that was the end of it. She made me see that a real choice was involved. So I made it.

We live where we love, and when the chips were down, Christ was my love.

— *Once Caught, No Escape*

"You shall have no other gods before me" —
Exodus 20:3.

The human heart can only have one supreme affection at its center. An idol is a rival affection, and while the rival occupies the affections, our interests and activities go along with it. I loved Christ, but my daily interests had been around the girl. When at last, on one of those train journeys, I made the decision and dropped the girl, a sudden new thought took possession of me. I was soon going to be with a crowd of men and any of us might be dead in a year. I had found the gift of eternal life. I had better see that some of them find it.

Though previously I had spoken of Christ only in a casual comment to a friend, it now was a life's obsession. I had really found my life's calling, and life's meaning for me — that others should find the Christ I had. But I could not see this, it could not dawn on me, while my affections and interests were in another direction. Christ must be Lord as well as Savior. A Rubicon was crossed, really the second stage of the new birth. I fear it must have hurt the girl and was without the meaning it had for me, except the realization from her point of view that I had become a fanatic; but of course it had to end sometime as we were not contemplating marriage, and she has now long since been married.

— *Once Caught, No Escape*

"If you confess with your mouth, 'Jesus is Lord,' and believe in your heart that God raised him from the dead, you will be saved" — Romans 10:9.

I enjoyed my army years, five of them. We had a year's training at home, and we surely needed it. What must a callow youth straight from school, with no experience of the world and mighty little of soldiering, have seemed like to the forty men in my charge as my platoon — men between eighteen and maybe thirty-five, who had been wage-earners in the world probably from age sixteen onward? They must have had some laughs behind my back! But my interest was in speaking to all about Christ, and it cost me everything to do it.

I hated broaching the subject, and it had to be like repeated jumps off the deep end. One of my first and crudest attempts was on a wet and muddy day when we were under canvas. I heard the clink of coins in a tent as I passed. I knew that meant gambling, which was against army regulations. So gathering up my courage, I opened the fly of the tent, popped my head in and said, "I say, you men, I can tell you something better than gambling, and that is to have Jesus Christ." And on I went! I would talk to the sergeant marching beside me on our route marches, or to my fellow-officer, even my company commander *en route* to a parade, and that cost something. And many of those I spoke to were dead a year later.

The first man I ever helped to accept Christ was a fellow-subaltern named Hone. It had cost me, when lying outside our tents on a Sunday afternoon, to open my Testament and read. He saw me, made some interested comment, and accepted Christ.   — *Once Caught, No Escape*

> *"Even though I walk through the valley of the shadow of death . . . you are with me"* — Psalm 23:4.

We were occupying an isolated forward trench in full sight of the Germans, about 1,000 yards away. From this trench a small communication trench led to an observation post 100 yards in advance. I was occupying this post with signallers and orderlies. In the morning the Germans laid a barrage on our main trench, but not on the forward post. Suddenly a clear word came to me, "Get out of your post and go back to where they are being shelled." I said to the others, "I'm going back to the trench. You fellows do what you like." I broke all regulations and did not even strap on my equipment and revolver, but just went down the communication trench followed by the others. No sooner had we arrived than a shell fell plumb on the post and buried all our equipment and would have buried us. We had to return later and dig our stuff out.

One night my platoon was digging a trench about 100 yards in length. Suddenly the Germans dropped a series of crumps, as we called their 5-inch shells, right at one end of this trench line. You don't feel like going and standing where the shells have just dropped with their acrid smell, but something said to me, "Move over from where you are standing (at the other end of the trench) and go where the shells have just dropped." I did so, and a moment later the next set of crumps fell exactly where I had been standing.

— *Once Caught, No Escape*

"Who, then, is the man that fears the Lord? He will instruct him in the way chosen for him" — Psalm 25:12.

[Hospital chaplain] Gilbert Barclay, passing my bed one morning, quite casually dropped on it a little magazine called *The Heart of Africa*. It contained the accounts of C. T. Studd's penetration into the then Belgian Congo, opening the first center of this infant mission, which he called "The Heart of Africa Mission," at Niangara, the geographical center of the continent. No sooner had I begun to read than as clear an inward voice as ever I heard in my life said, "That's where you are to go." I had received my life's call and knew it.

I wrote to Mrs. Studd. She invited me to come up and stay with them whenever I could get to London. About two weeks later, while I had begun to move about on crutches, a summons came to attend an investiture by King George V at Buckingham Palace to receive the Military Cross from him. So I came and stayed with Mrs. Studd.

There I met Pauline. My fate was sealed, and the net closed on me the very next day when traveling up to the Investiture. Pauline had a war job in a London office, but as we traveled in the train together she began to tell me about what the Bible teaches on Christ's Second Coming. So ignorant was I of my Bible and its contents that I had not heard of this, and I realized that I was with a very beautiful girl and one who knew more of the Lord than I did. I was done for.

— *Once Caught, No Escape*

"Fear of man will prove to be a snare, but whoever trusts in the Lord is kept safe" — Proverbs 29:25.

[On entering Cambridge University] I decided that I should seek to give a witness to every man in my college, Trinity. I hated and dreaded the idea. However, I went to each man's room and knocked, always hoping there might be no reply.

The captain of the college tennis and soccer teams, and one of the top mathematicians in the university, was an undergraduate named Carey Francis. With special fear I knocked at his door. He was in. I handed him the card and said much the same as to the others and left. A year or two later, when I was in Africa, I heard that Carey Francis was now a witness for Christ and a don at Peterhouse College, Cambridge. So when I came home on my first furlough I visited Cambridge and called on him.

I caught him just going out to a lecture. He did not recognize me at first, but when I introduced myself he burst out laughing and said, "Well, when I last saw you, I don't know who was most frightened — you or I. But after you had left, I said to myself, 'That fellow has something about his faith in Christ that I obviously don't have. I had better look into this.'" And as a result, Christ not only found him, but Carey later left his secure position in Cambridge to start a high school in Kenya. When he died, years later, all his pallbearers were Kenyan cabinet members or in big business positions, bearing their tribute to what he had meant to them.

— Once Caught, No Escape

"You will receive power when the Holy Spirit comes on you; and you will be my witnesses in Jerusalem, and in all Judea and Samaria, and to the ends of the earth" — Acts 1:8.

I felt convinced that, before I left [the University], I should go around to all my friends or acquaintances and I should pull no punches. This was the last time I would see most of them, and I must tell them exactly what my inner convictions were about how they stood with God.

Man after man, some sixteen of them, faced up to the need of accepting Christ, or getting something right which was a block. It was a revival on a small scale.

But the outcome which really mattered was a sudden flash which I can only call an inspiration. If God was working like this at Cambridge, and there was a small start at Oxford, should not every English university have a Christian Union, and then out to the universities of America and the world? Why not have an Inter-Varsity Conference in London as a start? I shared my vision with two friends, Clarence Foster, who in later years was the greatly loved and honored Secretary of Keswick and head of the Scripture Union, and Leslie Sutton, who has had a major part in the founding and development of Lee Abbey, which has been such a spiritual power in the Church of England.

We agreed together that this was of God and we would get going in arranging this conference around Christmas. The result was the first Inter-Varsity Conference (I.V.C.) with a good group from Cambridge and a few from Oxford, London, and Durham. That was all. But it was the beginning of what has now actually spread to the ends of the earth.   — *Once Caught, No Escape*

"Who is my mother?" — Matthew 12:48.

[When we reached Congo we met C. T. Studd,] Pauline's father, my father-in-law, whom I then saw for the first time. In himself he was all that we expected: in his loving welcome, the old aristocrat now accustomed to living the African way; always scrupulously clean, in simple khaki shirt and shorts and stockings, with his long beard and somewhat bent frame, aquiline nose and keen piercing eyes.

But we were ill at ease. Without realizing it ourselves, we had been the petted and pampered "fine young Christians" in the homelands, and now we were going out (even the Executive Committee told us this!) to bring help, refreshment and encouragement to the tired little band in Congo. Tired little band! They were not looking for any to bolster them up. All they wanted were some more fellow-soldiers! We found C.T. had no time for special welcomes and favors for a daughter or special preference for a new son-in-law. He stood where Jesus stood. "Who is my mother or my brethren? Whosoever shall do the will of God, the same is my brother, my sister and mother."

I think, without recognizing it ourselves, we were puzzled and hurt that we did not get any better reception than any other new recruits. There was no let-up with this man — no diversions, no days off, no recreations. The zeal of God's house had eaten him up, and souls were his meat and drink.

— *Once Caught, No Escape*

"For we who are alive are always being given over to death for Jesus' sake, so that his life may be revealed in our mortal body" — 2 Corinthians 4:11.

A friend of Pauline's, Dr. Isa Lumsden, was sending her a little paper called *The Overcomer*, published by Mrs. Penn-Lewis, well known in England as a Bible teacher. But what she wrote about didn't make sense to us. She was not speaking about Christ dying for us, but of our being crucified and dead with Him, and risen with Him. That was all new to us.

The full moon was out and it was all quiet in the banana plantation except for the usual chorus of insects, with the moon shining between the great banana leaves. So we took the two little camp chairs and sat outside in the moonlight. We had decided together that we would wrestle this thing out with God and specifically claim then and there that we should be filled with the Spirit. It was only later that we got our theology more in line — to discover that He in His fullness had always been there, His Spirit joined to ours since we had been born again, and that what we needed was not a filling from outside but a witness borne to the existing living relationship. We took Galatians 2:20 to be the fact by faith: "I am crucified with Christ, nevertheless I live: yet not I, but Christ liveth in me," and we went to our camp beds around 4 a.m., having accepted the matter as settled by faith. We awoke no different; but I took a postcard and drew a tombstone on it, and wrote "Here lieth Norman Grubb, buried with Jesus."

— Once Caught, No Escape

"Christ in you, the hope of glory" — Colossians 1:27.

Two years later I was at home and visiting this same Mrs. Penn-Lewis whose little magazine had first awakened our interest. I had gone to her to talk over our perennial problem of tensions on the field, but I think she must have observed that beneath this I had my own need, for instead of talking about the problem she told me what happened when she had been "baptized with the Holy Ghost," as she called it, and the power of God had come on a group of young people with whom she talked that night. As she talked, it was like a great light lit within me, bringing the inner awareness which has never left me since, of Christ living in me; and living in such a sense that it was not I really doing the living, but He in me, in His Norman form. The scripture against which I had written my name and date that next morning in Bangbani's village had become permanently alive to me — this great Galatians 2:20.

There was a great deal I had not yet gotten into focus; those clarifications had to follow later; but one tremendous fact had become fact to me, and the passing years and deepening understandings have only underlined it as the fact of facts — that the secret of the universe, and the key to my own life, is simply the Person Himself in me; as Paul had put it, "The mystery hid from ages and generations but now made manifest to His saints . . . which is Christ in you."

— Once Caught, No Escape

"Do you not know that your body is a temple of the Holy Spirit?" — 1 Corinthians 6:19.

This had become the central fact of our lives — Pauline's and mine — which has to become so in every life, call it by what name we like: the Second Blessing, Entire Sanctification, the Baptism of the Spirit, the Fullness of the Spirit, the Second Rest, the Exchanged Life. We can only live by what becomes part of us, not by something imposed from without.

We have to go through our "wilderness" experience, all of us, redeemed but still regarding Him as separate from us; and we seeking to live the new standards of Christian living as best we can, but with constant failures, self-disgust, strains and stresses we cannot handle.

In the new birth, Christ has become real and personal to us as a Savior, the Spirit has borne inner witness with our spirit that we are the children of God. So again in this second realization, Christ has become known to us, not merely as the Savior from our sins but also as the One who is living our lives. We had a first collapse when we recognized our guilt as lost sinners and came to Him for salvation. We have a second collapse when, now redeemed, we discover our helplessness. First we had learned we *had* not done what we should. Now we learn that we *cannot* do what we should. And so, as after the first collapse we were conditioned to see and affirm His blood replacing our sins, now, after the second collapse, we are conditioned to see and affirm Himself replacing ourselves.

And the way into this full realization is by faith.

— *Once Caught, No Escape*

*"We were . . . buried with him through baptism into
death in order that, just as Christ was raised from the dead,
. . . we too may live a new life"* — Romans 6:4.

I am sure there are many redeemed people who, as I was,
have not moved into the fixed and final act of faith that
Galatians 2:20 is *the* fact in their lives (whatever way they
may verbalize to themselves their inner eternal union with
God) and He is the One living their lives. Or, if they have, it
does not seem real to them, and they doubt whether they
really have. But having once taken the step, the fact is the
fact without any inner consciousness of it. Even the desire
for an inner witness we have to die to, for it is a final form of
self which wants to have for itself. *I* know. *I* want to know.
And that very desire to know is the final form of unbelief,
because it means "I am not really sure and need to know."
So faith needs to take its stand on fact, not even by inner
witness: "If I make my bed in hell, Thou art there."

Yet it is the changeless law of faith that what we take
takes us; so when we no longer finally hang the validity of
our faith on the need of knowing, by some means we shall
become inwardly and fixedly aware of the Union. When we
no longer seek the awareness (the witness), we shall have it,
because then we are safe from immediately turning it into a
final form of self-exaltation: "Now *I* know." After we have
ceased to seek the awareness, we shall have the awareness.

To both Pauline and me this experience stands out in
our lives as next in importance to the time when we found
Christ.

— *Once Caught, No Escape*

"Make every effort to keep the unity of the Spirit through the bond of peace" — Ephesians 4:3.

I was very clear — and I believe it to be the New Testament principle — that a functioning fellowship of God's people, be they a church or a society, should manage their own affairs without outside control; and that this was the only basis of total fellowship, when all who have given themselves to a work have the same rights of unitedly exploring, discussing and deciding on their courses of action. The division between managers and managed is deadly and means death to total heart fellowship in freedom unless the managers are merely members of the managed, voluntarily chosen for management, and there be open opportunities for all concerned to thrash things out together.

So we began the system in which all full-time WEC* workers at the home base or on furlough from the fields form the executive staff for the affairs of that home base. We met one evening weekly and came to any necessary immediate decisions. As we expanded we had quarterly meetings, lasting for two or three days. The length of time gave us plenty of opportunity unhurriedly to seek God's mind, which is impossible if the Committee consists of a few busy people who can only meet for an hour or so. It also meant that our staff meetings could be for times of spiritual refreshment with the first hours given to unhurried prayer, sharing and fellowshiping around the Word.

— *Once Caught, No Escape*

*Worldwide Evangelization Crusade, now re-named WEC International.

"And my God will meet all your needs according to his glorious riches in Christ Jesus" — Philippians 4:19.

[After visiting my friend Rees Howells,] I was to go on to some meetings in a town about 200 miles away. I had only a sixpence in my pocket, but I felt sure God would send some money for the fare, probably by a letter. No letter came, but I knew I should stick to my appointment, and the money for the ticket would come somehow.

On the way to the station with Mr. Howells, we stopped at the post office and there was one letter — for him. We arrived at the station and he remained at the back with my bag while I went to the booking office. I had by then a shilling or two more, and what I intended to do was to ask how far that amount would take me. But being accustomed just to ask for a ticket to a place, I mentioned the place and asked for the ticket. Immediately I saw I was caught, and here the man was clipping the ticket. As he did so, and was handing it to me through the window, a hand reached over my shoulder and a voice said, "Here, pay the ticket with this," and there was a pound note. It was Mr. Howells. I said nothing, but wrote and told him later. He then told me that he also had nothing, but there was a pound in that letter. He thought he would slip that pound into my hand when we shook hands as the train left; but instead the Lord's word came plain to him, "Go up to the booking office and put down that pound for the ticket." That was as narrow a squeak as I have had.

— *Once Caught, No Escape*

*"Give, and it will be given to you. A good measure . . .
running over. . . . For with the measure you use, it will be
measured to you"* — Luke 6:38.

My first experience of receiving a personal gift when on
a deputation tour was in the earlier days when we still had
an English committee, and I was on furlough. I was sent for
a six months' tour of Canada in 1929. I was just then
learning and kind of experimenting in the personal life of
faith, and I asked the Committee for permission to take no
travel funds and to trust the Lord to supply *en route,*
sending home for the work any gifts, and looking to the
Lord directly for travel expenses. They did not like it too
well, and felt the mission would be let down if I were caught
somewhere penniless; so they insisted on my taking £5
(English money). The crisis moment came in Winnipeg,
when I had money I could send home for the work, but none
for my fare to Regina.

I was tempted to use the money. But to cut off the
temptation I took it to the post office and posted it.

As I put the letter in the mailbox, a car drove up and in it
was the treasurer of the church where I had been speaking,
and he said he was wanting to give me a check for the
mission and another for my travel needs — $85. I had never
before in my life received a gift like that!

The tour finished with all supplied, and as I boarded the
ship to return from Montreal, a friend put a £5 note in my
hand (or its equivalent). So I was able to return to the
Committee the £5 they had made me take!

—Once Caught, No Escape

"Whoever loves his brother lives in the light, and there is nothing in him to make him stumble" — 1 John 2:10.

We had heard from Edith Moules, our pioneer leprosy worker in the Congo, of the revolutionary change in her life and ministry through contacts with members of the Ruanda mission, so I had invited two of the missionaries, Joe Church and Bill Butler, to visit us in London for two days. This was followed later by a visit from two of the Africans, William Nagenda and Yosiya.

Both visits had a definite impact of the Spirit upon us. Their humility, simplicity and naturalness made a first impression. The hours spent with fifty of us were in simple fellowship, using the Scriptures with personal application to their own experiences.

Every new moving of the Spirit takes some new form and has both its adherents and critics. For myself, I began to see that what God was doing in Ruanda, and has continued to do, and which has spread to thousands around the world, is restoration at the heart of normal church life of the free fellowship type of meeting — the house groups when "they that fear the Lord speak often one to another," and when the often quoted "not forsaking the assembling of ourselves together" is given the full content of that statement which goes on to say *"but exhorting one another."* Not the preacher-congregation relationship, the one speaking, the others silent: not the teacher-taught; but where all are free to participate if they want.

— Once Caught, No Escape

*"I want to know Christ and the power of his resurrection
and the fellowship of sharing in his sufferings, becoming
like him in his death"* — Philippians 3:10.

The third crisis of my inner life came unexpectedly. I
could only be a dabbler in my busy life, but one book I
picked up was William James' *Varieties of Religious Experience*. It hit me like a boxer's knock-out blow. As I read the
psychological explanation of Paul's conversion on the road
at Damascus, it suddenly struck me that perhaps this was
only some inner change in Paul's psychological make-up,
and that there is no reason to postulate a divine revelation;
and that perhaps there really is no God — just the human
race. I don't think James himself meant this (I should have
gone on to finish the book); but here was I, a missionary of
fifteen years' standing, and a secretary of a missionary
society, and I was questioning the existence of God!

Life blanked out on me. I was a year away in different
places, partly in a seaside home lent us on the coast at
Southwold, which gave me plenty of chances of walking on
those breezy sand dunes.

My answer came through the mystics — particularly
from Jacob Boehme, most difficult to read because he could
not easily put the depths of his illuminations into readable
form. Christ incarnated, crucified, risen and glorified is
central to him; but he gathered together into one all the
apparently twisted strands of the meaning of life as no one
else. He is a last word to me. How I reveled in him and
William Law.

— *Once Caught, No Escape*

> *"But he who unites himself with the Lord is one with him in spirit"* — 1 Corinthians 6:17.

The heart of the stabilizing revelation to me, and what has become the total answer to all life for me, has been that there is only One Person in the universe, and that the whole universe is His myriad forms of Self-manifestation. Of course I am immediately dubbed a pantheist and am often asked if I am. Those who ask that either don't understand what a pantheist is or don't understand what I am saying about my own beliefs. Pantheism, according to its Greek derivation, means that everything is God. I am saying that everything is a form by which He manifests Himself, much as my body is not exactly I, but an outward form of the inner me. This fact, gleaned through Boehme, confirmed through the writings of many others, and with the foundations in Scripture, has given me my anchor. It has moved me on from my separated concepts — and this I think is the weakness of evangelical teaching — of a God apart from His creation "making" His creation, much as a carpenter appears to be apart from the table he makes.

These men point out that God was from the beginning of time revealed as Spirit, confirmed by Jesus who said outright, "God is Spirit"; and Spirit is the Person within, as our human spirits are within our bodies. So He as the author of the universe is the inner life of it. He is "the beyond in the midst," the Transcendent in the Immanent.

— *Once Caught, No Escape*

> *"He was appalled that there was no one to intercede"* —
> Isaiah 59:16.

The central truth, which the Holy Ghost gradually revealed to Mr. Howells, and which was the mainspring of his whole life's ministry, was that of intercession. The Spirit can be seen leading him into this in all His dealings with him, from the time He took full possession of him in the Llandrindod Convention, until, in his dealings with the consumptive woman, the meaning of intercession became fully clear. From then onward the Spirit was constantly leading him both to gain new positions as an intercessor and to reveal the precious truths which he had learned to others able to bear them. It will be useful, therefore, to stop a moment and to look a little more carefully into what is meant by being an intercessor.

That God seeks intercessors, but seldom finds them, is plain from the pain of His exclamation through Isaiah: "He saw that there was no man, and wondered that there was no intercessor"; and His protest of disappointment through Ezekiel: "I sought for a man among them, that should make up the hedge, and stand in the gap before Me for the land ... but I found none."

Perhaps believers in general have regarded intercession as just some form of rather intensified prayer. It is, so long as there is great emphasis on the word "intensified"; for there are three things to be seen in an intercessor which are not necessarily found in ordinary prayer: identification, agony, and authority.

— Rees Howells, Intercessor

> *"I have often gone without food. . . . Besides everything else, I face daily the pressure of my concern for all the churches"* — 2 Corinthians 11:27-28.

On the completion of six months' intercession for Captain Gosset by Easter, 1910, Rees Howells was free to go back to a normal life. But the Lord gave him the offer of continuing in a hidden ministry for another four months to gain some other places of intercession, one being for the child widows of India, whose sufferings were so great under the prevailing system. He chose to continue the hidden life.

The Lord then pointed out to him that these widows were living on only a handful of rice a day, and reminded him of the law of intercession, that before he could intercede for them he must live like them. So his diet was to be one meal of oats (porridge) every two days.

"What pangs of hunger I had," he said afterward. "The Lord doesn't make it easy for you. He doesn't carry you through on eagle's wings, as it were. The victory is that you come up through it."

He saw that the point of fasting is to bring the body into subjection to the Spirit. "Each fast, if carried out under the guidance of the Holy Spirit, means that our bodies become more equipped to carry burdens."

It is a significant fact that with India's Independence and new Constitution in 1949, at least a legal change has been made in the laws of inheritance for the benefit of widows, and that a new day has dawned in the general emancipation of women.

— *Rees Howells, Intercessor*

"The spirit . . . in us tends towards envy, but he gives us more grace" — James 4:5-6.

One evening when his friend and he were speaking in the open air, the friend preached first, and the Holy Ghost so used him that Mr. Howells began to wonder how he would ever preach after him (he was not a gifted open-air speaker), and that grew into a thought of jealousy. "No one knew it," he said, "but that night the Holy Ghost whipped me and humbled me to the dust. He showed me the ugliness of it and how the devil would take advantage of such a thing to damage the souls of those people. I never saw a thing I hated more than that, and I could have cursed myself for it. 'Didn't you come out to the open air for these souls to be blessed?' He said. 'And if so, what difference does it make through whom I bless them?' He told me to confess the sin to my friend.

"From that day on I have not dared to cherish a thought of jealousy, because not once did the Holy Ghost go back on His word to me. Whatever warning of punishment He had given me, if I disobeyed, I had to pay the full penalty. A person might think it was a life of bondage and fear. It would be to the flesh, but to the new man in Christ it was a life of fullest liberty. At first I had a tendency to pity myself and grumble at the penalty for disobedience, but as I saw that I must either lose this corrupt self here or bear the shame of its exposure hereafter, I began to side with the Holy Spirit against myself, and looked on the stripping as a deliverance rather than a loss."

— *Rees Howells, Intercessor*

"*Religion that God our Father accepts . . . is this: to look after orphans*" — James 1:27.

One night by his bedside he found God's love pouring into him — His love for the fatherless. There were no bounds to it. It went out towards the four little orphan children he knew — nothing now could stop him going to live with them. He felt that they had a claim on him. He put it this way: "Any child without parents has a claim on God to be a Father to him, so these four orphans had a claim on the Holy Spirit who was to be a Father to them through me." But divine love could not be limited to four. He said, "I felt I loved every little child in the world that had no one to look after it. It was the love of God flowing through me."

However, on the very day that he was to go and offer to care for them, three sisters of their mother said they would like to take them and give them a home. The Lord showed him that that was His provision for them, but that he had gained the position of "a father to the orphans."

The proof of the reality of this was to be seen in the coming years. No one could live with Mr. Howells in his later days in the Bible College and see him and Mrs. Howells taking and loving children of missionaries and Jewish refugee children, some in their own home, and many in the happy home for missionaries' children nearby, without realizing the extent to which God had indeed given them the father and mother heart, which could gather, not four, but seventy, under their wings.

— *Rees Howells, Intercessor*

"I am the Lord who heals you" — Exodus 15:26.

An incident took place which Mr. Howells always considered to be one of the greatest experiences of his life. Up on the Black Mountain, his invalid Uncle Dick was still living at Pentwyn, the grandparents' old home. On New Year's Day, before going to visit him, Rees Howells ran upstairs to his room. It was his habit before going out to ask the Lord to shelter him under the Blood and to lead him to anyone who needed his help. But that morning, quite unexpectedly, the Holy Spirit spoke to him: "It is the Father's will to restore your uncle." It seemed "too good to be true, and too great to believe" — that after all these thirty years his uncle should walk again as other men.

When he arrived at Pentwyn, his uncle, who was always eagerly awaiting his weekly visit, asked him the usual question: "Anything new from the Lord?" "Yes," answered Mr. Howells, "and it is about you." "About me!" was the surprised reply. "Have I done anything wrong?" "No, but the Lord has told me that it is His will to heal you." We can only imagine what that news must have sounded like in his ears. All he could say was that he must go out and see the Lord about it. After a quarter of an hour in the little garden at the back, he returned with his face radiant. "Yes," he said, "I am to be healed in four and a half months; that will be on May 15."

— *Rees Howells, Intercessor*

"Everything is possible for him who believes" —
Mark 9:23.

Two weeks before the date of the healing, the Lord made it known to Mr. Howells that he was to leave home for a few months, and that after telling his uncle, he was not to visit him again until after the healing, because it was not God's will that any man should take praise from it. When he went down to Pentwyn, his uncle asked, with the glory of the Lord on his face, "Has the Lord told you why He said four and a half months, and May 15? It will be Whitsunday. And He is healing me in memory of Pentecost. He has told me that I am to be healed at 5 o'clock in the morning and I am to walk to chapel and back (a distance of three miles) for the first time in thirty years!"

On the night before Whitsunday, his uncle was as bad as ever. Every night between 1 and 2 a.m. he had to get up, being unable to remain lying down, and he had to do it that morning. It was the last attack of the enemy, who whispered, "It is all up. You are just the same now as any other night." But one minute is quite long enough for the Lord. He went back to bed, and a deep sleep came over him. The next thing he heard was the clock striking five, and he found himself perfectly restored. He called the family and there was such a solemn awe in the house that they were afraid to move, realizing that God Himself had done that great act that very hour.

He arrived at the church, and they had "another cause for thanksgiving on that Thanksgiving Sunday."
— *Rees Howells, Intercessor*

"I have become all things to all men so that by all possible means I might save some" — 1 Corinthians 9:22.

The Spirit led His servant more and more into the secret of intercession — the identification of the intercessor with the ones for whom he prays. Now He called him to share in the physical sufferings of the destitute, which would touch his body.

The Government lodging houses provided two meals a day for tramps, and the Lord told Rees Howells to live in the same way — on two meals of bread and cheese and soup.

He had one meal at 6:30 in the morning, and the other at 5:30 in the evening after his day's work in the pit and before he started for the village. It was a battle at first, both physically and mentally, eating at the same table with the others and having different food. "There was great suspicion about where this new thing would end," he said, "and what my object was in doing it. Neither they nor myself had ever seen a man called to fasting, and they thought the 'experiment' would soon come to an end. But in less than a fortnight the Lord had so changed my appetite that I preferred those two meals a day to the four I used to have. That craving for food was taken out of me, and through the whole period my health was better than anyone else's. I never had a shade of a headache, and my body was as fit as could be." He lived like that for two and a half years.

— *Rees Howells, Intercessor*

"When a man's ways are pleasing to the Lord, he makes even his enemies live at peace with him" — Proverbs 16:7.

It is hard to realize that throughout these three years of intense conflict and many triumphs of the Spirit, Rees Howells was working daily at one of the hardest jobs a man can do — down the mine, cutting coal. His was no sheltered, monastic life, but a walk in the Spirit right in the world, though never of it. During the "spell" down the mine — a period of ten to fifteen minutes when the men got accustomed to the darkness — if he was there, not an obscene word would pass their lips.

The impression he made on many of those young fellows down the pit can best be gauged from an incident about ten years later, when he returned to Brynamman from the African mission field. At a crowded meeting in his home church the front row was filled with those same men, many of whom seldom came near a place of worship. One young miner, Mr. Tommy Howells, who had recently been converted, was so touched by the practical realty he saw in that life "full of faith and the Holy Ghost" that in that meeting their hearts became knit together as Jonathan's to David's, and for all the years that followed "Tommy" became his devoted co-worker and prayer-partner.

— *Rees Howells, Intercessor*

"God is able to make all grace abound to you so that in all things at all times, having all that you need, you will abound in every good work" — 2 Corinthians 9:8.

There came a further call, which was to loosen him yet more from his old moorings. He was out on his favorite Black Mountain, where the silent spaces were so often the gate of heaven to him, and the Lord spoke: "For seven hours a day you are earning two shillings an hour," He said, "but you need not work for an earthly master any longer. Would you like to give these seven hours a day to work for Me?"

Rees Howells was standing on a small wooden bridge across a little stream, and the Lord asked him, "Will you give your word to Me that you won't look to another person to keep you? If so, put up your hand and repeat, 'I shall not take from a thread to a shoe-latchet from any person, unless the Lord tells me.'"

[He did so and also added:] "I do believe You are able to keep me better than that mining company." It was no mean stand of faith, because Mr. Howells had long since ceased that active ministry in the mission which might have led people to give to him. The moment he made this vow, the Lord drove home the reality of it to him by saying, "Remember this: you must never take a meal at home without paying for it, or your brothers could say they were keeping you." It was not that the family would have minded helping him, but the Lord was impressing on him that the real life of faith meant receiving all that he needed from God and paying his way, while using all his hours for God.

— *Rees Howells, Intercessor*

"*Having nothing, yet possessing everything*" —
2 Corinthians 6:10.

[Before leaving Wales for South Africa, Mr. Howells wrote:] "We went out to breakfast with some friends at Llanelly, and then walked back to the station still not with sufficient money. And now the time for the train had come. The Spirit then spoke to me and said, 'If you had money what would you do?' 'Take my place in the queue at the booking office,' I said. 'Well, are you not preaching that My promises are equal to current coin? You had better take your place in the queue.' So there was nothing I could do except obey. There were about a dozen people before me, passing by the booking office one by one. The devil kept on telling me, 'Now you have only a few people in front of you, and when your turn comes, you will have to walk through. You have preached much about Moses with the Red Sea in front and the Egyptians behind; but now you are the one who is shut in.' 'Yes, shut in,' I answered, 'but like Moses, I'll be gloriously led out!'

"When there were only two before me, a man stepped out of the crowd and said, 'I'm sorry I can't wait any longer. I must open my shop.' He put thirty shillings in my hand! It was most glorious. After I had the tickets, the people who came with us to the train began to give gifts to us, but the Lord had held them back until we had been tested. We were singing all the way to London!"

— *Rees Howells, Intercessor*

"After they prayed, the place . . . was shaken. And they were all filled with the Holy Spirit" — Acts 4:31.

In the meetings that Mr. Howells took he continued to speak to them about Revival, and in six weeks the Spirit began to move upon the Christians. We have Mr. Howells's own account of the days that followed:

"The Sunday was October 10 — my birthday — and as I preached in the morning you could feel the Spirit coming on the congregation. In the evening, down He came. I shall never forget it. He came upon a young girl, Kufase by name, who had fasted for three days under conviction that she was not ready for the Lord's coming. As she prayed she broke down crying, and within five minutes the whole congregation were on their faces crying to God. Like lightning and thunder the power came down. I had never seen this even in the Welsh Revival. I had only heard about it with Finney and others. Heaven had opened, and there was no room to contain the blessing. I lost myself in the Spirit and prayed as much as they did. All I could say was, 'He has come.' We went on until late in the night; we couldn't stop the meeting. What He told me before I went to Africa was actually taking place, and that within six weeks. You can never describe those meetings when the Holy Spirit comes down. I shall never forget the sound in the district that night — praying in every kraal."

— *Rees Howells, Intercessor*

"My ears had heard of you but now my eyes have seen you. Therefore I despise myself and repent in dust and ashes" — Job 42:5-6.

From the time of special dedication on March 29, 1936, when so many of the College,* both staff and students, laid their lives on the altar as intercessors, the Spirit was at work. Dr. Kingsley C. Priddy, M.B., B.S., D.T.M. and H., a member of the staff and later Headmaster of the School, gives the following account of those days:

"He did not come like a rushing mighty wind. But gradually the Person of the Holy Ghost filled all our thoughts, His Presence filled all the place, and His light seemed to penetrate all the hidden recesses of our hearts. He was speaking through the Director in every meeting, but it was in the quiet of our own rooms that He revealed Himself to many of us. We felt the Holy Spirit had been a real Person to us before; as far as we knew we had received Him; and some of us had known much of His operations in and through our lives. But now the revelation of His Person was so tremendous that all our previous experiences seemed as nothing. There was no visible apparition, but He made Himself so real to our spiritual eyes that it was a 'face to face' experience. We said like Job, 'I have heard of Thee by the hearing of the ear; but now mine eye seeth Thee'; and like him we cried, 'Wherefore I abhor myself and repent in dust and ashes.'

"In the light of His purity, it was not so much *sin* we saw as *self*. Lust and self-pity were discovered in places where we had never suspected them."

— *Rees Howells, Intercessor*

*The Bible College of Wales, founded by Mr. Howells.

> *"Everything is possible for him who believes"*
> — Mark 9:23.

There is a school of faith, and there is a life of faith. At school we are private individuals: we learn, we experiment, we try things out by ourselves and on ourselves, we gradually grasp a technique. In life we take responsibility, we are in the public eye; other lives depend on us; we are supposed to know our job and apply our knowledge; the wheels of our particular industry are kept going by us. My years in the school of faith lasted till 1931, my thirteenth year as a missionary.

As I now look back, I can see quite clearly when that transition took place in my experience; the school was left (although in another sense we are very much permanent pupils), the life of faith begun.

With the key to my inner problems in my hands, through the grace of God and illumination of the Spirit a clear-cut position of faith was taken in a certain matter, under pressure of the Spirit, involving my wife and myself to our financial limit. There is no need to go into details, which were comparatively trivial. The duration of the test was six months. The day of crisis came in the middle, when I almost succumbed and was only saved by walking to the post office and sending off a letter which once again staked everything on God's faithfulness. The deliverance actually began to come to me within ten minutes, on the pavement outside that post office, starting with a trickle and rising to a flood. It was all very mundane, but to me it was a landmark.

— *The Law of Faith*

Faith

"Anyone who comes to [God] must believe . . . that he rewards those who earnestly seek him" — Hebrews 11:6.

Ninety-nine per cent of life consists of God's endless giving. One per cent consists of taking. Both are essential, but in that proportion. We are here stressing faith, for our object is to analyze and examine the way man receives and uses what he is given. That is not meant to give glory to faith or credit to faith, as if faith produced anything. Faith supplies the 1 per cent. That is all. God supplies the 99 per cent — to Him is the glory, in Him is the grace, for Him is our love. (Indeed, properly speaking, the 100 per cent is His, for faith itself is a God-given, natural faculty.) Our consideration is only centered round the 1 per cent, yet that must be considered — because experience shows that so many Christians flounder not because they do not know the grace of God revealed in Christ but because they do not know how, steadily, consistently, to appropriate, use, and apply what they are given, according to the set laws of appropriation — of faith.

God made man in His image, free in will and choice, able to accept, able to reject; for God seeks the worship, love and service of willing hearts. He gives, He presses all upon us — His gifts, His Son, Himself. But we must take. Food He provides, but we must take and eat. Air, but we must breathe.

— The Law of Faith

"Jehoshaphat resolved to inquire of the Lord" —
2 Chronicles 20:3.

Jehoshaphat "set himself to seek the Lord." He separated himself by fasting from all that would distract, publicly reasoned with God as to why He should help, and with a final admission of helplessness and bewilderment asked God to work.

Those who would walk in any degree a sure path of faith must learn to do the same. The habit of retirement must be acquired. No matter how busy the life, time must always be found — and can be found, for men will always find time for what they really want to do. And in that quiet corner each situation must be weighed. We may appear to do the talking and God the listening, as with Jehoshaphat. We may spread the matter before God. We may reason as to why He should act for us. We may search into motives. We may make supplication. But really it is God getting His own mind through to us, the Spirit helping our infirmities, for we know not what to pray for as we ought; until gradually or suddenly assurance is ours, boldness is ours, heaven is open to us, the throne is a throne of grace, and we are seated with Him in the place of plenty and authority. The Spirit has prayed through us according to the Father's will. The circuit is complete: from the Father to our minds by the Spirit; from our minds back to the Father by the Spirit. The hidden power is released.

— *The Law of Faith*

"We have gained access by faith" — Romans 5:2.

The pull of faith, its attraction and fascination, never left me. It had become a deep inner conviction. I had glimpsed and tasted. It is my belief that in each member of Christ's body, from the time of the new birth, the Holy Spirit begins to develop some special characteristic through which God may be glorified in a particular way, some aspect of His grace and truth through which the whole body may be edified and enlightened. Such are the gifts of the Spirit, about which more will be said later.

In my own case, I humbly believe that it was God who maintained in me this special thirst and attraction for the way of faith, this readiness to absorb all light concerning it, and to venture my life in the exercise of it. Real opportunities were bound to come, as well as real enlightenment, at the right moment, and that moment was when I was ready to see and take them. For the real fact was that those intervening years had first to be spent in internal adjustments; the secrets of faith had to be discovered and applied in the solution of my own inner problems, in the satisfaction of my own soul-thirst, in the snapping of the chain of my own self-centeredness, in the transference of oppressing heart burdens to the One who had given Himself to bear them.

A faith that works first in our own lives can then, and only then, be applied to the problems around us.

— *The Law of Faith*

"Against all hope, Abraham in hope believed" —
Romans 4:18.

The best analysis of laboring and resting faith in the
Bible is the description given in Romans 4:16-22 of Abraham's pioneer act of faith. We there see the process outlined.
We see faith's beginning and foundation in a discovery of
the will of God; in this case it was a word from God: "So
shall thy seed be." For faith always comes by hearing, and
hearing by the word of God.

The second stage is the counter-attack of the visible — in
this case his and Sarah's age and physical condition. This he
countered by turning his back on the visible; a deliberately
considered act, for "he considered not his own body now
dead, neither yet the deadness of Sarah's womb." This is
described as being "not weak in faith"; he did not just lie
down under existing circumstances.

In the third stage, he passes from occupation with things
earthly to things heavenly. "He staggered not at the promise
of God through unbelief." Now the muscles of his faith are
rapidly gaining strength.

At the fourth stage, a radical change takes place: the
burden and struggle is replaced by a burst of praise "giving
glory to God."

At last, at the fifth stage, the topmost rung of the ladder
of faith is reached: full assurance, "being fully persuaded
that what He had promised, He was able also to perform."
Now he *knows*, now he *has*; perfect faith has come.

— *The Law of Faith*

"By faith Abraham . . . by faith Moses" —
Hebrews 11:8,24.

The right and full use of faith is the mainspring of every spiritual achievement. Preeminently this is so, of course, in the attaining of spiritual objectives, in the salvation of souls, in revival, in all concerns of the church of Christ. But by no means exclusively so. Faith is shown to be the principle of effective action, of supply, of the solution of all problems, in every single thing, small or great, temporal and material, in the home or in the business, at work or at play, that affects a Christian's daily life. It is necessary to say this because many people have got the idea that victories, deliverances, or the supply of need by faith are privileges confined to those set apart for the Christian ministry and not to be experienced in the ordinary home and the everyday life.

Watch the men of the Bible and it will be seen how central faith is in all their actions and attitudes. That unique chapter, Hebrews 11, the only approximation in the whole Bible to a biographical outline of Bible characters, clinches the matter for us. It is written for the one purpose of showing that faith was the dynamic of all they did. Abraham's whole life centered around obtaining the heir through whom was to come the promised race, and the birth of that son was simply and solely an achievement of faith. Moses, in leading the revolt against the Egyptian oppressor, was but a straw fighting against a millrace until he learned the secrets of faith.

— *The Law of Faith*

"I have not found such great faith even in Israel"
— Luke 7:9.

Most significant is the name that John gives Jesus: "The Word." The Word which created all things. "The Word made flesh." Nowhere does the authority of the spoken word of faith come out so clearly as in His life, which was a constant series of such spoken words with their miraculous results. To the waves: "Peace, be still." To a fever: a rebuke. To the fig tree: a curse. To the evil spirit: "I charge thee, come out of him." To the nobleman: "Go thy way, thy son liveth." To the cripple: "Rise, take up thy bed and walk." To the centurion: "As thou hast believed, so be it done unto thee." To the leper: "Be thou clean." At the grave of Lazarus, to His Father: "I thank Thee that Thou hast heard me"; then, to Lazarus: "Come forth." No wonder they were amazed at the authority with which He spoke. No wonder we echo the officers' words: "Never man spake like this Man."

The centurion seemed to be the one person who sensed the power that resided in that word, when he so boldly broke through the customary idea that the physical presence of the Savior was necessary and suggested that He need not come in person to his house, but just speak the word and his servant would be healed. It was a penetration into the secrets of faith which just thrilled the Savior, and brought those words of highest commendation to His lips: "Verily I say unto you, I have not found so great faith, no, not in Israel."

— *The Law of Faith*

"God said, 'Let there be light'" — Genesis 1:3.

If it is asked why there must be such emphasis on the spoken word of faith, the answer may be partly beyond our reach. It is hidden in the mysteries of creation. All we are told is that the Son is the Word, and that by the Word all things are made — The Word, presumably, of the Father. Therefore we know that the spoken word (not the deed) is the creating power; the word is antecedent to the deed, and therefore more powerful and more important. Indeed, the word produces the deed. Thus the first act of God of which there is record is a spoken word which began the creating process: "Let there be light," and there was light. And this was followed by six other "words," each of which produced a corresponding new state in creation.

Now a word is a crystallization of a thought. Thought is fluid, unformed. We turn things over in our mind. The word gives definition to the thought. The spoken word, given in the form of a command or decision, expresses the idea in the mind, digested, clarified, authoritative. A man's word, we say, is his bond. A general's word is his command, after he has weighed all the various possible disposals of his forces. An architect's word is his plan. An engineer's word is his blueprint. It is final, creative. It sets action in motion. James tells us of the power for good or evil of the spoken word which sets the course of nature on fire.

— *The Law of Faith*

"The word is near you, . . . the word of faith" —
Romans 10:8.

When Peter commented on the withered fig tree to
which [Jesus] had said the day before: "No man eat fruit of
thee hereafter forever," He told them to "have faith in God"
and they could do the same. In other words, that the way He
performed His miracles was by this word of faith, which
they could use just as much as He; but He then went on to
make clear that it was a *spoken word* of faith, and not just
an aspiration, request or hope; for they were to *say* to a
mountain "Be thou removed," and not to doubt in their
hearts, and they would have whatsoever they said. He
explained at the same time that such a spoken word of faith
was the central act that mattered in the prayer life, for He
divided the process of prayer into four component parts —
desire, request, faith that the thing is done, and realization;
but all is made parenthetic to the central emphasis, the
summit of the mountain: "Believe that ye receive" then and
there. On one other occasion He stressed the same truth
when He said that with faith as a grain of mustard seed they
could "say" the word of command to a sycamore tree and it
would obey.

The actual expression "the word of faith" is used by Paul
(Romans 10:8) when expounding the faith that justifies; and
here he brings out exactly the same truth: that faith is
something which must have plain-spoken expression. Hope
or desire is not enough. The prayer of request is not enough.
Not even the belief in the heart. What is believed in the inner
man must issue from the mouth.

— *The Law of Faith*

> *"When Jesus saw their faith, he said, 'Friend, your sins are forgiven!'"* — Luke 5:20.

Nothing could be more remarkable than [Jesus'] constant efforts to stimulate faith in His disciples and to impress upon them its working principles. It was to faith that He attributed His "mighty works"; not *His* faith, but that of the suppliants. To the centurion who asked Him not to come to his house but just to speak the word, He said: "I have not found so great faith, no, not in Israel." To the woman who touched the hem of His garment: "Daughter, go in peace, thy faith hath made thee whole." When the four men let their paralyzed friend through the roof, Jesus pardoned and healed him "when He saw their faith." To blind Bartimeus it was: "What wilt thou that I shall do unto thee?" And then, "Go thy way. Thy faith hath made thee whole." By the Syrophenician woman He allowed Himself to be compelled into action with the comment, "O woman, great is thy faith: be it unto thee even as thou wilt." Others He stirred into faith. He asked the two blind men: "Believe ye that I am able to do this?" To Jairus, when the servants came to say that his daughter was dead, He said: "Fear not, only believe." He told the father of the lunatic son: "If thou canst believe, all things are possible to him that believeth"; and afterwards told the disciples that they had failed to cure the boy because of their unbelief.

— *The Law of Faith*

"Abraham reasoned that God could raise the dead" —
Hebrews 11:19.

There is a laboring faith and there is a resting faith.
What Jesus called little faith, for instance, was the action of
the disciples in the storm, when He lay asleep on a pillow in
the boat and they awoke Him, crying out: "Master, carest
Thou not that we perish?" The disciples believed that He
could save them but doubted if He wanted to! There was
faith, but of a very watery consistency.

Great faith was what Jesus called the attitude of the
centurion, for he not only believed that Christ's word was
with saving power, but that He would speak if asked to. He
believed Christ could and would. But perfect faith is the
description given of Abraham's sacrifice of Isaac. There it is
seen that when God told Abraham to go and offer his only
son as a burnt-offering upon one of the mountains of
Moriah, Abraham obeyed. It is plain that he had full intention of carrying out God's word to the letter, for he not only
bound his son and laid him on the altar, but also raised the
knife to plunge it in him; and not till then, in the last split
second, did God withhold his hand.

And the comment in Hebrews 11 is that so sure was he of
God's promise of seed through Isaac that he knew if he slew
him at God's word God would raise him up again. In other
words, the faith of Abraham always *had* his son and never
let him go. God not only could and would, but could and
would and had. It was all settled before he started out. He
and the lad would come back.

                                              — *The Law of Faith*

Faith **April 12**

> *"Jesus said, 'My kingdom is not of this world'"*
> — John 18:36.

If faith honors God, it also puts sinews into man; as great liners have stabilizers for foul weather, so faith gives the apparently frail ship of God its even keel in the stormy ocean of a chaotic world.

The life of faith, however, has an uncomfortable shock for comfort-loving flesh. The history of the early church, the testimony of the apostles, gives no ground for equating earthly prosperity with Christian discipleship; and we have learned through these years that a life of faith by no means gives over-abundance or even simply an abundance. It is much more of a shoestring walk. Those who have not actually walked this way but have theoretical ideas about it seem surprised and suspect that a person lacks faith if all that is needed does not pour in as a continuous stream. The truth is that the true reward of faith is not material supplies, but Christ as its treasure both in ourselves and transmitted to others. This is the abundance and superabundance we seek, and which the New Testament promises. To us this is both Scriptural and logical. "My kingdom is not of this world"; "choosing rather to suffer affliction with the people of God, than to enjoy the pleasures of sin for a season"; "esteeming the reproach of Christ greater riches than the treasures in Egypt"; "strangers and pilgrims."

— The Four Pillars of WEC

"There is one body and one Spirit, . . . one Lord, . . . one God and Father of all" — Ephesians 4:4-6.

An important product of the faith life is a total dependence upon God. Each person remains inviolably as an individual before God. To a certain point, individual independence is voluntarily surrendered to make communal interdependence a possibility. Teamwork demands team loyalty, team discipline, team leadership. But that is only a relative horizontal relationship, never to rival the absolute vertical relationship between the individual and God; and living by faith preserves the sacredness of the latter.

Money is power. He who controls finances, controls lives. If down underneath, the heart reliance of a servant of God is on his board or denomination for his livelihood and daily bread, then there is bound to creep in a human subservience. If down at the grass roots God alone is the provider, ultimate allegiance is rendered only to Him. It puts a freshness into mission relationships — not the dullness of compulsory duty, but the spontaneity of freely rendered service. It is a preservative against the danger of mission magnification. If the Society is our life-center and life-security, we shall magnify the organization and seek its prosperity. If God is our life-center, we shall not make too much of any human organization, ours or others, for we shall only boast of one real membership — in the universal church of Christ.

— *The Four Pillars of WEC*

*"By faith Abraham . . . obeyed and went even though he
did not know where he was going"* — Hebrews 11:8.

The "way of faith" is the only unfettered, unconquerable
principle of advance. If with God's plan God's supply can be
taken for granted, we need have only one concern — what is
His plan? That is plain enough in all the biographies of the
men of faith in the Bible. Once they had heard God's voice,
the very principle of faith demanded that they act independ-
ently of visible human resources. They must call the things
that be not as though they are. For faith is an absolute; what
Paul calls faith unfeigned, and Jesus calls the single eye.

If it is faith in God, and God is the invisible source of all
that is visible and both creates and manipulates His visible
creation to His own ends, then unfeigned faith in God
confines the believer to God. It shuts the door on reliance
upon what are only God's creatures or on changing human
events of which God is in ultimate control. The man of faith
breathes the fresh air of eternity away up above the fogs and
mists of time. He moves in the freedom of the heavenlies.
The consequences are obvious. The human spirit, in union
with God's Spirit, in disunion with any other kind of spirit,
leaps out in the vision and commission of the Eternal. What
it sees, it declares with the word of faith — against all
appearances. What it declares, it sets about doing.

— *The Four Pillars of WEC*

"Unless a kernel of wheat falls to the ground and dies, it remains only a single seed" — John 12:24.

Faith is the whole man in action; therefore it involves our bodies, and there is a sense in which we answer our own prayers. "It all depends on God and it all depends on me" has truth in it. That is the faith James speaks of which without works is dead: "I will show thee my faith by my works." Having spoken the word of faith, we expect to be involved to any limit in fulfilling it. Salvation was by the offering of the *body* of Jesus. If love belongs to need, and we are an expression of that eternal love, then it will involve our time, our money, our physical labors, our homes, our earthly security.

There is a law, a principle at work in this, to which Jesus referred when He said, "Except a corn of wheat fall into the ground and die, it abideth alone; but if it die, it bringeth forth much fruit." Whatever form it may assume, this we take for granted — that the whole of us will be involved. Not by self-effort, not by pressing ourselves to get into action, but we shall find ourselves compelled: "the love of Christ constraineth me." We have to, and love to, right in the midst of the cost of it. For the joy set before us, we too endure our cross. Faith works by love in action. Yet through it all we know it is not our efforts, our so-called sacrifices, which bring the results. It is the faith which even through years of waiting has already declared the outcome.

— *Once Caught, No Escape*

"It is with your mouth that you confess and are saved"
— Romans 10:10.

Inner belief must be translated into outer action by "the word of faith." We confess with our mouth the Lord Jesus. We plainly and publicly state, as our God leads on the suitable occasions, what is our new relationship in Christ. We give Him the glory by "the sacrifice of praise," that is, the fruit of our lips giving thanks to His name. It is a sacrifice of self to praise and testify to our death and resurrection with Him when we may not feel any different!

Paul puts remarkable emphasis on what he calls this "word of faith." He makes it the central act of believing, for faith is a trinity of thought, word and deed. We first think a thing over and come to a conclusion about whether we believe it and want it. We then crystallize our thinking by a decisive "word." This is the central act of faith. We see it in the blueprint of the draftsman, the plan of the architect, the orders of the commanding officer. In each case it is their "word of faith" which commits them. There is no going back now: it is the creative word, for as is the plan, so will be the house; as are the orders, so will be the battle. It is the one way of creation from eternity.

— *The Liberating Secret*

"We live by faith, not by sight" — 2 Corinthians 5:7.

We must "labor to enter into that rest." Through faith and patience we inherit the promises. By every means in his power Satan will seek to cut the lifeline of our still flimsy faith. He will trip us into sudden sin and then mock our newly-made confessions of identification with Christ. He will lie to us that we are not different. He will tempt us through all our appetites and faculties, and then tell us to stop talking such foolishness as that we died with Christ.

But we must learn to "walk by faith." Not just to take the first step of faith but to take a million steps, and then another million! For faith, as we have already pointed out, is a God-given natural faculty. Just as every natural action is taken by faith, so every human attainment is gained by faith but only gained painfully and slowly. The first steps in learning a trade or a language are very hesitating. Often it seems to us we shall never get hold of it. The thread of our faith often wears very thin, but it must not snap. If it does, we give up. If it doesn't, we crawl on, until, almost unrealized by ourselves, a natural miracle has taken place. What we were seeking to get hold of has got hold of us! Effort and strain have disappeared. A long series of separate efforts have changed into a natural habit. That is the process of faith.

— *The Liberating Secret*

"Faith is being sure of what we hope for" —
Hebrews 11:1.

Faith does not vaguely desire a thing, it makes it its own. "Faith is the substance of things hoped for." To it the unsubstantial becomes substantial, and aspiration becomes realization. "Faith is the evidence of things not seen." To it the invisible becomes visible. In the natural realm, to have faith in a thing means that we already believe in it, and set about using it. We have an armchair in our room. We can argue till doomsday that it will or won't hold a person who sits on it. Either "belief" may be true, but quite useless. Then we sit on it. That is faith, and that ends all argument. Our faith makes our belief substantial. It does hold us and we know it. The chair was always a substantial fact whether we believed it or not. But it was our faith that made it substantial to us. The chair was always capable of doing the job for which it was made, but it was only our faith which gave us personal evidence of that fact.

So faith is not the fact in itself. Facts ARE, whether we accept them or not; but faith alone makes them facts in our personal experience, and therefore proven facts to us. We *must* use faith. We *do* use faith. No man has ever lived his life without it. Faith alone makes all the facts of life, known and unknown, facts of personal experience to each of us. We breathe by faith, and the air is ours; we eat by faith, and the food nourishes us.

— *The Liberating Secret*

"His incomparably great power for us who believe"
— Ephesians 1:19.

Belief is mental acceptance. We believe in thousands of things as realities, but that belief does not produce in us a personal experience of them. Experience is a product of a deeper level. That comes from the center of our personality, our human spirits, our ego, where knowledge and desire combine to motivate acts of will. That is freedom in action. That is faith in contrast to belief. Something is available —take the simplest —food, air, a chair; my belief takes me that far. But if I am to choose something, I must desire it. So to availability is added desirability; and we humans are so made that we are a continual stream of desires, for we are made of love.

Now when a thing is available and desirable, is it reliable? At that spot we have to stop short. Nothing in the universe can be proved by reason and observation to be reliable. Reason can take us up to the edge. It can make things appear the nearest thing to a certainty; but it cannot prove things as a certainty. No one can prove that the food I eat will agree with me, or the chair I sit on will hold me, or the house I buy will suit me.

Now comes the moment — the moment of faith, the moment of freedom in action. I have to leap into the unknown. I have to go beyond reason. From the center of my personality, called in the Bible my spirit or my heart, I have to make a deliberate choice, a leap into the dark.

— *The Spontaneous You*

"Before they call I will answer" — Isaiah 65:24.

We fallen humans, while we mistakenly regard ourselves as in such a distant relationship to God, look on faith or prayer as a desperate means of getting God to intervene in a situation. We call on Him, or with a great effort put faith in Him, as if He were asleep regarding our need and we must awaken Him to send the supply! But the real truth is that He is awake and we are asleep! He is busy awakening us by putting us in the place of need. It has always been the Father in action, the One with the eternal love-purpose of manifesting Himself in some new forms of goodness. Like air presses on us so many pounds to the square inch, so He presses Himself through His sons, and not they getting or arousing Him into action. The sons let the Father through; and they do it by speaking the word of faith. By that word, the Spirit brings the Father into some new form of visibility. So, "Let there be light, and there was light," and "The Spirit of God moved upon the face of the waters." Just as by our human word our human spirits go into action.

That is why faith is effortless, not sweating at it; for, as we say, faith is not our trying to drag God on to a scene to get Him to supply a need; that comes from our illusory concept of God at a distance and we by ourselves in a tough spot. But it is recognizing that He is there with the supply before there is the need: "Before they call, I will answer"! We as sons speak that word of faith, "Let there be" — and the manifestation comes in His way, not ours.

— *Who Am I?*

"Faith comes from hearing the message" —
Romans 10:17.

Certain facts are presented to us through the revelation of God's Word. The birth of faith is the inward conviction that these are truth for me. Therefore I receive and believe them, and in doing so transcend all natural doubts either about the truth of them or their efficacy in my own life. I transcend the doubts by replacing them by deliberate faith; actually, their opposition is what gives sinews to my faith.

The subtlest form of doubt will be psychological, the questioning in my own mind whether these things are really so since I don't feel or see their effect on me, because they still appear unreal to me, and so on. But I learn by these very pressures that what has appeared at first to be *my* faith in these facts was in reality a faith imparted to me — God's faith — without which I should never have been able to perceive or receive these facts as facts. Therefore I relax in the midst of such doubts and questionings, not trying to believe, but affirming that it has been taken out of my hands. God has done the believing in me; then leave Him to it, for the facts are that He Himself now lives His own life in me.

— *God Unlimited*

> *"Let us . . . make every effort to enter that rest"* —
> Hebrews 4:11.

But it is possible that you are not really believing in God's impossible word. You think you are, but you are really believing in what you think about that word. I told you that it costs everything to believe. "Let us labor therefore . . . lest any man fall after the same example of unbelief." Faith crosses an unbridgeable gulf into the invisible, unknowable, impossible. It crosses just by believing it has crossed, because He says so, and He is the bridge. To everything on the human side of the gulf it looks as unbridgeable as ever, and that there is no other side! If therefore, without realizing it, you are basing your faith on a single personal reaction to your faith, then you are still on the human side of the gulf. You are really believing in yourself, not in Him who takes you to the Other Side.

A man said to me, "Please help me. I feel a barrier between myself and Christ." I investigated and found that he had faith in an indwelling Christ, and also had no immediate barrier of uncleansed sin. So I said, "You are wasting your time asking for help from an illusion. There is no barrier except that you have transferred your faith back from Him to yourself — what you feel about your relationship to Him. Get back where you were — to faith without a shred of human assistance."

— God Unlimited

"See to it . . . that none of you has a sinful, unbelieving heart" — Hebrews 3:12.

Faith is built on doubt. Doubt is its lifeblood. Let us not be mistaken about that. Faith is doubt absorbed, doubt conquered. Unbelief (unfaith) is doubt accepted. Unbelief is an act of will as much as faith. Doubt is not an act of will, but is the only attitude we humans can have towards anything external to us until we decide whether to accept it or reject it. The uncertainty, the doubt, is the very element which gives stimulus and passion to the decision. Faith then is built on doubt.

Every smallest action is conquered doubt. You eat food. How do you know it won't poison you? You sit on a chair. How do you know it won't collapse under you? You go to visit a certain home. How do you know it will be there when you get there? Action, therefore, on every level is conquered uncertainty. You make up your mind that there is every possible likelihood that a thing is what it appears to be and will react as you expect it to, and then you act — by faith. The more uncertainty there is, the more passion in your decision of faith, for there has been a bigger doubt to conquer. Should you or should you not marry that person? Should you move over there and accept that new job? Should you invest in that company?

— *God Unlimited*

"Fight the good fight of the faith" — 1 Timothy 6:12.

Do not let us forget, faith begins by being a labor (Hebrews 4:11) or fight (1 Timothy 6:12), although it is consummated in a rest (Hebrews 4:3). That is to say, the first stage of faith is always the battle of taking hold by the will, heart and intelligence of some truth or promise which is not real to us in experience, and declaring it to be ours in spite of appearances. We do not appear to be dead unto sin and alive unto God. We are told to believe it, and so we dare to do so and declare so. A thousand times, maybe, faith will be assaulted and fall. Unbelief will say "nonsense," and we shall belie our declaration of faith; but the fight or labor of faith means that we deliberately return to the assault. Once again we believe and declare it. This we persist in doing. As we thus follow in the steps of those who "by faith and patience" inherit the promises, a new divine thing will happen within us.

The Spirit will cooperate with our faith (as He is invisibly doing all the time), and to faith will be added assurance; labor and fight will be replaced by rest. The consummation of faith has been reached. What was once an effort to attain or maintain now becomes as natural as breathing. Such is the law of faith, whether exercised in sanctification or in any of the later and higher reaches of Christian experience.

— *Touching the Invisible*

"If anyone says to this mountain . . " — Mark 11:23.

We have learned in the WEC that we have one great enemy of faith — within us, and not in our circumstances: fear of the visible. We know the inward urges of the mind of God to some certain end. We know the next step: not to ask for faith, but to exercise it (why ask for what we already have? — if the Author and Finisher of faith is within us, all faith is there already for the using). We must declare that what we desire (His desire in us) will come to pass — add the word of faith to the thought of faith. Then the battle is joined. The fear of some visible giant paralyses us. An opposing government, the need of funds, the hardness of a fanatical people, the grip of an illusion: the vision of the flesh lusts against the vision of the Spirit.

In Jesus' name we break through. We declare the word of faith: "That government will give way," "That area will be opened," "That money will come," "Those souls will be saved." The word, if we are rightly abiding, is spoken in the same power and through the same Person who made the declaration at the earliest dawn of history "Let there be light." It is repeated again and again as occasion arises; not prayer, nor aspiration, nor hope; but praise, declaration, quiet reception of a supply already given, a calling of those things that be not as though they were. As we do that, the manifestation of the thing believed comes to pass as surely as the harvest follows the sowing.

— Touching the Invisible

"According to your faith will it be done to you" —
Matthew 9:29.

One responsibility lies with man — only one, but so
pivotal that all the outcome is attributed to this one activity.
Man must carry out the process of faith. Fallen man has to
arise and grasp the heights and depths of the fact that he is a
son in Christ, together with the Son, and that he is now to
cooperate with this re-creative process of the Godhead. At
regeneration, by the mercy of God he "believes." God's
thoughts of sin are revealed to and in him; God's word of
salvation, Jesus, is declared to him; God's creative work by
the Spirit is wrought in him — all by his simple act of honest
reception, his first elementary exploit of faith.

But if he is to go on himself to be God's co-worker, he
has to be trained in the laws of the divine working. A
knowledge of God's acts may suffice for the personal
redemption of the children of Israel: but Moses, to be a
redeemer as well as a recipient of redemption, must know
God's ways (Psalm 103:7). It is the difference in usefulness
between the passenger and the driver of a car. God's servant
has to learn, not merely how faith gives entrance into the
heavenly life, but also how faith maintains as a reality the
indissoluble union between man's regenerate spirit and
God's Spirit, that region of abiding in a simple, single-eyed,
pure-hearted relationship, where God's thoughts are inwardly revealed, Christ's word of authority spoken through
human lips, and the Spirit's mighty works manifested
before all the world.

— *Touching the Invisible*

*"Seek first his kingdom and his righteousness, and all
these things will be given to you as well"* — Matthew 6:33.

The gift of Pat Symes, our first representative to
Colombia, was especially remarkable. He received definite
guidance from the Lord that he was to remain at Headquarters and prove that God was calling him to this new work by
receiving a gift of £100.

I asked him to go and collect some further information
on Colombia from a friend living ten miles away on the
other side of London. He never told me that he only had six
pence in the world, but went on his errand. Four pence was
spent on getting there, partly by bus and partly on foot. On
the return journey he walked to the Thames Embankment,
intending to get a twopenny tram ride from there. A "down
and out" accosted him and asked the price of a cup of coffee.
Pat refused. But the Spirit told him to go back and speak to
the man about his soul. Pat went back, but found that he
could not speak about his soul and do nothing for his body,
so the two pence changed hands and Pat walked the eight
miles home. Meanwhile I had a visitor from the Midlands.
She felt God wanted her to leave £100 toward the opening of
a new field!

Pat arrived back weary and perspiring. I opened the
door to him with the check of £100 in my hand just at the
same time that the Devil had been hard at work telling him
that the life of faith was a poor business!

— *After C. T. Studd*

"If anyone . . . does not doubt in his heart but believes"
— Mark 11:23.

Unless we differentiate between the external doubts of the mind and the central faith of the heart, we get into difficulty. When Jesus said, "Whosoever shall say unto this mountain, Be thou removed . . . ," He added "and shall not doubt in his heart, but shall believe that those things which he saith shall come to pass, he shall have whatsoever he saith."

He said, "shall not doubt in his heart," not his head. There is the difference. Our reasons and emotions are what the Bible calls our soul, and they are the external means by which we express our true inner selves, which is our spirit. Our reasons express our inner knowledge; our emotions, our inner love. But both reason and emotion are open to influences from without as well as controlled from within, therefore they vary.

But in our spirits, our hearts, our fixed choices are made. That is where, spirit with Spirit, we are united with God. Now an act of faith is made there in our heart, our spirit. It is a free, definite, fixed choice. We have confirmed it by our word of faith. Therefore, we do not move. But doubts will recur any time. That is normal in our contact with the world of appearances, which seem to run clean contrary to faith. If we have discerned between soul and spirit, and, therefore, between the variable thoughts of our minds and the invariable, fixed choices of our hearts, we shall not accept false condemnation.

— *The Spontaneous You*

"We live by faith, not by sight" — 2 Corinthians 5:7.

The position of authority [in prayer] has been proved hundreds of times over to be equally the secret for obtaining supplies, moving governments, saving souls, transforming characters, and the like.

Written on a river steamer in the interior of South America, these are but scrappy jottings on this "lost chord of Christianity," but, I trust, sufficient to put a seeking reader on the trail. To one who asks, "But how can we realize this as a personal experience?" we answer, as God answered Moses in the incident at the beginning of this article, "Awake. Arise from your deluded condition as if you are still fallen, still separated by sin, still weak. Realize your equipment, the mystery hid from ages and from generations: CHRIST IN YOU. Declare it, as the prophets of old: 'I am full of power by the Spirit of the Lord.' Cease to live bound up in those old graveclothes of 'judging by appearances,' 'walking by sight.' You appear weak, you appear to be without the presence of Christ, you appear loveless, of little faith, and all the rest of it. You still live in the devil's lies of the have-not life. But you have — all things. All is within, if Christ the Savior is within. Burst through those bonds of feelings. Say, 'Though all men and devils say I have not, I say I have, on the authority of God's Word.'"

— Throne Life

"I will do whatever you ask in my name" — John 14:13.

Faith is the whole man in action, but primarily the inner man. We must know, therefore, how to win our battles within before waging them without. Indeed, every battle is in fact won from within, and the spoils of victory gathered outside.

I should look back very differently on past years if I had not learned and applied some of these principles of faith. I learned them largely from a great man of God, Rees Howells of the Bible College of Wales. For years we have practiced them in our missionary crusade, individually and in our home base fellowships, in every conceivable kind of need, problem and challenge. It is authority. "Concerning the work of My hands, command ye Me." How do we talk this language and have faith become substantial? As intercessors we are mouths without teeth, arms without muscles, if we have all the rest but have not the word of authority.

The first step must be knowing the will of God. There can be no ifs about the word of authority. When we are sure of His will we can be sure of our word of faith. How can we know? For us it necessitated changing the start of our prayer times from talking to God to listening to Him. If we understand that prayer is not our bringing our needs to God but God moving us by His Spirit to be His channels of supply (Romans 8:26-27), then we form the habit of finding out first what supplies He is planning to send.

— *The Spontaneous You*

"Those God foreknew he also predestined to be con-formed to the likeness of his Son" — Romans 8:29.

Our relationship to our fellow Christians radically changes when we know who we are, for then we know who *they* are. I first see my brother just as a human person, who may or may not appeal to me. I always start like that, but then the change. I know who I am, so I know and see who he is. He is *Christ* to me, even in his human form. More than that, we all have mannerisms, habits, ways of saying and doing things in which we are different from each other, and this can rub each other the wrong way. But since I know that I am as God *means* me to be, warts and all, so I know my brother is as God means *him* to be, and we love and accept each other as we are, for we are Christ to each other.

He will be taking care of any changes that are needed. We are all being "conformed to the image of His Son." My part is to have it fixed in my faith that God *is doing* that in my brother, as I see Christ perfect in him. That saves me from being judgmental of him. The time may come when the Lord gives me the freedom to talk things over with him. This is where what Jesus said about the mote and beam takes effect. If I have the beam in my eye, it means that I am seeing my brother's weak spot more vividly than enjoying Christ in him. I cannot then take out his mote. But if my love and esteem of my brother is greater than any lesser shortcom-ings, and he senses that, then he is likely to hear me about his mote. So this is the beautiful way in which our brother is always Christ to us in his human form; and whenever he is less than that to me and the clay feet are obsessing me, *I* am the one off-center more than he.

— *Yes, I Am*

"Make my joy complete by being like-minded, having the same love, being one in spirit and purpose" — Philippians 2:2.

The team of Christian Literature Crusade workers in each home base is really God's day-to-day miracle more than any material supply; hours of work given daily to the Lord without remuneration, extending to months, years, and a lifetime, is a daily miracle in a self-loving, self-seeking world. Just as big a miracle is when we humans, each different from anyone else, each with our obvious weaknesses as well as strengths, can live in the closeness of a communal life and love one another. That is no static automatic relationship — once achieved and never again disturbed. No indeed. Brotherly love is a daily walk, a daily adventure. Personalities are meant to differ. That makes the wheels of life and progress go round. Each has different gifts, different characteristics, different outlooks.

The interflow and interaction of a team in fellowship is the manifestation of Christ in His body. It is the outgoing of Christ to the world, drawing all men by the attractiveness of people loving one another. Such an interlove is neither gained nor maintained easily. The appeals of the Apostle Paul to "be of the same mind" demonstrate that. There never will be a fellowship in perfect love on earth without a weak link in the chain; but a standard of spontaneous fellowship can be a fact. This is of another dimension than what the world can know, for we can see and reckon on Christ in each other.

— *Leap of Faith*

"If we walk in the light, as he is in the light, we have fellowship" — 1 John 1:7.

There is one other way, the healthiest of all, to maintain fellowship in personal relationships, as well as the freshness of the walk in Jesus. We learned lessons which have much affected many of us over the past fifteen years through our friends from Ruanda, East Africa. From these, missionaries and Africans, we caught the reality of the walk in the light, not only with God but with one another.

Our first contact with them came through Edith Moules, the founder of the Leprosy and Medical department of WEC. She had noted the quality of brotherly love and fellowship between missionaries and Africans, beyond anything she had seen before, and a way of walking in the Spirit together which could be called brokenness, openness, and challenge. That is to say, they were quick to repent when they slipped, calling sin sin, and to claim the cleansing blood of Jesus. This was the walk in the light according to 1 John 1, which they spoke of as brokenness. But they were also open and sharing with each other where the Spirit had convicted them and the blood of Jesus had cleansed them. They would do this not only on the spot in their daily contacts but in their open fellowship meetings at night. This was down-to-earth reality.

— *The Four Pillars of WEC*

"Let us love one another, for love comes from God" —
1 John 4:7.

Edith Moules* stood at her husband's deathbed crying, and, mighty woman of faith as she was, maybe temporarily questioning God's dealings in so suddenly taking her husband. One of the Africans standing by the bedside discerned that her tears were more of questioning than of faith, sorrow of the world rather than godly sorrow as Paul said, and he boldly challenged her: "Lady, if your husband is with Jesus, why are you crying like that?" She left the room filled with indignation at being spoken to like that, and that by an African, one of those whom she was supposed to have come to teach. But there in her room with the same sensitiveness to sin which she had seen around her, responding to God's light, God showed her her own pride and anger, and took her back to the many times she had been hot-tempered herself while in the act of pointing out the faults of her leprosy patients. He reminded her of the saying of the Africans that when you point one finger at your neighbor, the other three fingers of your closed hand are pointing to yourself. Follow the three first! So she did, and began this same walk of brokenness and openness.

When later she returned to Congo and told her leprosy patients the same thing, a move of the Spirit began among them also.

— *The Four Pillars of WEC*

*Missionary of the (then) Worldwide Evangelization Crusade.

"The blood of Jesus, his Son, purifies us from all sin"
— 1 John 1:7.

Only true openness brings heart into true unison with
heart. When barriers are really down, and fellowship has
gone below the surface to where we are living our daily lives
and meeting our daily temptations, there is a sense of brotherhood and understanding nothing else can give. Such fellowship in the light, costly though it is, gives us all a new
understanding of one easily missed truth — that He fashioned our hearts alike and that we are all men of like
passions. One of the devil's commonest lies to us is that I am
the only person who would do or think such a thing. If my
brethren knew, wouldn't they be horrified! And I am shut
up in a prison of secret shame, and maybe struggle against
some temptation which I imagine assaults no one as it does
me.

But when we walk in the light, how different we find it to
be! We are all alike. There is level ground at the foot of the
cross. Like temptations come to all of us, and we all need the
same cleansing blood. Here we find unity indeed. Not in
some artificial attempt to claim some special standard of
spirituality, but as fellow sinners all rejoicing daily in the
same Savior.

— *The Liberating Secret*

"If we walk in the light, as he is in the light, we have fellowship with one another" — 1 John 1:7.

"If we walk in the light . . . we have fellowship one with another." Now we have seen that this walk demands quick recognition of sin, followed by confession and cleansing. But this also means that when the sin has affected a brother, the confession must include him. That is really obvious, and we but mention it in passing. A repentance before God which said, "To You I confess, but not to my brother" needs no comment on its unreality.

David called repentance "brokenness." That leaves no place for establishing my own righteousness. Down I go before God, and before man where necessary. A bent tree can spring into place again, a broken one cannot. That is repentance. This is no light challenge to face, for so many sins I commit affect my neighbor: an untruth, irritability, harsh criticism, stress and strain, an unquiet spirit, even the heaviness of unbelief, affect home, church or business. I must be ready to confess, and under God's guidance will often do so. Yet confession to man should be under His guidance. Satan can whip God's saints and drive them from behind to unwise action, whereas the Spirit gently leads and goes before. There are times when confession can do more harm than good. There are earnest folks who embarrass by their constant reference to their failures. I must be truly willing. That is the point. The rest we can leave to God.

— *The Liberating Secret*

"Why do you look at the speck of sawdust in your brother's eye and pay no attention to the plank in your own eye?" — Matthew 7:3.

Whenever I see faults in my brother as something bigger than the fact of Christ in him, I am sinning. When my eye is single, it is full of light. In looking on my brother, my eye is single when I am seeing Christ in him, and only then. In God's sight that is all He sees, for "by one offering He hath perfected forever them that are sanctified." My eye is evil when it is so fixed on faults and failings in my brother that they obscure my clear sight of Christ in him. And how easy it is to do that! It is the beam in my eye which hinders me from taking out the mote from my brother's eye. Motes are there (as also in me), but they are fiddling compared to my sin in making more of them than Christ in him. He is the apple of Christ's eye.

Let me therefore get my sin out of the way by confession and cleansing, and if led, by confession to my brother. Then let me renew my faith in the One within him who is busy conforming him to His perfect image. That is perfect love. It is not blindness concerning those motes, but it is clear-sighted faith and love. It surrounds the brother with love and contributes a living faith to the fact of a transforming work of the Spirit going on in him. That is the difference between criticism and discernment. Criticism sees the flesh or devil in a brother. It tears down and condemns. It has self-superiority at its roots. Discernment sees Christ in a brother. It edifies. It combines loving appreciation of the present with hope for the future.

— *The Liberating Secret*

"Since God so loved us, we also ought to love one another" — 1 John 4:11.

To live in free, open, happy relationships with others is an achievement of the highest spiritual order. [But what if fellowship is broken?] Recognize frankly the unpleasant feelings. Do not be condemned by them; just recognize that that person has that effect upon you (and you may be sure that you have that same effect on him). Go a step further. Go to the secret place; spread the matter before the Lord. Go to get His point of view on your neighbor, even as you get His point of view on a difficult situation. What does He say or think about him? Ah, that takes on a different aspect, for God does not see us all clothed in our pettinesses, in those little selfishnesses and idiosyncracies which annoy. He sees us in Christ and Christ in us. He sees His Beloved Son and us in Him.

Now that makes all the difference. We look again at our neighbor. We see Christ in that life (supposing him to be the Lord's). We see the changes Christ has wrought. We praise and love, for Christ in us unites with Christ in him. It does not mean that the faults are not there, but it means that the greater fills our vision and the lesser retires to its proper place; for nearly all disunity comes through magnifying the lesser and minimizing the greater in a person.

Now we go out to begin again. By God's grace we are going to reckon on Christ in our brother, rather than see the flesh or even the weak human. Real love means we *trust* our brother.

— *The Law of Faith*

"Let us consider how we may spur one another on toward love and good deeds" — Hebrews 10:24.

One other aspect of fellowship in the light is mutual exhortation. Twice over in the letter to the Hebrews we are told to "exhort one another," with particular reference to the danger of unrecognized backsliding. "Take heed, brethren, lest there be in any of you an evil heart of unbelief in departing from the living God. But exhort one another daily . . . lest any of you be hardened through the deceitfulness of sin." And when we are told not to forsake the assembling of ourselves together, it is again "to exhort one another; and so much the more as ye see the day approaching." We are to help each other to the highest. But we at once recognize the dangers and difficulties of such reciprocal challenging. On the one hand, we could do it in a wrong spirit, as a form of retaliation — to put a person right, to give them what we think they deserve. We can be certain that no one is in a position to challenge another on something in their lives or attitudes who is not equally ready to receive a challenge themselves. Only those who readily and continually "break" and admit their own sins are in a place to point out those of others.

On the other hand, it is truly costly to be faithful to a brother. It is much more comfortable to pass things by, say nothing, and thus not risk disturbing the peace. A challenge may not always be accepted in the spirit in which it is intended. It is costly to give, costly to receive.

— *The Liberating Secret*

"Man looks at the outward appearance, but the Lord looks at the heart" — 1 Samuel 16:7.

I must not keep my believing, as I have done for so long, on outward appearances. I must not lump together all the people involved in some combined action I disapprove of (and my disapproval of the action may be largely because I don't understand) as just a crowd of prejudiced or self-seeking people: but I must see them as individuals, in each of whose hearts God is working as He is in mine. Equally I must not look with a jaundiced eye on individual outward behavior or appearance of which I don't approve. I must practice this same principle of transferred believing, transferred to who each person really is — a created and loved human in the being of God, really therefore a form of God, a human expression of God, gone wrong — that he may be made right; and God in His Spirit of love is as busy working in him, disturbing his false beliefs, as He has been on me through the years.

Then I love my neighbor as myself. Just as I always find tolerance for myself, so I can for my neighbor. In fact, I must get this habit, of which my African friends always spoke, of realizing that when I point one finger at my neighbor, the other three fingers are pointing back at me! Follow them first! And I must be sensitized to my real sin, which is believing flesh rather than spirit, believing in what I outwardly dislike in my neighbor instead of believing and seeing him as one in God's own being, in whose inner center God is continually working in mercy.

— *Who Am I?*

"Is Christ divided?" — 1 Corinthians 1:13.

Fresh fellowships in Christ — fresh in love, in zeal, with some Spirit-revealed emphasis of "the truth as it is in Jesus" which may have become overlaid in older groups — are the lifeblood of the growing church. Just as we go to annual flower shows to delight in the new varieties and combinations of blooms produced by modern horticultural methods, [let us delight in *them*]. They are all the one church, the only church recognized in God's Word.

The problem is not in plenty of variety and the constant rebirth of the church in new forms and under new names; we are fools if we think we can stop that and time-wasters if we attempt it, for men cannot stop the seeding of grace any more than of nature. The mistake on the one hand is to be occupied in uniting the outward church instead of affirming the permanent unity of the one inner church, and fostering all means of fellowship between those who hold the Bible faith once delivered to the saints; or, on the other hand, to be so provincial in outlook that instead of seeing the one Christ in the one body worldwide and throughout the whole length of history, we see minute fragments of the church of history and almost call them *the* church, usually because they are the one fragment in which we have grown up or through which we have gained light. Without realizing it, maybe, we have then slipped into a dual loyalty to which we seek to give equal allegiance, and that is idolatry. Our loyalty is single, eternal, unchangeable — to a Christ who is Head and body complete.

— The Deep Things of God

"There is one body and one Spirit" — Ephesians 4:4.

The whole history of the church of Christ in the vigor of its expansion has been progress by fission rather than fusion. The birth of the church was out from Judaism, and the great movements of the Spirit through the centuries have been dynamic outbursts which could seldom be retained in the existing organizations. If that has been so up to the present, we are foolish if we think the pattern will now change. It is really a form of unrecognized pride when the present-day large denominations, which were themselves small, persecuted and despised schismatics in the views of the established churches of their day, now in their era of consolidation point an equally contemptuous or critical finger at new movements and perhaps speak of them as "the sects" or even "the fringe sects," or "the lunatic fringe," or "the religious underworld."

Opposition to the start of new movements is natural on the part of the older ones, who may be losing members and who will not be seeing eye-to-eye with the newer brethren on the reasons for their new start. It is just here that the single eye is tested out. Can we feel the human hurt of such losses, yet squarely recognize that the church is always and forever one, and that no minor differences affect that? Can we act as one, and find means to bridge in fellowship a parting in organization?

— *The Deep Things of God*

"Our fellowship is with the Father and with his Son, Jesus Christ" — 1 John 1:3.

Fellowship rather than individualism needs emphasizing as the pattern for the believer. We do not live merely on a vertical plane, but also on a horizontal. All our vertical relationships of faith in God through Christ are consummated by our horizontal relationships with each other: "that ye also may have fellowship with us: and truly our fellowship is with the Father and with His Son, Jesus Christ." One does not properly function without the other. This was plain in the early church, when their meetings were on the free sharing basis. We see them in their normal condition when Paul was checking the Corinthians for over-enthusiasm: "How is it then, brethren? When ye come together, everyone of you hath a psalm, a doctrine. . . ." Evidently the flow of the Spirit through the members of the body was such a normal experience that he had to urge them to quieten down a bit. This was horizontal fellowship; and we have to face the fact that the churches through the centuries have so changed their character that such a flow of fellowship is very much the exception as the regular characteristic of a church at worship.

The one-man ministry, which is almost universal today, results in the Lord's people meeting to be ministered unto, rather than to minister to the Lord and each other. It appears that the pattern of the early church was the Spirit manifesting the gifts through the members as He pleased.
— *The Deep Things of God*

*"You are a chosen people, a royal priesthood, a holy
nation, . . . that you may declare the praises of him who
called you out of darkness"* — 1 Peter 2:9.

One church — yes. Local church fellowships, yet part of
the one church — yes. But the church does not exist for itself
but for those outside of it. A church which is not a propagat-
ing church is a swamp, not a river. It *must* witness or die.
Those Roman Catholic worker-priests in Paris, Abbe
Godin and the others, who were later suppressed by the
hierarchy, were appalled at the way the average Roman
church functioned as a feather-bed for the faithful, while the
mass of Parisians around them were totally indifferent to
any religion. The same may be said of us Protestants. A
church of the Holy Spirit, who came to point the world to
Christ, cannot rest without finding means of reaching its
neighborhood. That is the spearpoint of its fellowship life.
We know of churches on the mission fields which in their
zeal to reach the outsider give up the use of their church
buildings for certain weeks each month on the Lord's day
and go to hold their services in neighboring towns in order
to reach the unchurched.

That again is the dire danger of a one-man ministry.
How easy for the "layman" to say, "Why should I do his job
for him?" How can the "laity" (a word which in itself shows
how far we have drifted from the pattern of the New Testament Ecclesia) be retaught that *they* are the church and the
ministers?

The whole church in action — a royal priesthood — that
is the New Testament norm.

— *The Deep Things of God*

> *"I know that nothing good dwells in me, that is, in my flesh"* — Romans 7:18 (NASV).

The new self redeemed in Him is to be what it was created to be — a willing, loving, dependent manifestor of the Christ living within. But, not yet having attained the final goal of the union which will be ours, by grace, with the resurrection of the body, we are still mingled with a self-reliant world, and we are always liable in our new dependent selves to be diverted from Christ within to some form of self-reliance. In doing that, we enter again into the old conflict of the law with its demands on self, back in the struggling, striving and failing realm; for the new I, which delights in the law of God after the inward man, has to learn and re-learn its utter helplessness, according to the law of its creation, apart from Christ in it, and therefore its total defeat the moment it moves out of the shelter of "Christ in me." We have to learn, and learn deeply, that the new I, the "good" I, is as helpless as the old I, and is a slave to sin the moment it tries to manage its own affairs.

The law, then, fulfills two purposes. By it we receive a twofold ministry of condemnation, first as guilty sinners (Romans 3:19), with the guilt removed in the blood of Christ; then as failing saints (Romans 7:18) with the wretchedness removed by the new walk in the indwelling Spirit (Romans 7:24; 8:2-4); so that we too can say with Paul, "I thank God through Jesus Christ our Lord," for "Christ is the end of the law for righteousness to every one that believeth."

— The Deep Things of God

> *"God is greater than our hearts, and he knows every-thing"* — 1 John 3:20.

John perceived the oversensitiveness of the redeemed human heart and its tendency to false self-condemnation, which would prevent it from acting easily and naturally in the Spirit, and would always make it afraid of itself, fearful of presumption, over-suspicious of selfish motives, causing a paralysis of bold faith and prayer. So he added a passage in his letter on this specific point in connection with believing prayer.

He here said that our normal condition should be one of confidence before God, confidence in prayer that what we ask for we get. But unfortunately, he said, we get so easily under self-condemnation and are tortured by it. "Our hearts condemn us," and then we hardly dare believe that Christ still indwells us, much less that He grants our desires; so John adds that God is greater than our hearts, and knows the real truth and acts according to that truth, and not according to our wrongful self-condemnation.

But, all the same, a self-condemning heart, he says, does make it impossible for us to enjoy His presence, to be bold and free and happy in our acts and attitudes, or to declare the word of faith. And so in a later chapter he again refers to this false and tormenting fear and self-accusation, and gives the remedy for it. Do you love God? Does God love you? Well then, stand in that love. Realize that such love has no fear in it. Refuse the fear that torments. Revel in the perfect love; then dare to count on it and act on it.

— *The Law of Faith*

"If I make my bed in the depths, you are there" —
Psalm 139:8.

Life in the human must always be a tension, a constant propounding of problems with no adequate solution, a constant oscillation between the pleasurable and the painful. But when we raise our sights from the human to the divine, the whole picture changes. All started with God, all ends with God, and there is only One with whom He has to do: from eternity to eternity all is centered in Christ. Therefore whatever intervenes in history, whether pleasant or unpleasant, must be caught up into the stream of His purposes of grace in Christ. If the devil appears on the scene, then the devil must be His agent. If the fall of man adds to the chaos, then we learn that He had already foreseen that and the fallen first Adam was to be only a type in reverse (Romans 5:14) of the last redeeming Adam. This same Christ would Himself embrace the consequences of sin, atone for it, conquer it, and then produce out of the wreckage of fallen humanity a new race of sons to occupy the highest position in the universe, to share the throne of Him who is made "higher than the heavens," better than the angels, seated at the right hand of the majesty on high.

Evil, then, would be to Christ an agency for good; not that evil comes from God, or is anything but evil, but faith utilizes it for good, because faith understands that God reigns in the darkness as well as in the light (Psalm 139:12), and that God fulfills His own purpose through adverse circumstances which expose to man his inability and spur him on to the receiving faith which liberates God to work.
— *The Deep Things of God.*

"When I am weak, then I am strong" —
2 Corinthians 12:10.

Faith means that we turn our attention from the need to the Supplier who is already supplying that need, and who allowed the need because He intends to supply it to His glory.

Paul's thorn in the flesh is a perfect illustration of this. Though a "messenger of Satan," *God* sent it, for it was "given" him for a deliberate purpose — to keep him from the subtle inroads of self-esteem, leading to self-reliance. The trial was deep and prolonged (probably increasing blindness). At first he thought that the One who had done physical miracles in other bodies through him would do the same in him. But no. After three separate appeals, we may suppose with intervals between each, God's word came clear to him. He was to prove the power of God *in* his weakness, not *from* it; not by deliverance from it, but by constant ability to transcend it. The Supplier had met his need — this time as abounding spiritual supply overflowing an ever-present physical need. A seeking faith became a praising faith, and reaching out over all the unending trials and sufferings of his pioneer life, he gathered them up in one embrace of praise and thanks for all of them (2 Corinthians 12:10).

Our trials are *God's* trials, *given* us for a purpose, exactly suited to us. Our lacks are *God's* lacks, our perplexities are *God's* perplexities. Before the trials, God has already prepared the deliverance and sends us the trials that He may manifest Himself through them.

— *The Deep Things of God*

"God has bound all men over to disobedience so that he may have mercy on them all" — Romans 11:32.

The law was to challenge man with the only principle of righteous living, and at the same time open his eyes to his own unrighteousness. "By the law is the knowledge of sin." "For God has shut up all into disobedience, *that* He might have mercy on all" (Romans 11:32 — literal translation). It was what Paul called "the ministry of condemnation," "the ministration of death," which yet was "glorious" because it was the first stage in God's glorious work of redemption; for the gift of God's law was a gift of His grace, sent not to condemn but to save; for the law was to be "our schoolmaster to bring us to Christ." But so far from this massive presentation of the law of God being the means of condemnation to a law-breaking people, coupled with the means of grace through the sacrifices, for the most part the subtle egoism in man turned these into an exclusive religion of self-righteousness.

The law plunges its knife of conviction and condemnation right into the heart of our self-righteous selves, and produces one or other of two effects. Most, both in Israel and throughout the history of the church, hastily pluck out the knife and seek to heal the wound by the medicaments of self-justification, even to the point of using the worship and sacraments of the church as a covering of good works, anything indeed which will save them from the self-immolation of a broken and contrite heart and will preserve their precious selves.

— *The Deep Things of God*

"You also died to the law through the body of Christ"
—Romans 7:4.

[Christ] erased the very existence of a codified external law for all believers. When He arose from the dead, He left behind Him on the cross the whole entangling body of law with its demands as well as penalties, "abolishing in His flesh the law of commandments contained in ordinances," "blotting out the handwriting of ordinances that was against us, and took it out of the way, nailing it to His cross." For an external law is only in existence where there are those who do not fulfill the law by nature, but who can and may and do break it: "the law is for the lawless" (1 Timothy 1:9). When people live the law by internal instinct, there is no outward law (Galatians 5:23). External law only came into an existence when humanity began to live by its false god, the god of lawlessness, of independent self — "that wicked one." The moment, therefore, that humanity is restored to its predestined relationship of inner union with God, external law ceases to exist for it.

And this is what Christ did for us, making us "dead to the law by His body" (Romans 7:4). Being made sin for us, He died as sin-infected humanity. He arose as the new humanity who had died to sin, and this new humanity consists of all human beings who receive Him. He, then, who is the Living Law, becomes their life within, and lives the law within them. For them, therefore, the external law is buried. It is the old husband who has died in the crucified Christ (in Paul's bold symbolism of Romans 7:1-6) that we might be married to another, the risen Christ.

— The Deep Things of God

"I have the desire to do what is good, but I cannot carry it out" — Romans 7:18.

The fact that we are dead to the external law by the body of Christ does not mean that external law has ceased to exist in the world. We live in the midst of it, surrounded by it, for we live in a world under judgment, under law. It is very easy for us, therefore, to respond to the demands of the law.

Self-effort in the new man comes perilously easy to us just because we want to please God and delight now in His law, His standard of life. What more natural, then, than to set about living by it? And at this point we have our new lesson to learn. We have discovered our guilt; now we must discover our helplessness. The new self is exactly as helpless as the old! It was created helpless, and never can be anything else! The only difference is that the old self, infected by the spirit of egoism, did not want to fulfill the laws of God, but the new self does. But neither can do it, nor are made to do it!

Romans 7:14-24 opens to us the helpless bondage of the new self the moment it moves out of the vine-branch relationship and endeavors to meet any claims on itself by itself. Not only can it not do so, but it finds another principle or law terrifyingly operative in itself. Self-effort *is* sin; it is self acting as its own god. Therefore, self-effort is immediately conscious of the domination of the selfish, lustful demands of its own appetites and instincts, and being helpless by nature cannot resist them.

— *The Deep Things of God*

"What a wretched man I am! Who will rescue me?" —
Romans 7:24.

Man's first and deepest instinct is not lawlessness, but
law. That is to say, his first form of self-consciousness is
responsibility. It was the first word spoken to him in the
garden: "You must do this; you must not do that." It is the
basis of personality.

If he turns to Christ and finds relief from the condemnation of the law, there law still stands with its unchanging
demands. If now as a new man in Christ, ignorant of the true
grounds of his new life, he still tries to obey the law, he is
aghast to find that he still cannot obey it and still is
enchained by the contrary impulses of the flesh — till at last
he echoes Paul's cry, "O wretched man that I am, who shall
deliver me from the body of this death?" His basic problem,
then, the problem of the new self, is not sin but law. How
can he escape these absolute standards confronting him? He
cannot. How can he fulfill them? He cannot. So what? At
last his eyes are opened. These are absolute standards.
These are demanded eternally of him. But he has forgotten
the first law "imposed" on him, the law (principle) of grace
—that he should *receive* the grace of God, not that he
should *do* anything of himself; and the grace of God is
nothing less than the indwelling Law-giver and Law-keeper
keeping His own perfect law in the believer, the One who
imposes the absolute standards on man being Himself the
One who maintains them in man, so that the only responsibility that man has is to receive Him, abide in Him, walk
after Him.

— *The Deep Things of God*

> *"He has given us his very great and precious promises,*
> *so that . . . you may participate in the divine nature" —*
> 2 Peter 1:4.

It would be good to underline the danger of constant condemnation through the law, of which warning is given in Romans 8:1. It is probably the most prevalent cause of unhappiness and ineffectiveness among God's people. For we do "come short of the glory of God," and do so daily. What are we to do about it?

First, there is the big lie of the Accuser of the brethren. He will cast doubts on our crucified position in Christ, and try to tell us that our "old man" is still very much alive in us. That is a falsehood. But many accept it, and drag their feet through life on the false assumption that they have a divided self, a divided heart, a divided nature. Their conception of Christian living is a continuous struggle, a losing battle between their old nature and their new: "the flesh lusteth against the spirit, the spirit against the flesh; these are contrary the one to the other: so that ye cannot do the things that ye would."

But that does not mean two co-equal natures battling in the believer one against the other. We have only one nature at a time; we cannot have more, for our nature is our very self. We *were* by nature the children of wrath, we *are* partakers of the divine nature. That is the death and resurrection in Christ. No half measures about that! The old nature is the old man which has been crucified with Christ. The new nature is the new man, which is we risen with Christ and Christ living in us.

— *The Deep Things of God*

"My God will meet all your needs according to his glorious riches in Christ Jesus" — Philippians 4:19.

God permits needs in our lives *that* He may *now* supply them in Christ. Needs, shortages, problems are summonses to *faith*. That is why they are God's will. They are His necessary way of compelling us flesh-bound humans to recognize our earthly limitations, to be dissatisfied with them, to seek the way to transcend them, and to become agents of redemptive faith. He says, "I am the answer, I am the supply. I have come to you in Christ. Receive Me in this situation." For need is a shadow. And what casts the shadow? The light. No light, no shadow. The light of God's fullness shines on this world. The oppositions of Satan, to which we add the sin of unbelief, have interposed themselves and cast the shadows of the lacks of this life. Christ has come to destroy that intervening barrier. Then to those who believe Him, it is no longer a barrier but a bluff — a challenge to faith.

That may or may not mean that the actual material situation is changed. Very often it is. But it means that we look at all situations with God's eyes. We see that in reality they are *His* situations, into which He has deliberately put us that He might be glorified in them. Therefore before we call, He is already answering, because He Himself has instigated this actual situation with His answer all prepared. Our calling is His stirring of us to feel the need and recognize that here is a situation in which God is going to do something.

— *The Deep Things of God*

"I shall lack nothing" — Psalm 23:1.

Judgments are pointers to grace — signposts — and not to a grace which has to be sought somewhere or manufactured, but which was there long before the judgments; and the judgments are only the necessary way of getting the grace through to us, conditioning us to accept it.

Long before there was a condition of need God had completed His work of perfect creation. The Fall and its consequences have been an apparently tragic interlude, but that was foreseen and provided for in "the Lamb without blemish and without spot; who verily was foreordained before the foundation of the world." Therefore, as we have already said, God has always had His fullness in readiness to replace our emptiness, His perfection our imperfections, His light our darkness, His life our death. He has always intended, planned and provided total supply for every human need, and the supply has always been there. It is not that our need initiates the demand for its supply and must somehow call the attention of the Father to it and persuade Him to supply. No indeed. HE initiated the need so that we might find all our supply already there in His and our Christ! The need is the proof that the supply is there, and is merely God's means of conditioning us to be agents of faith. It is God who confronts us with every kind of problem, inability, difficulty, that, in our weakness, He may flash the spark of faith into our hearts.

— *The Deep Things of God*

"A good measure, pressed down, shaken together and running over, will be poured into your lap" — Luke 6:38.

Give to men and men give to us. By some means, we know not how, the Spirit moves in men's hearts so that the response to the giver is far greater than the gift he gave. Not, indeed, response from the actual recipient of the gift. The way the Spirit seems to work is that, when we receive a gift, we are moved to show our gratitude. Often we cannot in any way recompense the kind donor; it may not be either seemly or possible. But the spirit of recompense is stirred within us and a way opens up to recompense another, really as an act of gratitude to God for the former gift; and thus giving and receiving, receiving and giving, flow on around the world. Giving is really like the circulation of the blood. It comes back to the starting-point. What we give comes back, only in greater abundance. What we hold unnecessarily to ourselves chokes the inflow. Give, to receive, to give again, to receive again, to give again, and so it goes on. All the industrial problems of our day, the inequality of possessions, the poverty, have their ultimate source in the fact that this golden secret was lost in the Fall, when grab and keep, in place of give and receive and give again, became man's only method of getting provision and security. A simple rule is: If in need, give.

— *The Law of Faith*

"This man was handed over to you by God's set purpose and foreknowledge" — Acts 2:23.

How can I include the workings of an evil power, of which the world and people are so full, as an expression of the one power which is God, who is love? God called the heathen king who would destroy Israel "Nebuchadnezzar, *My servant"* (Jeremiah 43:10)! The Assyrians God called "the rod of My anger" (Isaiah 10:5).

Peter, in a startling statement in his speech on the day of Pentecost, when referring to the greatest crime in history, told the crowds, "Jesus of Nazareth . . . Him, being delivered by the determinate counsel and foreknowledge of God, ye have taken, and by wicked hands have crucified and slain" (Acts 2:22-23). *Determinate counsel* — no "permissiveness" there!

We all know about Joseph, and he went even further. He left no room for us to say that God "permits" evil things to happen but does not direct them; for, even though he had suffered thirteen years by being sold as a slave by his brethren and then being thrown into prison because of the false accusation of Potiphar's wife, still he told his brethren, "Ye thought evil against me, but God meant it unto good" (Genesis 50:20). *Meant* it! To "mcan" is not to "permit." It is direct purpose and planning. However, God is not the doer of evil. As freedom involves the necessity of making choices, He created [men] with the possibility of choosing the opposite to Himself — the evil — and they did.

— Yes, I Am

> *"Through Christ Jesus the law of the Spirit of life set me free from the law of sin and death"* — Romans 8:2.

We have to learn not to accept the big lie of our return to a permanent old condition, just because we are caught out by the flesh on occasions; nor to live in the bondage of a false but very commonly held conception of being two people at once, with a civil war within, a good and bad nature. No. Let us confess with the same assured voice as Paul that "the law of the Spirit of life in Christ Jesus hath set me free from the law of sin and death."

But then equally we must not stay, even temporarily, under condemnation, when Satan has caught us out. It is the easiest thing to do, and our distressed feelings are really self-pity and pride. It is not so much that we have grieved *the Lord* that disturbs us as that *we* have failed. The acceptance of condemnation is a form of self-righteousness. *God* has told us, when we sin, to get quickly to the light, recognize and confess the sin, and then He is faithful and just to forgive us our sins and to cleanse our consciences from all sense of unrighteousness. "The cleansing fount I see, I see; I plunge, and oh, it cleanseth me." To remain in condemnation, therefore, is really disobedience and hurt self. We can learn many lessons from simple believers who keep short accounts with God. They are tripped up, they humbly recognize it, they claim the cleansing blood, and go on their way rejoicing; and often they use their testimony to such daily simple experiences to be a blessing to others.

— *The Deep Things of God*

"What I want to do I do not do" — Romans 7:15.

Now, said Paul in Romans 7, watch the effect of being "under the law." It says to you: You do this. We say we will and want to (we delight in the law after the inward man). But we find a contrary principle at work in us, compelling us to do the things the flesh wants to do, not the Spirit — and we follow the flesh. We find we are "sold under sin," and that "sin dwells in me." How is this? Because, not having yet fully understood ourselves, we have not yet grasped the fact that self-reliant self *is* sin. That is what Satan is; and self-reliant self can only desire to please itself. That is the power of sin in it. But in Christ we are no longer self-reliant selves; instead, we are containers of Him. We are not in the flesh but in the Spirit. He who is love is Himself *the* law, and He lives that life of love through us.

Then what has happened? If that is so, why do we experience the bondages and defeats of Romans 7? Because not having completely learned, or easily forgetting, the basic helplessness of self, and its only function to be the container of the Spirit, we are constantly assaulted by temptation to be something or do something or not do something. Obey those commands, pray more, give more, witness more, be more patient, don't lose your temper, get rid of those evil thoughts, struggle against your lusts, and so on. The real answer to all these is Christ within. He is the Person like this, and I boldly reckon on Him to live like that in me.

— *God Unlimited*

"If a man remains in me and I in him, he will bear much fruit; apart from me you can do nothing" — John 15:5.

We are not made capable of thinking of two things at once. When we are doing something, we put all we have into it. We cannot, therefore, be thinking directly of Christ at the same time, or consciously communing with Him. We have a sub-conscious realization of His presence, like the flow of an underground stream, and we refer to Him momentarily at any time; but the great percentage of our daily lives is spent, not directly in touch with Him, but immersed in our own affairs.

So we are freed to act as normal men and women, living normal lives; yet it is not really we living, but He; that is our special secret, shared with those who know what we are talking about. We pray, we read the Scriptures, but we are not in bondage. We do not even depend on these, for we are joined irrevocably to Him; and even if pressures mean that we can't get the times with Him we would like, again we don't come under condemnation or fall into the false imagination that therefore we are spiritually dry or disarmed. No, not even prayer or the Scriptures are our living water or our armor; these are His changeless self, the real Self in us. As we learn to recognize Him in us at all times, fellowship and communion with Him will spontaneously become the heartbeat of our lives.

— *God Unlimited*

"God cannot be tempted by evil, nor does he tempt anyone" — James 1:13.

God does not sin, nor is He responsible when we sin. He created *freedom*, and it is in freedom that there must be this possibility of the alternative choice, and thus in that sense alone He created evil. Satan himself was God's created being of the highest order. In his freedom he rebelled and founded the kingdom of darkness of which he is the god. But he is still forever *God's* Satan, and God deliberately used Satan, for instance, to bring Job to the final end of himself (as He uses him in all our lives!).

In that sense, then, the Bible says that God "intends" the consequences of evil, whether referring to its corruptions within our personal lives or to all its horrors of disease, disasters, death, cruelties, "man's inhumanity to man." To think that God is taking pleasure in these things, however, is utterly untrue. We know that our fallen, evil condition so pierced His heart that, to redeem us from it, He came in the person of His Son to be perfected in suffering, right up to "tasting death for every man."

But it is necessary that we do recognize that, in another sense, He *does* "mean" evil in all its tragedy, and understand why He means it. Only by that recognition can we be firm and strong — and praising! — when the storms of evil are blowing around us. If, when distressing conditions hit us or our neighbors, we only can say that God "permits it," we seem to imply a weakness in God as if He is sorry about such things but can't help it.

— Yes, I Am

> *"You will receive power when the Holy Spirit comes on you; and you will be my witnesses in Jerusalem, and in all Judea, and Samaria, and to the ends of the earth"* — Acts 1:8.

C. T. Studd's testimony about consecration:

"I found that God had promised to believers a peace which passeth all understanding, and a joy that is unspeakable. We then began to examine ourselves earnestly, and we found that we had not got this. But we wanted the best thing that God could give us, so we knelt down and asked Him to give us this blessing.

"I was very much in earnest about it, so when I went up to my own room I again asked God to give me this peace and joy. That very day I met with the book, *The Christian's Secret of a Happy Life*. In it was stated that this blessing is exactly what God gives to everyone who is ready and willing to receive it. I found that the reason why I had not received it was that I had not made room for it, and I found, as I sat there alone thinking, that I had been keeping back from God what belonged to Him. I found that I had kept back myself from Him, and had not wholly yielded.

"As soon as I found this out, I went down on my knees and gave myself up to God in the words of Frances Ridley Havergal's Consecration Hymn:

> *Take my life and let it be*
> *Consecrated, Lord, to thee.*

"I found the next step was to have simple, childlike faith, to believe that what I had committed to God, He was also willing to take and keep."

— *C. T. Studd*

"Anyone who loves his father or mother, . . . son or daughter more than me is not worthy of me" — Matthew 10:37.

"I realized that my life was to be one of simple, childlike faith, and that my part was to trust, not to do. I was to trust in Him and He would work in me to do His good pleasure. From that time my life has been different, and He has given me that peace that passeth understanding and that joy which is unspeakable.

"It was not very long before God led me to go to China. I had never thought of going out of the country before. I had felt that England was big enough for me. But now my mind seemed constantly to run in the direction of the Lord's work abroad. I went one day with my friend Mr. Stanley Smith to Mr. McCarthy's farewell, and I shall never forget the earnest and solemn way in which he told us of the need of earnest workers to preach the gospel. I thought, however, that I would not decide at once, because people would say I was led by impulse. I therefore resolved that after the meeting I would go and ask God. I prayed to God to guide me by His Word. I felt that there was one thing alone which could keep me from going, and that was the love of my mother; but I read that passage, 'He that loveth father or mother more than Me is not worthy of Me,' after which I knew it was God's will, and I decided to go."

— *C. T. Studd*

"'My food,' said Jesus, 'is to do the will of him who sent me and to finish his work'" — John 4:34.

Then came the big test. He met with the strongest opposition from his own family. It had been shock enough to the whole family circle when his father had been converted, but that one of them should become a missionary was the last straw. Every persuasion was used, even to the extent of bringing in Christian workers to dissuade him. Even a relation, whose witness had been a great blessing to him, said to him one evening, "Charlie, I think you are making a great mistake. You are away every night at the meetings and you do not see your mother. I see her, and this is just breaking her heart. I think you are wrong." But C.T. was not again to be moved by human advice.

"I said, 'Let us ask God. I don't want to be pigheaded and go out there of my own accord. I just want to do God's will.' It was hard to have this one, who had been such a help, think it was a mistake. We got down on our knees and put the whole matter in God's hands. That night I could not get to sleep, but it seemed as though I heard someone say these words over and over, 'Ask of Me and I will give thee the heathen for thine inheritance, and the uttermost parts of the earth for thy possession.' I knew it was God's voice speaking to me, and that I had received my marching orders to go to China."

— *C. T. Studd*

"If you love me, you will obey what I command"
— John 14:15.

At Leicester [C. T. Studd and Stanley Smith] met F. B. Meyer, who wrote later: "The visit of Messrs. Stanley Smith and Studd to Melbourne Hall will always mark an epoch in my own life. Before then my Christian life had been spasmodic and fitful; now flaming up with enthusiasm, and then pacing wearily over leagues of gray ashes and cold cinders. I saw that these young men had something which I had not, but which was within them a constant source of rest and strength and joy. Never shall I forget a scene at 7 a.m. in the gray mist of a November morning, as daylight was flickering into the bedroom, paling the guttering candles, which from a very early hour had been lighting up the Scriptures and revealing the figures of the devoted Bible students, who wore the old cricket or boating blazer of earlier days, to render them less sensible to the raw, damp climate. The talk we had then was one of the formative influences of my life. 'You have been up early,' I said to Charlie Studd. 'Yes,' said he, 'I got up at four o'clock this morning. Christ always knows when I have had sleep enough, and He wakes me to have a good time with Him.' I asked, 'What have you been doing this morning?' And he replied, 'You know that the Lord says, "If ye love Me, keep My commandments"; and I was just looking through all the commandments that I could find and putting a tick against them if I have kept them, because I do love Him.'"

— *C. T. Studd*

"Thomas said to him, 'My Lord and my God!'"
— John 20:28.

F. B. Meyer continued:

"'How can I be like you?' C. T. Studd replied, 'Have you ever given yourself to Christ, for Christ to fill you?' 'Yes,' I said, 'I have done so in a general way, but I don't know that I have done it particularly.' He answered, 'You must do it particularly also.' I knelt down that night and thought I could give myself to Christ as easily as possible. I gave Him an iron ring, the iron ring of my will, with all the keys of my life on it, except one little key that I kept back. And the Master said, 'Are they all here?' I said, 'They are all there but one, the key of a tiny closet in my heart, of which I must keep control.' He said, 'If you don't trust Me in all, you don't trust Me at all.' I tried to make terms; I said, 'Lord, I will be so devoted in everything else, but I can't live without the contents of that closet.' I believe that my whole life was just hovering in the balance. He seemed to be receding from me, and I called Him back and said, 'I am not willing, but I am willing to be made willing.' It seemed as though He came near and took that key out of my hand, and went straight for the closet. I knew what He would find there, and He knew too. Within a week from that time He had cleared it right out. But He filled it with something so much better!"

— *C. T. Studd*

"But seek first his kingdom and his righteousness, and all these things will be given to you as well" — Matthew 6:33.

"May 26. [Studd writes from China to his younger brothers Reggie and Bertie at Eton.] We were overrun with rats who during the night would take away our socks, nibbling off our legging tapes, taking away our blotting paper, and putting them at the bottom of the boat in their nest. They caused us a good deal of annoyance, so we thought of setting traps for them; but we decided not to do so, but simply to ask the Lord to rid us of the grievance. Since that time we have had no further trouble with them.

". . . I do not say, don't play games or cricket and so forth. By all means play and enjoy them, giving thanks to Jesus for them. Only take care that games do not become an idol to you, as they did to me. What good will it do to anybody in the next world to have been even the best player that ever has been? And then think of the difference between that and winning souls for Jesus. Oh! if you have never tasted the joy of leading one soul to Jesus, go and ask our Father to enable you to do so, and then you will know what real true joy is. The time is so short, such a little time to rescue souls from hell, for there will be no rescue work in heaven. . . . I have written earnestly because I know the joy there is in Jesus and because I well know the innumerable temptations you are exposed to in a Public School life."

— *C. T. Studd*

"For whoever wants to save his life will lose it, but whoever loses his life for me will save it" — Luke 9:24.

So far as he could judge, Studd's inheritance was £29,000. But in order to leave a margin for error, he decided to start by giving £25,000. One memorable day, January 13, 1887, he sent off four checks of £5,000 each and five of £1,000. As coolly and deliberately as a business man invests in some "gilt-edged" securities, as being both safe and yielding good interest, so C.T. invested in the Bank of Heaven. This was no fool's plunge on his part. It was his public testimony before God and man that he believed God's Word to be the surest thing on earth, and that the hundredfold interest which God has promised in this life, not to speak of the next, is an actual reality for those who believe it and act on it.

He sent £5,000 to Mr. Moody, expressing the hope that he would be able to start some Gospel Work in North India. Moody hoped to carry this out, but was unable to, and instead used the money to start the famous Moody Bible Institute in Chicago, writing, "I will do the next best thing and open a Training School with it."

He sent £5,000 to Mr. George Mueller. He also sent £5,000 to George Holland, in Whitechapel, "to be used for the Lord among His poor in London," and £5,000 to Commissioner Booth Tucker for the Salvation Army in India. This £5,000 arrived just after they had had a night of prayer.

— *C. T. Studd*

"Provide ... for yourselves a treasure ... in heaven that will not be exhausted" — Luke 12:33.

In a few months he was able to discover the exact amount of his inheritance. He then gave some further thousands, mainly to the China Inland Mission, leaving another £3,400 in his possession. Just before his wedding he presented his bride with this money. She, not to be outdone, said, "Charlie, what did the Lord tell the rich young man to do?" "Sell all." "Well then, we will start clear with the Lord at our wedding." They then wrote the following letter to General Booth:

"July 3, 1888

"My dear General, I cannot tell you how many times the Lord has blessed me through reading your and Mrs. Booth's addresses in *The War Cry* and your books. And now we want to enclose a check for £1,500. The other £500 has gone to Commissioner Tucker for his wedding present. Besides this I am instructing our Bankers, Messrs. Coutts and Co., to sell out our last earthly investment of £1,400 Consols and send what they realize to you. Henceforth our bank is in heaven. You see we are rather afraid — notwithstanding the great earthly safety of Messrs. Coutts and Co. and the Bank of England — that they may both break on the Judgment Day. And this step has been taken not without most definite reference to God's Word, and the command of the Lord Jesus, who said, 'Sell that ye have and give alms. Make for yourselves purses which wax not old.'"

— *C. T. Studd*

"Husbands, in the same way be considerate as you live with your wives, and treat them with respect" — 1 Peter 3:7.

"I did not marry her for her pretty face; I married her for her handsome actions toward the Lord Jesus Christ and those He sent her to save. In fact, I can well remember the afternoon when I was talking to a missionary in Taiyuen and he twitted me on being engaged to the prettiest girl in all Shanghai. Now that was an absolute shock to me, for certainly I had never thought of her pretty face. I verily believe that of all God's many good gifts, the least of all is good looks."

Miss Stewart's version is this:

"If C.T. were here, he would tell you I had proposed to him. I did not; as a matter of fact, for certain reasons I refused him. And when I tell you his answer, you will see it is just characteristic of the man. His reply was 'You have neither the mind of God nor the will of God in the matter, but I have. And I intend to marry you whether you will or not, so you had better make up your mind and accept the situation.' That is the reason why I am Mrs. C.T. today."

She kept his love letters, and in one of them we find this:

"July 25, 1887. After eight days spent alone in prayer and fasting, I believe the Lord has shown me that your determination is wrong and will not stand, and that you yourself will see this presently, if the Lord has not shown you already. . . ."

— *C. T. Studd*

"Wives, submit to your husbands as to the Lord" —
Ephesians 5:22.

"July 25. It will be no easy life, no life of ease which I
could offer you, but one of toil and hardship; if I did not
know you to be a woman of God, I would not dream of
asking you. It is to be a fellow-soldier in His army. It is to
live a life of faith in God, a fighting life, remembering that
here we have no abiding city, no certain dwelling place, but
only a home eternal in the Father's House above."

"October 8. I just want to beseech you, darling, that we
both make the same request every day to our Father, that we
may give each other up to Jesus every single day of our lives,
to be separated or not just as He pleases, that neither of us
may ever make an idol of the other.

"I must write and tell darling mother this mail, and others
too, for I cannot keep it secret; only I do laugh when I think
of how little I know of or about you, my own darling, not
even your age or anything; only it is more than enough for
me that you are a true child and lover of the Lord Jesus.

"I love you for your love to Jesus, I love you for your zeal
towards Him, I love you for your faith in Him, I love you for
your love for souls, I love you for loving me, I love you for
your own self, I love you forever and ever. I love you
because Jesus has used you to bless me and fire my soul. I
love you because you will always be a red-hot poker making
me run faster."

— C. T. Studd

"When I called, you answered me; you made me bold and stout-hearted" — Psalm 138:3.

"The last of our supplies was finished, and there was no apparent hope of supplies of any kind coming from any human source. The mail came once a fortnight. The mailman had just set out that afternoon, and in a fortnight he would bring the return mail. The children were put to bed. Then my wife came to my room. We had looked facts in the face. If the return of the postman brought no relief, starvation stared us in the face. We decided to have a night of prayer. We got on our knees. I think we must have stayed there twenty minutes before we rose again. We had told God everything that we had to say in those twenty minutes. Our hearts were relieved; it did not seem to us either reverence or common sense to keep on talking to God as though He were deaf.

"The mailman returned at the appointed time. We were not slow to open the bag. We glanced over the letters; there was nothing, and we looked at each other. I went to the bag again, took it by the corners and shook it mouth downwards; out came another letter. I opened it and then began to read. We were different after the reading of that letter from what we had been before, and I think our whole lives have been different since. This was the letter — I looked at the signature first, one wholly unknown to me — 'I have,' he said, 'for some reason or other received the command of God to send you a check for £100.'"

— *C. T. Studd*

*"Do not get drunk on wine, which leads to debauchery.
Instead, be filled with the Spirit"* — Ephesians 5:18.

[They returned home in 1894. In 1896 Studd was invited
to the U.S.A. and remained there eighteen months.]

"Knoxville, June 24, 1896. I have had such a good day
today, early up and a quiet time for most of the day and the
Lord has been opening up the Word. I am generally awake
and reading and praying soon after 4 a.m."

"Lincoln, Nebraska. December 5. Hallelujah! Just
caught a fish. I was coming back here to the hotel when a
student met me and began to talk to me in the street about
his soul. We stood and talked. He was miserable, and began
to have tears in his eyes, so I said, 'Come to my room and do
business with the Lord.' He came, gave himself utterly away
to Jesus, saw that Jesus must have taken him because He
can't lie, thanked, asked for the Holy Ghost, received by
faith, on the same principle that Jesus can't lie: He must give
the Holy Ghost to him who asks. Then I turned to him and
told him he was to let the Holy Ghost do the work in him
and through him. He seemed to understand a bit, but face
unchanged, dark and unhappy. I said to him, 'Does a man
generally keep a dog and then go barking himself?' He
laughed, his face changed in the twinkling of an eye and he
burst into praising God. 'Oh, I see it all now'; and then he
laughed and rejoiced and prayed all at the same time."

— *C. T. Studd*

*"Yet when I preach the gospel, I cannot boast, for I am
compelled to preach. Woe to me if I do not preach the
gospel!"* — 1 Corinthians 9:16.

"That church is a place to be avoided unless a man means
to get converted." The remark was made about Mr. Studd's
church at Ootacamund, South India, where for six years,
from 1900 to 1906, he went to be Pastor of the Union
Church.

His work lay among all types: the planters in the out-
lying districts of Mysore and Madras, among whom he took
long and arduous journeys; the population of "Ooty,"
European and Eurasian; the soldiers in the neighboring
Soldiers' Home, with whom he was tremendously popular;
the officers and their families, and Government officials,
who crowded to this lovely hill station in the hot months,
including the Governor of Madras and his wife, Lord and
Lady Ampthill, of whom they saw a good deal, as Lord
Ampthill was an old Etonian. They were often invited to
Government House.

As usual he went straight out for souls, both at the
Union Church and amongst the planters, and found responsive hearts in unlikely quarters. A good number professed
conversion, and Mrs. Studd once wrote home, "I don't
think a week passes here that Charlie does not have one to
three conversions." But the pull of the world was very strong
in this popular station, and only those stood who really
went the whole way with God, and who got a salvation
which took the love of the world out of their hearts.

— *C. T. Studd*

"But the cheerful heart has a continual feast" —
Proverbs 15:15.

Studd describes the baptism of his daughters:
"The time for our leaving India came in sight, and the girls wanted to be baptized. We belonged to the Union church, of which I was Pastor, so we were neither Church of England nor Church Missionary Society. The churchman was high, the missionary was low, and somehow we must have fallen between the two stools, or underneath. Consequently I had to baptize the children myself. But where? There was no satisfactory place, so I ordered the gardener to dig up one of the biggest flower beds to a substantial depth, and then I went down to one of the commercial houses and purchased the biggest zinc-lined case I could find and fitted it into the flower bed. Meanwhile I stood outside the box in a similar hole, but without water. The weather was very cold, so the morning of the baptism saw a stream of black boys carrying kettles and saucepans of all dimensions, full of hot water, which they emptied into the box. They had to keep at it pretty persistently, because at the last moment we found that there was a leak.

"One by one the girls went in and came out again, while appropriate singing was going on. I am afraid my girls, trained in such an extraordinary school as ours, where my wife was headmaster and I was matron, imbibed the spirit of fun that possessed us. At any rate, after the ceremony the girls got it off on me that I had baptized two of them with the wrong names."

— *C. T. Studd*

"Again, if the trumpet does not sound a clear call, who will get ready for battle?" — 1 Corinthians 14:8.

[Upon the Studds' return to England,] ministers and workers among men awakened to their golden opportunity of using an outstanding converted sportsman to reach men.

He gripped and stirred his great audiences to their depths, and many were the decisions for Christ. His method of speaking dead straight as man to man, no mincing matters, using the ordinary language of the people, coupled with his humor, made a tremendous appeal to men. A Birmingham newspaper which had a reputation for speaking slightingly of missionary and religious work surprised its readers by the following comments:

"Mr. Studd is a missionary to emulate. And so all that band of college men from Handsworth thought, as they cheered him to the echo — this man with the red tie and slim athletic body and the young face. After more than twenty years in harness he is bubbling over with life and humor; no pessimism about him, no lukewarmness; he loves and he follows, he teaches what he believes, he keeps a brave sunshiny face through all. His faith is as brave as his speech is clear and straight."

An instance of the way he started a talk to men was the following at a businessmen's luncheon:

"Gentlemen, you've had a rich dinner, you will be ready for plain speaking. I am not going to tickle you with a pulpit or academic display of language. I shall speak in ordinary language. . . ."

— *C. T. Studd*

"Not everyone who says to me, 'Lord, Lord,' will enter the kingdom of heaven" — Matthew 7:21.

Studd's testimony:

"I once had another religion: mincing, lisping, bated breath, proper, hunting the Bible for hidden truths, but no obedience, no sacrifice. Then came the change. The real thing came before me. Soft speech became crude salt. The parlor game with the nurses became real cricket on the public ground. Words became deeds. The commands of Christ became not merely Sunday recitations, but battle calls to be obeyed, unless one would lose one's self-respect and manhood. Assent to creed was born again into decisive action of obedience. Orthodoxy became reality. Instead of saying 'Lord, Lord,' in a most reverent voice many times and yet continuing deaf to the simplest commandments, I began to look upon God as really my Father and to rely upon Him as a real Father and to trust Him as such. Instead of talking about fellowship, I enjoyed it. Instead of being unnatural and constrained, I became natural and unconventional. I talked of God and Jesus Christ as Real Living Personal Friends and Relations. *They* have never chided me for it. If a man is willing to obey and sacrifice, he soon learns what is the blessed reality of the fellowship of God's Son Jesus Christ — familiar and social intercourse. In other words, I dropped cant and ceremony and became a Christian. Reverence, I observe in the New Testament, is not apparent politeness and manifest disobedience, but filial or childlike obedience, trust and love."

— *C. T. Studd*

"He said to them, 'Go into all the world and preach the good news to all creation' " — Mark 16:15.

We are now coming to the last and greatest era of Mr. Studd's life — China, then India, and now the heart of Africa. The call came very suddenly, while he was still contemplating returning to India. He was in Liverpool in 1908 and saw such a strangely worded notice that it immediately caught both his attention and his sense of humor. *"Cannibals want missionaries."* "Why, sure they do, for more reasons than one," said he to himself. "I will go inside and see who could have put up such a notice as that." As he thought, it was a foreigner, Dr. Karl Kumm. But God was in that chance impulse, for in that meeting He called C.T. to the great work of his life.

"Karl Kumm had walked across Africa [writes C.T.] and was telling his experiences. He said that in the middle of the continent there were numbers of tribes who had never heard the story of Jesus Christ. He told us that explorers had been to those regions, and big game hunters, Arabs, and traders, European officials and scientists, but no Christian had ever gone to tell of Jesus. *The shame sank deep into one's soul.* I said, 'Why have no Christians gone?' God replied, 'Why don't you go?' 'The doctors won't permit it,' I said. The answer came, 'Am I not the Good Physician? Can I not take you through? Can I not keep you there?' There were no excuses, it had to be done."

— *C. T. Studd*

"Anyone who does not take his cross and follow me is not worthy of me" — Matthew 10:38.

He had no money. At fifty years of age, after fifteen years of ill health, how could he face tropical Africa?

As C.T. presented this challenge and his willingness to pioneer the way, it was taken up by a group of businessmen who formed themselves into a committee to back the project — but on one condition. He must be passed by the doctor. Then things came to a dead stop. The doctor's report was absolutely against him.

Penniless, turned down by the doctor, dropped by the Committee, yet told by God to go, what was he to do? "The only honest thing." Once more he staked all on obedience to God. As a young man he staked his career, in China he staked his fortune, now he staked his life. A gambler for God! He joined the ranks of the great gamblers of faith, Abraham, Moses, etc. in Hebrews 11, and the true apostolic succession, "Men that have hazarded [gambled with] their lives for the name of our Lord Jesus Christ" (Acts 15:26). No wonder he once wrote, "No craze is so great as that of the gambler, and no gambler for Jesus was ever cured, thank God!" His answer to the Committee was this: "Gentlemen, God has called me to go, and I will go. I will blaze the trail, though my grave may only become a stepping stone that younger men may follow." He carried out His Master's word to the letter: "He that shall lose his life for my sake and the gospel's shall find it."

— *C. T. Studd*

"Now faith is being sure of what we hope for and certain of what we do not see" — Hebrews 11:1.

He was due to sail in about three weeks and had no money. What was he to do? The very next day he had a meeting in Birmingham, speaking on the same platform as Dr. Jowett.

"I landed on the platform without knowing what I could say under the circumstances. While the chairman was speaking, a sudden thought came. It was the voice of God: 'Why are you not going?' I replied, 'Where is the money?' 'Can you not trust Me for it?' was the answer. It was like the sun bursting through the clouds. 'Of course I can,' I replied. 'Then where lies the difficulty?' came the answer. The chairman ceased speaking, and I got up and spoke exactly as I would have spoken had the Committee not withdrawn the funds.

"The next day I went up to Liverpool to hold the week-end meetings at the Linnacre Mission. We had a good time. On the Monday morning when taking leave, a friend who had been a complete stranger to me before that weekend put into my hand £10. Imagine my excitement and joy. I had to pass through Liverpool to reach London. On my way through I told the cabby to stop at the Bibby Office, and on the strength of the £10 I booked my passage to Port Said, wiring to the Committee what I had done. Of course the £10 would not take me to Port Said, much less to Khartoum and a thousand miles south and back again, but God sent in supplies in a wonderful way, with the result that I went."

— *C. T. Studd*

"But I am a worm and not a man, scorned by men and despised by the people" — Psalm 22:6.

A letter to his wife:

"December 20, 1912. Somehow God tells me all my life has been a preparation for this coming 10 years or more. It has been a rough discipline. Oh, the agony of it! The asthma — what has not that meant, a daily and nightly dying! The bodily weakness! The being looked down upon by the world folk! The poverty! And have I not been tempted? Tempted to stop working for Christ! Doctors! Relatives! Family! Christians! Who has not declared I tempted God by rising up, and 'going at it' again? It has not been I, it has been Christ who has carried me through.

"This is a poor weak worm of a creature that God has chosen to put into the fiery furnace and walk with Him, and bring him out gain. And now! Ah, yes, He seems to be pouring health and strength into me, and a burning, consuming desire to live, to live for Christ and men. Glory! Jesus is my chief love and my Chief. And now, Scilla darling, all this separation is for our good; and what is far better, it is for God's glory and Christ's honor. I believe this assuredly: (1) Your health shall be restored. (2) You shall become a bigger firebrand for Jesus than ever you have been, and a far greater power than poor weak I could ever be. (3) Our girls shall be white-hot Christian warriors, and to God be all the glory.

"I think and think, and all upon the same line — *a New Crusade.*"

— *C. T. Studd*

> *"Therefore go and make disciples of all nations. . . . I will be with you always, to the very end of the age"* — Matthew 28:19-20.

He proceeded to outline the principles of the New Crusade.

"Believing that further delay would be sinful, some of God's insignificants and nobodies in particular — but trusting in our Omnipotent God — have decided on certain simple lines, according to the Book of God, to make a definite attempt to render the evangelization of the world an accomplished fact. For this purpose we have banded ourselves together under the name of 'Christ's Etceteras,' and invite others of God s people to join us in this glorious enterprise. We are merely Christ's nobodies, otherwise Christ's Etceteras. We rejoice in and thank God for the good work being carried on in the already occupied lands by God's Regular Forces. We seek to attack and win to Christ only those parts of the devil's empire which are beyond the extremest outposts of the regular army of God. Christ's Etceteras are a union mission; a Christian and, therefore, international brotherhood; a supplementary Worldwide Evangelization Crusade.

"Our method is to search and find out what parts of the world at present remain unevangelized, and then by faith in Christ, by prayer to God, by obedience to the Holy Ghost, by courage, determination, and supreme sacrifice to accomplish their evangelization with the utmost despatch.

"The Head, the Commander, the Director of this Mission is the Triune God."

— C. T. Studd

"I will extol the Lord at all times. . . . My soul will boast in the Lord" — Psalm 34:1-2.

The parting from his wife seemed even harder this time. But she was now with him in making the sacrifice, although the harder part was to be hers — to remain at home, never knowing from month to month what news she would receive of her husband.

[The night before C.T. left] she read Psalm 34: "I sought the Lord, and He heard me, and delivered me from *all my fears.* This poor man cried, and the Lord heard him, and saved him out of *all his troubles.*"

[She relates:] "I just felt every fear was gone — all my fears, all my troubles, all that 'left alone' was going to mean, all the fears of malarial fever and the poisoned arrows of the savages; and I went to bed rejoicing. I just laughed 'the laugh of faith' that night. I rose from my knees and wrote the experience to my husband and posted it to Marseilles, though he had not yet left this country."

On the eve of their parting, in a flash of inspiration, C.T. put the thought of both their hearts into a sentence, and that sentence became the motto of the Crusade. A young fellow sat talking with them and remonstrated with C.T. He said, "Is it a fact that at fifty-two you mean to leave your country, your home, your wife and your children?" "What?" said C.T., "have you been talking of the sacrifice of the Lord Jesus Christ tonight? *If Jesus Christ be God and died for me, then no sacrifice can be too great for me to make for Him.*"

— *C. T. Studd*

"If that is how God clothes the grass of the field, . . . will he not much more clothe you, O you of little faith?" — Matthew 6:30.

In a letter to Dr. Wilkinson he told of the fire burning within him in characteristic style:

"The Committee I work under is a conveniently small Committee, a very wealthy Committee, a wonderfully generous Committee, and is always sitting in session — the Committee of the Father, the Son and the Holy Ghost.

"We have a multi-millionaire to back us up, out and away the wealthiest person in the world. I had an interview with Him. He gave me a check book free and urged me to draw upon Him. He assured me His Firm clothes the grass of the field, preserves the sparrows, counts the hairs of the children's heads. He said the Head of the Firm promised to supply all our need; and to make sure, one of the Partners, or rather two, were to go along with each member of our parties, and would never leave us or fail us. He even showed me some testimonials from former clients. A tough old chap with a long beard and hard-bitten face said that on one occasion supplies had arrived and been delivered by black ravens, and on another, by a white-winged angel. Another little old man who seemed scarred and marked all over like a walnut shell said he had been saved from death times untold, for he had determined to put to proof the assurance that he who would lose his life for the Firm's sake should find it."

— *C. T. Studd*

"Trust in the Lord and do good, dwell in the land and enjoy safe pasture" — Psalm 37:3.

[C. T. Studd and his companion Alfred Buxton] gained their heart's desire, and reached Niangara, the very heart of Africa, after nine months' arduous traveling and living mostly in tents, during which, as he said afterwards, "We got into so many tight corners, but always found God there, that we began to look out for, nay, even desire, tight corners to get into, that we might see how God would extricate us from them." It was remarkable how God led them on to this place, for it had not been their original plan. They had thought to start work at Feradje, ten days from Niangara.

After crossing the river at Dungu the scene changes, vegetation becomes luxurious, grassland gives place to the giant trees and the tropical forest; everywhere are little groups of grass-thatched huts, surrounded by plantations of bananas and palm trees. They had entered the fringes of the great tropical forest which stretches for hundreds of miles to the south, and contains, though unknown to them at the time, the biggest population of the whole of Congo. Added to this, God had in His own wonderful way given them favor with this Government official of high standing, who not only directed them to all these strategic centers but enabled them to get concessions in them. The first stage of this venture of faith had been crowned with success beyond their dreams.

— *C. T. Studd*

"Endure hardship with us like a good soldier of Christ Jesus" — 2 Timothy 2:3.

C.T. had many tests but the severest of all came by news from home. Shortly after he sailed Mrs. C.T. was suddenly taken severely ill on a journey to Carlisle. Her heart was found to have extended out several inches. For days she was kept alive only by stimulants, until, after a visit from Lord Radstock, and the prayer of faith, she turned the corner. But even then her recovery was but partial, and she remained an invalid with no likelihood of further improvement. The doctor's verdict was that she "must live quietly in every sense of the word for the rest of her life." She had to go to her room each night at seven and not come down the next day until lunch time.

No doctor's verdict, however, could now stop her from joining in the New Crusade. She had the example of her husband before her, and his victory of faith over all bodily weakness. More than that, she had God's call. She now knew that it was God who had led her husband to start the Crusade, and that He was calling her to the fight side by side with him. So she took up the reins at the home end. At first she kept to the doctor's instructions in hours of rising and retiring, but broke all rules in the amount of work she did. Later she took the whole plunge.

From her bed and invalid couch she formed Prayer Centers, issued monthly pamphlets by the thousand, often wrote twenty and thirty letters a day, planned and edited the first issues of the *H.A.M.* Magazine.*

— C. T. Studd

*Heart of Africa Mission.

"For I have not come to call the righteous, but sinners"
— Matthew 9:13.

[Back in England] C.T. went up and down the homeland, urging and pleading with God's people to rise up and fight and sacrifice for perishing souls.

He took the magazine in hand and issued the most stirring appeals that pen could write.

"Christ's call is to feed the hungry, not the full; to save the lost, not the stiff-necked; not to call the scoffers, but sinners to repentance; not to build and furnish comfortable chapels, churches, and cathedrals at home in which to rock Christian professors to sleep by means of clever essays, stereotyped prayers and artistic musical performances, but to raise living churches of souls among the destitute, to capture men from the devil's clutches and snatch them from the very jaws of hell, to enlist and train them for Jesus, and make them into an Almighty Army of God. *But this can only be accomplished by a red-hot, unconventional, unfettered Holy Ghost religion,* where neither Church nor State, neither man nor traditions are worshiped or preached, but only Christ and Him crucified. Not to confess Christ by fancy collars, clothes, silver croziers, or gold watch-chain crosses, but by *reckless sacrifice and heroism* in the foremost trenches.

"When in hand-to-hand conflict with the world and the devil, neat little biblical confectionery is like shooting lions with a pea-shooter. One needs a man who will let himself go and deliver blows right and left as hard as he can hit, trusting in the Holy Ghost."

— *C. T. Studd*

"And now these three remain: faith, hope and love. But the greatest of these is love" — 1 Corinthians 13:13.

On his final return to Africa, Studd wrote:
"May 31, 1918. The closer you live to these natives, the better. Keep them out of your house and off your verandah, and you will have as bad a time as you give them, and as bad an opinion of them as they have of you. Be thick with them, make them your friends, and they will be the most loving and joyful folks on earth.

"The other day I was far from fit, so kept my bed longer than usual. Some of our Christians from a neighboring village came in for early service. Seeing me from afar on my verandah in bed, they at once changed their route, and came to me in deep concern, which was only partly allayed when I assured them the name of my complaint was mostly 'laziness.' Thereupon they sat down around my bed. Conversation having come to an end, I wondered how I could get rid of these too loving folk without giving offence, and so be enabled to dress. Suddenly, to my consternation, I found the whole six kneeling around my bed, one after another letting out his heart in prayer for me. When the six had prayed, and before I could have my innings, the leader had pronounced the benediction, and a funny one it was too! But the humor of it cleared the lump from my throat and mopped my eyes, so fortunately, being extra unconventional, I took my innings after the benediction. They may be weak or fail in the possession of many talents; but I knew that they possessed the greatest of all God's gifts, *love!*"
— *C. T. Studd*

> *"The entrance of your words gives light; it gives under-*
> *standing to the simple"* — Psalm 119:130.

In spite of the enormous amount of work he was already doing, he determined also to translate the New Testament into Kingwana. It was a marvelous intellectual feat for a man of nearly seventy. He worked at it night and day. "My days," he wrote, "are eighteen hours as a rule, and no meals but what I gulp down as I write." Much of it was done in the early morning between 2 a.m. and 6 a.m. Sometimes by the end of a day he had such a stiff neck through bending over the table that Jack Harrison, who was like a son to him, would have to come and gently massage it before he could sit up straight again. While he translated, Harrison typed. It was a deliberately simple translation, kindly published by the Scripture Gift Mission, made so simple that any bush native who learned to read could understand it.

He finished it, and later also the Psalms and extracts of Proverbs, but at the cost of his remaining strength. Heart attack followed heart attack. Several times he went right to the River's edge. In 1928 he was so ill for a week that it was not thought that he could live. At one time, as he lay hardly breathing and eyes closed, it seemed that all was over. But the missionaries managed to summon a Belgian Red Cross doctor, who treated him with various drugs, including morphine. He gradually recovered, but was so weak that he could not get off his bed, nor do any work, still less take meetings, without the aid of morphine.

— *C. T. Studd*

"Even though I walk through the valley of the shadow of death, . . . you are with me" — Psalm 23:4.

A close friend, Dr. A. T. Wilkinson, wrote about Studd's health:

"From early years C.T. had been perforce his own doctor, and, in China, dealt medically with others as well as with himself. He was a museum of diseases when he left China, and was afterwards hardly ever free. He understood himself as no other doctor understood him. That he kept himself alive for 70 years, and then did not die directly from any of his tropical diseases but from surgically unrelieved gallstones and their consequences, is a wonderful testimony to his medical skill. He was ever willing to learn from others and glad to have medical advice, but he also leaned back on the Great Physician; and as regards his hazardous missionary enterprises, did so when on every occasion medical advice was dead against the project. He was a man whom God loved and took care of.

"Chronic disease calls for chronic treatment. When a man has asthma and recurring malaria and dysentery and the chills and pains of gallstones ever with him in varying combinations, what can he do but take the drugs that the Lord himself has provided to relieve his symptoms, prolong his life, and so enable him to go on with his work? He fought as brave a fight against adverse conditions as Paul himself; and in consequence of this judicious treatment he was able to go on working not eight but eighteen hours a day. He was one of the finest Christians and the most heroic and lovable man I ever met."

— C. T. Studd

"Precious in the sight of the Lord is the death of his saints" — Psalm 116:15.

The end came suddenly. Mr. Harrison gives us the details:

"Ibambi, July 1931.

"On Monday (13th) afternoon, he asked me to give him an injection of quinine as he felt cold and thought maybe he had some fever hanging around, although there was no temperature at all. In the evening he felt still worse and I stayed with him all night until 4:30 a.m. During that night he had very much pain in the stomach towards the right side. He told me that evening that he suspected gallstones, and asked me to read up all I could about this complaint. I did, and to our amazement, we found that in every detail the symptoms agreed with his case. On Tuesday morning he was still weaker and in very much pain too; and in the evening still weaker and the pain ever so severe. . . . On Thursday morning (16th) he was easier and thought that the pain in the stomach had moved somewhat. He had become so weak and exhausted by this time that now his voice began to weaken. . . .

"He ceased to try to talk about anything and with each little breath he could spare he could only say 'Hallelujah!' 'Hallelujah!' It was amazing to see him passing out like this — quite conscious all through and just 'Hallelujah' coming every breath he had.

"At about 7 p.m. on Thursday he seemed to lapse into unconsciousness, and shortly after 10:30 p.m. passed to his reward. It was a fine going."

— C. T. Studd

"Create in me a pure heart, O God" — Psalm 51:10.

I remember when I first heard two from Ruanda* speaking very quietly and simply for two days in our London Headquarters to about ninety of our staff. At the last meeting they very quietly opened the door for any present to say anything that was on their hearts. Very soon one and another were bringing to the light areas in their lives where they had come face to face with sin unobserved by them before and were bringing them to the cleansing blood. I got a real shock at the end when one of the two quietly said, "I don't know if you realize it, friends, but this *is* revival!"

It began to shake me out of the misconception of years, that revival could only come in great soul-shaking outpourings of the Spirit. Thank God for such when they do come; they have been the great and precious hurricanes of the Spirit in the history of the church. But I saw the defeatism and almost hopelessness that so many of us had fallen into by thinking that we could do nothing about revival except pray, often rather unbelievingly, and wait until the heavens rent and God came down. But now I see that "revival" in its truest sense is an everyday affair right down within the reach of everyday folk, to be experienced in our hearts, homes, churches, and fields of service. When it does burst forth in greater and more public ways, thank God; but meanwhile we can see to it that we ourselves are being constantly revived persons.

— *Continuous Revival*

*The Ruanda Mission, East Africa.

"Guard your heart, for it is the wellspring of life" —
Proverbs 4:23.

Revival, as contrasted with a Holy Ghost atmosphere, is a clean-cut breakthrough of the Spirit, a sweep of Holy Ghost power, bending the hearts of hardened sinners as the wheat before the wind, breaking up the fountains of the great deep, sweeping the whole range of the emotions, as the master hand moves across the harp strings, from the tears and cries of the penitent to the holy laughter and triumphant joy of the cleansed.

They are fools who belittle such holy experiences and warn against "excessive emotionalism." Such do not even understand the make-up of "Mansoul," still less the ways of the Eternal Lover with His beloved. With sure sense of direction does the inspired Word always point us to the heart, not the mind, as the citadel of Man.

The mere mind of man, his views and ideals, his intellectual conceits and opinions, are but straw before the whirlwind in the grip of the real inner man of the heart when it holds the helm. And revivals reach that inner man and carry the mind along later as captive in its train. They move the deep springs of being, and all else follows; and they do it in earthquake fashion.

Of course there are the accompanying dangers: emotionalism that runs to seed, that remains content with pleasurable sensations instead of being the driving force of a new way of life; emotionalism that despises mental attainment instead of inspiring and directing the mind to lofty concepts in the Spirit.

— *Christ in Congo Forests*

*"If we confess our sins, he is faithful and just and will
forgive us our sins and purify us"* — 1 John 1:9.

Sin is a revelation. It is God who graciously shows us sin,
even as it is He who shows us the precious blood. Sin is only
seen to be *sin* — against God — when He reveals it; otherwise sin may just be known as a wrong against a brother, or
an anti-social act, or an inconvenience, or a disability, or
some such thing. Indeed, that is often the extent of the
message of a "social gospel."

God shows us sin. We do not need to keep looking inside
ourselves. This is not a life of introspection or morbid
self-examination. We do not walk with sin, we walk with
Jesus; but, as we walk in childlike faith and fellowship with
Him step by step, moment by moment, then if the cups cease
to run over, He who is light, with whom we are walking, will
clearly show us what the *sin* is which is hindering, what its
real name is in His sight, rather than the pseudonym, the
excusing title, which we might find it more convenient to
call it. Let us say again, it is so simple. God does not speak in
terms of general condemnation leading to despair of past or
fear of future. He speaks in simple, specific terms of any
actual sin in the present which is hindering the inner witness
of His Spirit.

What do we do then? Well, that is obvious. 1 John 1:9
says, "If we confess our sins. . . ."

— *Continuous Revival*

"The blood of Jesus . . . purifies us from every sin" —
1 John 1:7.

Where there is confession, we all know there is the word of promise, "If we confess our sins, He is faithful and just to forgive us our sins, and to cleanse us from all unrighteousness." We may say the cleansing is almost automatic, where there is the confession. That light which shines so unchangingly on the sin shines also on the blood. "If we walk in the light, as He is in the light," says John, "we have fellowship one with another, and the blood of Jesus Christ His Son cleanseth us from all sin." When walking in the light, we read, both sin and the precious blood are seen, the one, praise God, cancelling out the other. And it is important to remember that confession of sin does not deliver by itself. It is *the blood* that cleanses, and we must always pass on from confession to faith and praise for *the blood,* believing that the blood alone is what glorifies God and delivers us.

Folk often remain depressed and mournful, asking others to pray for them after confession of sin when they ought to pass straight on by simple faith to the blood ever flowing and cleansing.

Once again, where the blood cleanses, the Spirit witnesses, and where the Spirit witnesses, the cups always run over! So we are back again where we started — walking with Jesus step by step, brokenness, cups running over.

— *Continuous Revival*

"The sacrifices of God are a broken spirit" —
Psalm 51:17.

Brokenness is a picturesque word, a key word, indeed *the* key word in continuous revival. It is not a word that comes a great deal in Scripture, though more than we think if we examine a concordance; but it comes enough to show that it is a picturesque, as well as true, way of describing the sinner's only and constant relationship to his Savior. We first learn that salvation is only possible for lost men through a *broken* Savior: "This is my body which is *broken* for you"; "Reproach hath *broken* my heart." In Gethsemane He had a broken will, and on Calvary a broken fellowship even with His Father; for the One who is our Substitute and who was made sin for us had to take upon Himself the proud, unbroken ego of fallen man, and had to be broken at Calvary in his place.

But man also has to be "broken." He sees his sinful condition before God as he realizes the coming judgment and wrath, and as he is pointed to the slain Lamb he has to "break" at the foot of the cross. The proud, self-justifying, self-reliant, self-seeking self has to come just as a lost, undone sinner, whose only hope is a justifying Savior. David said it, when at the supreme moment of his own total brokenness, in Psalm 51, the Spirit caused him to comment, "The sacrifices of God are a *broken* spirit: a *broken* and a contrite heart, O God, thou wilt not despise."

— *Continuous Revival*

"If you confess with your mouth, 'Jesus is Lord,' and believe in your heart . . . you will be saved" — Romans 10:9.

All Christian relationships are two-way, not one-way. They are horizontal as well as vertical. This is to say, we are a two-way people. We are not just isolated units living in a vertical relationship with an isolated God.

"The word of faith," we read in Romans 10:8-10, is two-way, with the heart towards God and with the mouth before man. Indeed, it takes it farther and says that to experience in our hearts and lives the full benefit of our faith we *must* express it both ways, for "with the heart man believeth unto righteousness," that is to say, the heart-believer is accounted righteous before God; but it is "with the mouth" that "confession is made unto salvation," that is to say, we realize in our experience the joyful fact that we are saved. Confession before man does something in our hearts that heart-faith alone never does.

So saving faith, the attitude of brokenness, is a two-way activity, towards God and man, as are righteousness and love and indeed all the relationships of Christian living. Indeed, we can put it this way. We can liken a man to a house. It has a roof and walls. So also man in his fallen state has a roof on top of his sins between him and God; he also has walls up, between him and his neighbor. But at salvation, when broken at the cross, not only does the roof come off through faith in Christ, but the walls fall down flat, and the man's true condition as a sinner saved by grace is confessed before all men.

— *Continuous Revival*

"Live as children of light" — Ephesians 5:8.

Continued revival is continued brokenness; but brokenness is two-way, and that means walls kept down as well as roof off. But man's most deep-rooted and subtle sin is the subtle sin of pride: self-esteem and self-respect. Though hardly realizing it, while we are careful to keep the roof off between ourselves and God through repentance and faith, we soon let those walls of respectability creep up again between ourselves and our brethren. We don't mind our brethren knowing about successes in our Christian living; they can know if we win a soul, if we lead a class, if we get a prayer answered, if we get good things from the Scriptures, because we, too, get a little reflected credit out of those things. But where we fail, in those many, many areas of our daily lives — that is a different question!

If God has to deal with us over our impatience or temper in the home, over dishonesty in our business, over coldness or other sins, by no means do we easily bear testimony to our brethren of God's faithful and gracious dealings in such areas of failure. Why not? Just because of pride, self-esteem, although we would often more conveniently call it reserve!
— *Continuous Revival*

"My cup overflows" — Psalm 23:5.

We are to recognize that "cups running over" is the *normal* daily experience of the believer walking with Jesus, not the abnormal or occasional, but the normal, continuous experience. But that just isn't so in the lives of practically all of us. Those cups running over get pretty muddled up; other things besides the joy of the Lord flow out of us. We are often much more conscious of emptiness, or dryness, or hardness, or disturbance, or fear, or worry than we are of the fullness of His presence and overflowing joy and peace.

And now comes the point. What stops that moment-by-moment flow? The answer is only one — sin. But we by no means usually accept or recognize that. We have many other more convenient names for those disturbances of heart. We say it is nerves that cause us to speak impatiently — not sin. We say it is tiredness that causes us to speak the sharp word at home — not sin. We say it is the pressure of work which causes us to lose our peace, get worried, act or speak hastily — not sin. We say it is our difficult or hurtful neighbor who causes us resentment or dislike, or even hate — but not sin. Anything but sin. We go to psychiatrists or psychologists to get inner problems unraveled — tension, strain, disquiet, dispeace —but anything which causes the cups to cease running over is *sin*.

— *Continuous Revival*

*"Save me from bloodguilt, O God, . . . and my tongue
will sing of your righteousness"* — Psalm 51:14.

Initial brokenness was roof off, walls down. But now in
the daily life? Roof still off, but what about the walls?
Continued brokenness is continued revival, and continued
brokenness has implicit in it the continued two-way testimony. But here we want to watch carefully. The confession
that matters in the Scripture, and which is most referred to,
is the confession of *Christ*, rather than of sin (although there
are such verses as 1 John 1:9 and James 5:16, where in the
original text *faults* is *sins*); and it is to the constant confession of Christ that I am called. That is my duty. That is my
privilege. That is the way both to get blessing and to trans-
mit it. Indeed, perhaps the word *confession* has become so
misused through its use in the confessional that it is better
and clearer to use the word *testimony*.

As we entered the way of salvation by a two-way brokenness, we must continue in the daily walk. Something
comes in which stops the flow of the Spirit. It is seen to be
sin, however "small" we may like to call it (is any sin small
which crucified my Lord?); it is confessed and forgiven. But
brokenness is two-way. There is the testimony to give before
men, as God gives the opening. Nothing need stop me giving
it except that it would hurt my pride, my self-esteem. That is
how I glorify God — by testifying, as occasion arises, to His
fresh deliverances, the fresh experiences of the power of His
cleansing blood in my life.

— *Continuous Revival*

"You desire truth in the inner parts" — Psalm 51:6.

We remember that it was the confession of Christ before men that made Him so real to our own hearts. It did something for us, which mere heart-faith did not. Now it is just the same concerning the daily walk. The real reason why we are usually so insensitive to the "little" sins of our daily walk and why we pass them over without much concern is just because we are not too ashamed about them, or not too repentant, or even in some cases we have given up hope of any lasting deliverance.

And why so? Because, while we only walk with the roof off and deal in secret with God alone about our daily affairs, we have the convenient sense of a God of great mercy or a Christ who died for us, of our security in Him, of an easy-giving forgiveness, and so frankly we do not get too concerned about our present inconsistencies! But if we start walking in the light with others about the Lord's daily dealings with us, telling them when the shadow of sin has darkened our path and how God has dealt with us over it, we shall suddenly find two things: one, that we have an altogether new sense of shame for sin; and two, an altogether new sense of cleansing and liberation from sin.

— *Continuous Revival*

"O Lord, open my lips, and my mouth will declare your praise" — Psalm 51:15.

We know that the way salvation is spread is by our telling the unsaved what the Lord has done for us; it does something in their hearts, quickening a desire for the same experience. So it is with testimony among God's people. The joy and praise leaps from one heart to another when we hear what the Lord has done for another. The more direct, open, and exact the testimony, the more we rejoice. It does yet more. It convicts. Our hearts are fashioned alike. The way the devil tempts you is almost certainly the way he tempts me. When I hear you tell of the Lord's dealings down where you really live in your home relationships, in your business, and so on, it surely reaches me on some spot where I need the same light and deliverance. That is exactly how great revivals break out and spread.

Sin is suddenly seen to be sin in some life. Someone breaks down (brokenness) and doesn't mind who is present; he can only see himself as a sinner needing renewed cleansing. So out he comes, maybe with tears; public reconciliations are made; the conviction spreads, till dozens are doing the same thing. "Revival has visited this church," we say with joy. When there is a continuous sensitiveness to the smallest sin that stops the cups running over, when there is recognition of the sin in the light, confession, forgiveness, and the thankful public testimony to the glory of God, there is a daily revival.

— *Continuous Revival*

"Let us throw off everything that hinders and the sin that so easily entangles" — Hebrews 12:1.

Many of God's people, including the writer, know something of God's deliverances from sin; but there is some spot still in the life which may be given the name mentioned in Hebrews 12:1, "the sin which doth so easily beset us"; and at this "weak spot" we really give up any idea that God can really, fully, and permanently deliver. It may not be some big thing, as the world calls big; perhaps it is so hidden that it is just a mere touch of sin known only to the person himself ("the garment spotted by the flesh"), but hope of full deliverance is really given up.

Then we enter into this revival — walk in the light step by step. We are made sensitive as never before both to the reality and the shamefulness of sin. We find that as we walk brokenly with God and one another, sins which used to beset us easily lessen in their power and falls are fewer. Then it suddenly comes to us as light that this special spot of weakness, taken for granted through the years, can be dealt with and deliverance found, if recognized as sin to be faced and hated each time it arises.

However we can get into bondage of thinking that we are under strict compulsion to testify to the Lord's dealings on all or on fixed occasions. We must never allow ourselves to be driven.

— *Continuous Revival*

"Continue to live in him" ∽ Colossians 2:6.

In our evangelical and rightful zeal to bring sinners to the crisis of the new birth, and to lead the saints on to further crises of separation, consecration, sanctification, and the baptism of the Holy Ghost, we have often made too much of the crises and too little of the *walk*. But the Scriptures leave us in no doubt of their emphasis. In almost every Epistle the Holy Spirit leads us on through the crises, the way into Christ, to the *walk* with Him.

Now to walk is a step-by-step activity. Given the main destination, all that matters is the next step. Christian living is concerned, therefore, just with the implications of the present moment, not with past or future. But we tend to live in the past and thus to avoid the keen edge of the challenge of the immediate moment. Thus, as things arise in our hearts and lives which are not consistent with our Christian testimony, we say, or imply, "Well, I know these things are not right, but anyhow I have been born again, I have been cleansed in His blood, I have received eternal life, Christ lives in me." Thus I circle around the raw facts of my immediate condition by leaning back on my past crises. We make too little of the present walk.

Let us remember that all we are asked to do is to *walk with Jesus*, and that means simple concentration on things as they are with me just this moment, then the next, then the next, and so on.

— *Continuous Revival*

"There is now no condemnation for those who are in Christ Jesus" — Romans 8:1.

One of Satan's favorite weapons is false condemnation. He loves to make us look back at our past failures, or into the future at our probably equal failures (so he says), and then puts us into a tailspin of despair or depression. "Look at your pride, coldness, sensuality, worldliness, fruitlessness. You say you were born again or sanctified. Look at yourself! And if you have been that in the past, believe me, you will be exactly the same in the future!" In other words, Satan likes to talk in long-term generalities, based indeed on an element of truth, but built up into a huge lie; for God does not look on His children in a general sense as proud, cold, fruitless, and so on. He sees them in Christ, being conformed to the image of His Son.

The difference between Satan's condemnations and God's convictions is that where Satan uses generalities pointing back to the past or forward to the future, God sees past and future in Christ and just deals with the present, and deals specifically. We *walk* moment by moment, step by step with Him, the past under the blood, the future in His keeping. We are in Jesus, and He in us.

If our walk at this moment is beclouded with the rising up of some motion of sin in us, then God just points to that. "There," He says, "look at that, just that. Just get that right under the blood and then walk again with Me."

— *Continuous Revival*

"Anyone who claims to be in the light but hates his brother is still in the darkness" — 1 John 2:9.

Revival is the simple outcome of obedience to the light. But for many of us the brokenness to which we are now referring, including openness before men, starts by being really costly.

It is the walls of Jericho which have to fall down flat! I certainly found that, and so have many others. In my own case I found myself face to face in Central Africa with a brother whom I had met and disliked in England! Here I was in a revival company where dislike was only another word for hate which was faced and brought to the light as sin; and I was carefully pretending that I had brotherly love for a man whom in the white and black terms of 1 John, I "hated"! It was then I found how high those walls of pride are. I just could not bring myself to admit in public that I had the sin of dislike against him, and equally the sin of hypocrisy against all my brethren in pretending that I did like him. As a senior visiting missionary, I could not let on that I had such a "foolish" thing in my heart. But it was not foolish, it was sin.

At last, after two days under the constant inner compulsion of the Spirit, I just took the step of cold-blooded obedience, brought it into the light before the brother and all, and of course the blood reached me at once; there was cleansing, the love of God in my heart, and the joy of the whole company. I love and honor that brother today.

— Continuous Revival

"Let the word of Christ dwell in you richly as you teach and admonish one another" — Colossians 3:16.

There remains one further stage in revival fellowship, and a most important one. *Mutual exhortation.* The early church was first and foremost a fellowship. All took part, and there was such a flow of the Spirit through the believers that Paul had to write words of restraint. "How is it, brethren? When ye come together, *everyone of you* hath a psalm, hath a doctrine. . . ."

We have now replaced fellowshiping by preaching in our modern church life, and the reason is not hard to find. Fellowshiping necessitates a real flow of life in the fellowship, for each has to be ready to contribute his share of what the Lord is really saying to him; preaching is an easy way out for a not-too-living fellowship. Appoint the preacher and let him find the messages; we can sit still and take or leave what we hear, as we please! Probably the best balance was found in early Methodism, where John Wesley laid down that, besides the preaching and teaching meetings, there must be a weekly classmeeting, which was on a strictly fellowship basis. All who attended were required to tell of the Lord's personal dealings that week, whether concerning sins, or answers to prayer, or opportunities of witness.

— *Continuous Revival*

"Let us consider how we may spur one another on"
— Hebrews 10:24.

In the Scriptures it is also obvious that an important part of fellowshiping was to be mutual exhortation, not just public exhortation by a preacher. In Hebrews it distinctly says that the reason for such exhortation is to keep each other from becoming "hardened through the deceitfulness of sin" (3:13).

Such exhortations are not easy either to receive or give. To receive them with humility and a readiness to be constantly adjusted before God is one proof of continuing revival, for where we are not revived we almost certainly resent such challenges. To give them in grace and faithfulness costs perhaps even more. We are so easily tempted to "let well alone," or to say "It is not my business," because we recognize that to bring such a challenge might disturb the peace or disrupt a friendship. But in revival we see we are our brother's keeper, not for his sake, but for Jesus' sake. When a brother is not on top spiritually, it wounds the Lord Jesus, it grieves Him, it hinders the working of His Spirit; therefore it is part of our duty to Him to be faithful to the brother. Not to be so is sin. Of course such challenging has to be deeply in the Spirit, that is to say, its source must be godly concern for the brother in question, and the subtle danger watched against using such a method to "put a brother right," or even "to get our own back." It can only proceed from brokenness in ourselves.

— *Continuous Revival*

"Whoever hates his brother . . . walks around in the darkness" — 1 John 2:11.

One final word about the way revival starts. It begins by one person who sees from God what it is to walk in the light. But to walk with Jesus like this involves also walking in the light with one another horizontally as well as vertically, and that means at least one other person with whom to walk in open fellowship. Of course, as one brother said to me, "One would naturally start walking like that with the person nearest to you — husband and wife, brother and sister, friend and friend." In other words, revival starts with two people being revived, and starts at home!

The way to begin walking in the light in fellowship one with another in a more public sense is to do it. I have found it most helpful, after talking with a congregation on the subject, to suggest that we move straight on to a time of quiet open fellowship. There will be no pressure, no demands made on any, but just an opportunity given to any to say anything, if they know the Spirit is telling them to do so; if others have no special word from God in their hearts, they are right to keep silent. But revival comes through obedience. Indeed, revival is really just obeying the Holy Ghost. Where He tells to "break" and to testify to the light shining on sin in our life, and on the blood which cleanses from all sin, then let us obey, and we will find at once that the Spirit is loosed in revival in our heart, and is moving in revival in the company.

— *Continuous Revival*

"The prayer of a righteous man is powerful and effective" — James 5:16.

When the nationals were out in the forest in the mornings for communion with the Savior, things happened about which they could scarcely speak afterwards, experiences of the unutterable joy of His presence. Believers had now a new sense of the peril of unbelievers and their responsibility towards them. Each took up the call of his own neighbors or relatives and prayed as never before for their conversion, bringing them along when possible to the meetings. The early morning service took on another form. It opened as a prayer meeting for Christians only. After a time of worship, prevailing prayer, broken sometimes by sobs, ascended to the throne for the lost. They were mentioned one by one, by name. Men and women prayed as if they could not be denied, crying with tears, "O God, these people must be saved." When they had prayed through to a place of assurance, they confidently thanked God for the answer.

Then the drum was beaten as a sign to the waiting groups outside that they could enter. While they were pouring in, the Christians dispersed themselves over the church, allowing their unsaved friends to fill up the seats between; for the meeting that followed was for the bringing home of the prodigals. The others gave themselves to the ministry of intercession while the service continued, praying their brothers out of the far country. This resulted in conversions at almost every meeting; sometimes only two or three, sometimes twenty, thirty or forty.

— *Christ in Congo Forests*

"Love . . . from a pure heart and a good conscience and a sincere faith" — 1 Timothy 1:5.

As the service continued, quite a little crowd collected outside, mostly Christian people. They were trying to listen without being seen. By and by, one by one, they started creeping in and taking their places with the others — thirty, forty, fifty, sixty of them! When an opportunity was given for prayer and confession, the first break came with the station workmen. Consciences were very tender and the sense of sin deep and real. It was well understood that confession meant restitution, but the shame and humiliation of the uncovering of sin cost those proud Babudu people infinitely more than any material restitution.

Carpenters made confessions that they would not have made for any money and which no threat would ever have forced from their lips, of the stealing of timber, nails, screws and hinges. The house lad who had gone halfway the day before rose again and confessed to some minor thefts, such as taking salt from the salt box. "Is that all you have to confess?" he was asked from the platform. "No. That's not all," he said, recounting a few more instances. "And is that all?" Then he would add a few more. "You are a hypocrite," said Jack Roberts.* "You are confessing only what you think is known to me. But remember all is known to God." After that he confessed to gross sin. Young people told how they had been to all-night dances and drinking feasts.

— *Christ in Congo Forests*

*A Worldwide Evangelization Crusade missionary.

"You are being built together to become a dwelling in which God lives by his Spirit" — Ephesians 2:22.

The sense of the Lord's purity and love seemed to fill the air — just to be breathed in by souls, as their spiritual capacity invited its inflow. Men and women worshiped Him in the beauty of holiness, an experience so very new to most of them.

One early morning the Lord met Lily Roberts.* "Suddenly," she said, "I saw a vision. Heaven was opened. I saw the Lord Jesus and I saw myself standing close by Him. In between was a Mabudu woman I knew well, a lovely Christian; and near to her one of the evangelists, and a group of others behind them. The Lord Jesus spoke to me so clearly, reminding me how He had left His glory and humbled Himself to come to earth as the Son of Man, how He lived in me and lived in them; and yet I was keeping in my heart a difference between us. I was melted to tears by His rebuke and put my arms around the woman.

"I went to the early service with no message prepared. I just told them what had happened, that during the previous night God had reproved me for allowing in my thoughts a barrier between myself and them, that we were absolutely one in His sight because He was dwelling within. All of us seemed bowed with a sense of His presence. God graciously called us to know in some measure how He loved us, and we realized how we loved Him and each other."

— *Christ in Congo Forests*

*A Worldwide Evangelization Crusade missionary.

> *"Who can stand when he appears? For he will be like a refiner's fire or a launderer's soap"* — Malachi 3:2.

The breakthrough with the school children came last and was every bit as real. Many lads owned up to stealing animals out of other boys' traps. Older boys admitted attending heathen rites and being guilty of impurity. Even small children confessed to taking cooked food, hidden by their mother for the evening meal. With tears running down their cheeks, they would say, "I told mother I didn't take it, but I did." The girls' confessions were astounding — painting their bodies in black, white, and red, as a substitute for dress. Blackening their eyebrows, braiding straw hats with the object of making themselves attractive, wearing their hats obliquely over one eye with a feather stuck out at another angle to be conspicuous, running away from school, and going to dances on the quiet. Their confessions came from the breaking up of the deep wellsprings of the heart.

The blessed Holy Spirit was doing what He came to do — convict of sin and reveal the Savior. The words of Malachi were finding their fulfillment: "The Lord, whom ye seek, shall suddenly come to His temple. . . . But who may abide the day of His coming? . . . For he will be like a refiner's fire or a launderer's soap."

But if conscience had been deeply wounded, Calvary had healed the wounds of all who had found their way there.

— *Christ in Congo Forests*

*"The law of the Spirit of life set me free from the law of
sin and death"* — Romans 8:2.

The new man in Christ is basically the same person,
same self, same entity as the old man; formerly carnal, sold
under sin; now spiritual, sold unto holiness. The flesh (I
carnal) becomes the new man in Christ (I spiritual). It is the
Dr. Jekyll and Mr. Hyde of Stevenson's creation, the one
becoming the other by an imagined process of metamor-
phosis.

We see it most clearly when we are told to count ourselves "dead indeed unto sin but alive unto God through
Jesus Christ." The self is seen here to be the living center of
both the old man and the new. I am to count the self that was
once the old man as now dead unto sin — in other words,
immune from the power of sin as sharing the death of Christ
— and that same self now as the new man, alive to God as
sharing in the quickening life of the risen Christ. We are
then told to yield our *selves* unto God as those that are alive
from the dead.

"Who shall deliver me?" cries Paul. The glory of the
gospel is the answering cry of Romans 8:2: "He hath made
me free"; not "He shall," but "He *hath*." We are back again
to our old theme: all grace, as all nature, consists in the
givingness of God. He *has* given deliverance from the power
of indwelling sin — the law of the Spirit of life in Christ
Jesus which *has* set us free from the law of sin and death.
                                        — *The Law of Faith*

"Death is at work in us, but life is at work in you" —
2 Corinthians 4:12.

Where there is a dying there is a rising. As we by acceptance die to our hurt selves, we have a consciousness of Him living His life in us. We have a poise, faith, peace, liberty, which hurt self does not have. The life of Jesus is being manifested in our mortal body, and people see something different from the usual way of behavior in unpleasant circumstances. Then also, being freed from self-pity and self-hurt (though there is the constant hurt), we can now see along with God into something of His purposes in revealing Himself to others by us. We are freed to cooperate by the word of faith that God will do what He plans to do in the specifics He shows us in the situation. We are free to love those whose very antagonisms are proofs that they are really crying out for love, and to give acceptable witness as occasions arise.

The very hurts we so deeply feel become redemptive in stirring us to aroused human reactions which become a springboard for faith — this dying and rising with Him. God can come through to others where He could not come through unless He first had His dying and rising human agent. So, as Paul summed it up: "Death works in us, but life in you."

What was frustration is now adventure. But we are active agents, not passive recipients.

— *Once Caught, No Escape*

". . . from darkness to light, and from the power of Satan to God" — Acts 26:18.

Redemption has released us humans from our former taskmaster and joined us to our new Lord. The old man has become the new man. The same man (human) in both relationships, but the change of an old lord for a new one. In the light of this we can accept ourselves, with no single thing about our human nature which is not now for God-manifestation; and wherein we still have difficulty with aspects of our humanity, it is not for us to despise or smear ourselves, but to inquire how these same aspects can now be harnessed for new uses.

Let us also remember that the accuser of the brethren is a born, compulsive liar; therefore, one favorite weapon of his is to make us appear in our eyes a distorted, disgusting caricature of what we are in other people's eyes. Remember, God has chosen us exactly as we are; and if He is satisfied to do that, we can be satisfied.

Replace the waves of condemnation with boldness of faith. Long ago I learned that "the voice of the stranger" depresses, downgrades, and darkens. "The voice of the Shepherd" is always gentle, upbuilding and healing. Discern between soul and spirit, for the soul, which is the seat of the emotions and reason, is variable and can convey variable impressions to us. We live beneath the outer covering of soul, where our spirit is joined to His Spirit, and there the relationship is invariable and there He is in all His sufficiency.

— *The Spontaneous You*

"If we confess our sins, he is faithful and just and will forgive us" — 1 John 1:9.

We, the redeemed, though we do not live a life of continued sinning, do commit sins, usually sudden and unpremeditated. What should we then do? We have not broken our relationship with God, but we have interrupted fellowship from our side of the relationship. We have asserted our freedom by acting as if we were not one with Him but were once again our independent selves and going our own way.

The way back is as simple and plain as on our first coming to God. If there is quick sinning, there is quick cleansing. It has to start at the point of my personal freedom, where I went wrong, and I must express that freedom in honest confession. That is all I can do about it, but that I must do, and that means my brokenness. It may involve confession to man or restitution, but it certainly means admission to God of my sin. When I do that, it is as if God says to me, "Yes, you sinned, and honest confession and repentance were necessary. But as for the sin, I settled the whole sin question 2,000 years ago in the atoning death of My Son."

At this point we have to be careful not to add a second sin to the first. The first was the sin itself; the second and greater is my not believing at once that what God has cleansed He has cleansed. Not to believe in the efficacy of the blood of Christ is a worse sin than the first, for unbelief, Jesus said, is the only real sin (John 16:9).

— *The Spontaneous You*

"As he is, so are we in this world" — 1 John 4:17 (KJV).

Christ gives His life for those He disapproves, for below their hate and guilt and rebellion — indeed, because of it — He knows their dire need; and God lives to meet need and gives Himself without limit to do it. That is a different quality of love, and only God is this kind of love. What is God's joy? What is His pleasure? How does He complete Himself or express Himself (for, as we have said, a self must have self-completion and self-expression)? What is life, this eternal life, in its ultimate meaning?

The answer is given us in the God who has shown us exactly what He is in Jesus. It is in self-transcendence. God's life is others having life: God is blessed when man is blessed; God sorrows when man sorrows. God (in Christ) moves into man's earthly hell to get him out of it; Christ lives His life in man so that man in his turn now, through God in him, begins to live other people's lives. The gaiety of God, the seriousness of God, the joy of God, the sorrows of God, the song, the laughter, the eternal livingness of life, the total meaningfulness of eternal life — here it is.

And then John quietly writes: "For as He is, so are we in this world." Not "ought to be," or "could be," but "are." Of course we are; this new life is He in us. So we are now the eternal love. Exactly what He is, we are.

— *The Spontaneous You*

"He was delivered over to death for our sins and was raised to life for our justification" — Romans 4:25.

Jesus lays down His life on the cross by His own choice, and God raises Him from the dead. The whole of Scripture interprets this for us as the judicial removal of the inevitable separation of the human race from God for eternity, which is the consequence of us being law-breakers (sinners), guilty, cursed, condemned. This was completed by Himself voluntarily taking the place of separation from God on the cross in our place, "bearing our sins in His own body on the tree." His outpoured blood was the evidence of the completed sacrifice.

There would be no efficacy in the death of one man for another. That is why the root of our faith, John says, lies in the fact of the incarnation, "God manifest in the flesh" — so that this was God in human form, the source and upholder of the human race, being "the propitiation for our sins" in His death. The resurrection was the evidence that the atonement was so complete that all consciousness of sin and separation had disappeared forever, and we who believe are "justified" (Romans 4:25) — legally pronounced as like the risen Christ Himself with "no stain on our character." Forgiveness would not be enough, because though forgiven we remember what we did. Justification means we are as if the thing never happened.

— *Once Caught, No Escape*

"The mind controlled by the Spirit is life and peace" —
Romans 8:6.

Maybe by repeated failures, by the strain and stress of a
life we can't cope with, at last God opens our eyes, and we
see our mistake. The new man (the human part of it) is as
helpless as the old man! Neither was made to function by
itself, and never has and never will.

The old man was Satan in us: the new man Christ in us;
in both cases the human self is the container, the recipient,
the agent. At last we see it; and Romans 7 was as necessary
to our spiritual education as the backside of the desert was
to Moses and the years with Laban to Jacob. Now we know
how to avoid the pitfalls of that subtle chapter. We still pay
calls there, but we know where we are when we do, and we
know how to get out quickly.

Our normal life by grace is now in chapter 8, with the
occasional visit to chapter 7; only we must admit that for
most of us, and I include myself, the visits are too frequent.
We surely never get beyond the daily cleansing of 1 John 1.
— *God Unlimited*

"Who will rescue me . . . ? Thanks be to God — through Jesus Christ our Lord!" — Romans 7:24-25.

What is the deliverance I expect? Just this: I have a puny, poisoned, localized self, shut up to its mean "my" and "mine," lusting and having not, desiring to have and unable to obtain. It is alive in me in place of a God-expanded, God-indwelt self which can know all things, have all things, do all things.

It is the flesh of which Paul so often speaks, the old man, the carnal nature. Yet it is the very same self that came from the hands of my Creator — the same self, but seduced from its proper function as the hidden and willing servant of the Spirit in the kingdom of light, and taken captive by sin and Satan to be his agent in the kingdom of darkness. It is not something which was created evil and for which the only remedy is destruction or eradication. Such is an impossibility. The God-made self, a ray from His own self, is no more capable of dissolution or extinction than is God's own self. Rather, it is man's ego which has become enslaved, defiled, bedeviled, and must be released, cleansed and restored to its rightful Owner. It may be likened to the man who "had devils a long time and wore no clothes," who was later seen, "the devils departed out of him, sitting at the feet of Jesus, clothed and in his right mind." The same man in two totally different relationships, first to devils, then to Jesus.

— *The Law of Faith*

> *"When I am weak, then I am strong"* —
> 2 Corinthians 12:10.

Our weakness is our glory. It is that which necessitates the indwelling of God. That is our claim on Him, as new men in Christ. If He makes weak and ignorant humans, then He *must* be their strength and wisdom, for He only makes empty vessels to fill them.

It is, therefore, a great release when we realize that we are meant to feel our inability. Indeed, it should be our constant reaction to every situation. When it isn't, we are on dangerous ground. It is the wisdom of God which keeps us progressing from problem to problem, from one tight corner to another.

The most illuminating autobiographical account of a man who had learned this lesson is Paul's in his second letter to the Corinthians. It scintillates with this truth. It is Paul the human, thoroughly human, radiating Christ. The human sticks right out of chapter after chapter; but, mark you, it is not Paul condemning himself because he was human and feeling that he needs cleansing from it. It is Paul who has a redeemed humanity through the cross, and is now occupied with Christ coming through His humanity in risen and saving power. It is the Paul of Galatians 2:20, who has finished once for all with his self-centered humanity ("I have been crucified with Christ"); the Paul who is now a cleansed and renewed human ("nevertheless I live"); the Paul whose attention is centered on the Other Self operating through him ("Christ liveth in me").

— *God Unlimited*

> *"Each one should use whatever gift he has received to serve others"* — 1 Peter 4:10.

God's gifts are of His apportioning, who "divideth to every man severally as He will." We shall find that He will fit us into the type of life and ministry in which He expresses Himself through us by the gifts He gives us; and as we take our share in a living church fellowship, very often our brethren will see more clearly than we just where our gift lies. At any time God may pour out His Spirit on us in new ways. Let us put no limit on Him. We are told to "covet earnestly the best gifts" and to "desire spiritual gifts," so it is not out of place to look to Him for fresh enduements, just as those in the early church were filled and refilled with the Holy Ghost.

Sudden discoveries are sometimes made, such as that one or another has an unexpected gift of healing or teaching or preaching. Let us expect the Lord to lead us on from "waters to the ankles" to "waters to swim in." The gospel was preached in those early days "with mighty signs and wonders by the power of the Spirit of God" and "with divers miracles and gifts of the Holy Ghost," and should we not see the same today?

He in us now manifests Himself to the world in saving grace through the varied gifts with which He has severally endowed us. Our part, and it is a real part, is to be conditioned by the Spirit to recognize, receive and realize what He is to us, in us, and by us.

— The Deep Things of God

"I die every day" — 1 Corinthians 15:31.

This cross is not to be confused, as many do confuse it, with His cross and resurrection which we trusted in for our own redemption. What we are now talking about is not the cross for our redemption but for the redemption of others. This is adulthood, not adolescence. This kind of cross is constantly repeated in our daily lives whenever we are in situations which our human selves would be rid of; but instead of remaining in hurt self, we recognize them to be part of some redemptive purpose of God through us in others. So, Paul says, we accept them as something we have been "delivered unto," and our "dying" is our heart acceptance of them, though that may not be done lightly or easily any more than the Savior could accept His cross without a Gethsemane.

Here is a principle of constant "dyings," daily maybe, affecting every kind of normal situation in life. Anything which hurts, disturbs our *status quo* or challenges, be it what we may call small in our personal lives or big in some public affair, is a place of dying when we change from self's resistance to acceptance as a step in God's saving plans.

— *The Spontaneous You*

"I want to know Christ . . . and the fellowship of sharing in his sufferings, becoming like him in his death" — Philippians 3:10.

If I am Christ's, then voluntary "deaths" to the normal advantages in the flesh — comforts, loved ones, material advancement, enlarged income, pleasures, leisure — give me the right to claim and receive the harvest in the Spirit. Instead of regarding such as losses and deprivations to be endured if necessary but avoided if possible, we deliberately embrace them and glory in them as the way of the harvest. Equally we turn all life's unsought "trials" to the same use — tragedies, injustices, slights, insults, losses. As a matter of fact, although unsought, none are unsuited. Each comes because it just fits our case, and each is either resisted as an impudent gate-crasher or welcomed as friend and ally, with corresponding destructive or constructive effect.

"Awake, O north wind; blow upon my garden, that the spices thereof may flow out." By the practice of this principle of the cross, losses and trials, whether unsought or deliberately chosen, become positive weapons of offence in destroying the works of the devil and loosening his grip on humanity — even as Christ's death, thus embraced, destroyed him who has the power of death, and led captivity captive.

— *The Liberating Secret*

"Why are you crying out to me? Tell the Israelites to move on" —Exodus 14:15.

"Why do you ask Me to do it? Do it yourself," God was saying, in reality, to Moses. "Stretch out your rod and divide the sea." In other words, Moses had said to God "You do it," but God answered Moses, "No, you do it."

Man starts on the Christian highway with much of the graveclothes of the Fall still upon him. Separation from God has been a stark reality to him. He knows the weakness of the flesh. Visible lack and need are more concrete to him than invisible fullness and supply.

But to those who have ears to hear and hearts set to follow comes a new word: "Say not, I am a child." "Go in this thy might." Say not, I am weak, I am carnal, I am needy, I am earthy. Awake thou that sleepest and arise from the dead. Understand that the Lord is joined unto you, one spirit. Understand that you have the mind of Christ. Understand that the life of Christ is ever flowing in and through you as the sap of the vine through the branches. Do not keep asking for what you already have. Do not sing, "I need Thee, oh, I need Thee." Sing, "I have Thee, oh, I have Thee." Never waste breath by asking Him to be near you, who is already within you, joined to you in such a union that you and He are described as "one spirit."

— *Throne Life*

"I can do everything through him who gives me strength" — Philippians 4:13.

The Spirit is original in each of us, and He will get His original plan into action by you in some way which frees you from man-pleasing. A pastor through whom God is going to do His real work must die to what his people think he ought to be, and still more dangerously what his denomination can approve (if he is called to be a denominational man); and God does call many to be "stay-inners" as well as calling others to be "come-outers." But promotion in the Holy Spirit and with His mighty enduement comes not from east or west or from the human hierarchy but from God, and only death leads to life.

So we are back on the usual paradox: Do nothing which stems from self-effort. But in being a do-nothing you will actually be a do-everything, because the Real Doer whose aim is to get the world back to Himself will surely be busy by you in His own way and time.

There is no meaning to life for eternity other than that we are for others, because that is all God is. *That* at least is the whole meaning of being a person — a person for others. And the plain proof in ourselves is that when we can be some help to others, the bells always ring within us. Precisely! We are in tune with the Infinite, and therefore the inner music is harmony. Even a child finds a secret satisfaction when he shares something with his little brother, especially if it is something he values. Those bells are ringing!

— *Who Am I?*

"He settles the barren woman in her home as a happy mother of children" — Psalm 113:9.

None of us can tell in what surprising ways God may suddenly recommission us and involve us, with our hardly realizing it, in some wholly new enterprises of faith. For the Holy Spirit is at work in new ways in every generation, and we are on tiptoe for any participation in them, or for any new call to action which might come personally to us. He is always original, and may have some original calling for us. We have only to see some of His surprises today.

Who would have predicted the enormous uprise of home fellowships, like a return to church-in-the-house of the early days, where thousands upon thousands are meeting in homes for free interchange in Bible discussion, personal problems, and prayer sessions?

It is easy to greet new movements with suspicion and to take quick note of extravagances. But I believe that we who have been settled in our faith and convinced of our right foundations have always to be watchful lest we find ourselves to be the old wineskins that cannot stretch to contain the new wine; just as the Jews were warned by the prophets that "more would be the children of the barren than the children of the married wife"!

Every life is an adventure of faith, every life without exception, yours and mine; and every day has its own freshness and originality when we see it with the eyes of the intercessor.

— *The Spontaneous You*

"'Who will go for us?' And I said, 'Here am I. Send me!'" — Isaiah 6:8.

A commission is no passing thing. It is not a prayer I can take up and put down. It is not participating in various interests and activities. It is "*This one thing I do.*" It will be the main drive of my life until it is gained.

Then when conscious of the commission, I respond like Isaiah, "Here am I; send me." By that I mean my body is wholly available, which of course includes my soul with its emotions, and my concentrated thought-processes. And somewhere along that line is coming travail and death. There will be a *price paid* equivalent to a death; but there again, we do not seek that out or make it up. He brings us into it and through it. We may not even recognize the death process until we are well into it. It may mean literal sacrifice of all that goes with our body living: our time, our faculties, our possessions, our finances, our homes, and usually most costly and common of all, our reputation. Misunderstanding and even opposition may arise in our own family circle, among our friends, our social circle, our church fellowship, or right out to the public. As we go through or have gone through our intercession, we shall well know where we have died.

— Yes, I Am

"No matter how many promises God has made, they are 'Yes' in Christ. And so through him the 'Amen' is spoken by us . . ." — 2 Corinthians 1:20.

After Pauline and I returned to England in 1931 to carry on the home end, God's commission to our Worldwide Evangelization Crusade was to go to any unevangelized area of the world. It was our custom then for those at the home end to take a slightly larger share of what monthly money there was before it was apportioned to the fields, as it cost more to live in England than in Africa. But when we had practically nothing to send to the thirty-five missionaries (we were nearly penniless that first month), the Lord clearly said to Pauline and me, "Why not personally live by the injunction to 'take no thought for food and clothing . . . but seek first the kingdom of God and His righteousness,' and believe the promise that 'all these things will be added unto you'?"

We saw the point and accepted it from God, though to us at that time it was a big thing — having no earthly source of supply, not even from the mission — and we also thought at that time we should never get anyone else to join us in the work of the home end on those same conditions! But how way off we were, for our WEC co-workers (over two hundred of them at all our home bases around the world) all these years have taken no mission funds for personal needs, but have lived by the promises of God.

— *Yes, I Am*

He made known his ways to Moses, his deeds to the people of Israel" — Psalm 103:7.

The whole Bible and the whole Christian history attests the fact that if God's acts are to be made known to the world, it must be by people who know God's ways.

[The next few pages contain testimonies from workers of the Christian Literature Crusade — the publisher of this book.] Each testimony is equally a romance, a romance of faith. The human element sticks out all over the place, and is meant to: the fears, shrinkings, repulsions, perplexities; the weaknesses, the poverty, the impossibility, the constantly glaring contrasts between actual appearances and high-sounding objectives; and then — the gradual uprising of the building of God not made with hands, the work really done, the business efficiency; the books and pamphlets procured, printed, published and outpoured by the tens of millions; the finances supplied (and always just enough!), the necessary buildings and bookmobiles, supremely the dedicated personnel, the countries entered.

Yet through it all, the weakness and foolishness of faith is never to be replaced by the apparent strength and wisdom of human security and organization. Soren Kierkegaard, that great exponent of the paradox of faith, well said: "Spiritual existence is not easy; the believer constantly lies upon the deep, has 70,000 fathoms of water underneath him. However long he lies out there, that does not mean that he gradually comes to lie on land. He may become calmer, but to his last instant he lies upon a depth of 70,000 fathoms of water."

— *Leap of Faith*

"Offer your bodies as living sacrifices. . . . Do not conform any longer to the pattern of this world" — Romans 12:1-2.

George daCosta, Jamaica, writes:

"[Our small store had a souvenir department and a literature department.] We were believing that we could earn money and give to God. But God was wanting us to give *ourselves* to Him — not just our money.

"Soon God showed us clearly that what He wanted was lives fully given over to Him, surrendered to get His Word out. There was nothing like this in Jamaica before — very little Christian literature work at all. So we prayed about this matter again and the Lord impressed us with the thought of inviting John Davey, Caribbean Director of CLC, to Jamaica. He came and we took him all around.

"When he was ready to go, I said, 'Now, John, here's the point. We're in two businesses. We can't do both. We want you to take over the literature part of the work. We'll even give you the shop and get back into our old job or carry on our private business.' I shall never forget that night.

"John looked at me and said, 'George, CLC will never do that. We believe God has called *you* to this job and we are going to wait on God to show this to you clearly.'

"Soon after, the Lord made clear to us what we should do, so we went on our knees and told Him, 'We hand over everything to You now.' We wrote Ken Adams* and John and got rid of all the secular things in the shop. Then we handed over the rest to CLC, and the Lord began to pour out His blessing in a way that has been unbelievable."

— *Leap of Faith*

*International Secretary of CLC.

223

"I have chosen Bezalel . . . and I have filled him with the Spirit of God, with skill, ability and knowledge in all kinds of crafts" —Exodus 31:2-3.

Bonnie Hanson trained for a short period in an art school where the witness of the Inter-Varsity Christian Fellowship set her on her feet for Christ. Then, while at the Bethany Fellowship, Minneapolis, she heard Ken Adams speak on particular spheres of service in CLC which were right along her line of interest.

"Coming into the work full time, I had my battles," continues Bonnie. "When I first came I prayed that the Lord would mature me, and my, what storms came after that! But storms mature us. They drive our roots deeper and we learn to cling to God. Along with that the Lord gives us a generous dose of disillusionment with our co-workers, the people over us in the Lord, the mission and everything, until we are thoroughly cast on Him. Then we're safe because it's just us, the Lord and our commission.

"When I began my first issue of *Floodtide* magazine as editor, I realized how far 'over my head' I was, and how little I knew. The Lord gave me a word of encouragement and spoke so forcefully to my heart that it has been with me ever since: 'See, I have called by name Bezalel . . . and I have filled him with the spirit of God, in wisdom, and in understanding, and in knowledge, and in all manner of workmanship.' It was a marvelous revelation to me that the Lord did have a gift of workmanship and art in the Holy Spirit, and that what He had done for that man He could still do today."

— *Leap of Faith*

"For it is God who works in you to will and to act according to his good purpose" — Philippians 2:13.

Virginia Walton testifies:

"Though I was acquainted with WEC the Lord never seemed to quicken me about specific missionary service until the conference when Ken Adams spoke on literature. I knew then that this was for me. I saw for the first time the need for behind-the-scenes missionaries.

"When I arrived at mission headquarters I found a print shop with almost no workers and a backlog of work. My heart was immediately drawn to this phase of the ministry and I knew that this was His place for me. However, the Lord had a very basic work to do in me (as I suppose He has with all new candidates) — to let Him take over in my life instead of my helping Him out.

"I was first assigned to the task of housecleaning and any extra time I had could be spent in the print shop. Seeing the need in the print shop and my 'qualifications' for that, I didn't see why others couldn't do the housecleaning. Surely there was something wrong in the distribution of 'qualified' personnel. I stewed over this for some time, and when I got to the point of desperation He showed me that He didn't want my *service* for Him but my *fellowship with* Him, and was I going to work *for* Him or *with* Him? Wasn't it for Him to work *through* me in any way He saw fit? Was I willing for it? When I yielded to Him the work became a joy and I was ready to stay on housecleaning the rest of my days if He wanted it that way."

— *Leap of Faith*

"O my Strength, come quickly to help me" —
Psalm 22:19.

[Virginia continues:]
"One of the first jobs I helped Ken print was *The Calvary Road*. Because of shortage of personnel Ken was doing the printing in his 'spare' time. He was pushing through on this job as he had to leave for meetings the next morning. It took about three hours to print one plate and we had finished one about midnight. 'All right now,' he said, 'let's go on with the next one.' I questioned the hour but put the plate on the press and continued to work, a little rebellious in my spirit. The title of the chapter we were printing was 'Are You Willing to Be a Servant?' and as copy after copy came off the press, this stood out. The Lord really spoke to my heart through this, as He has done with many other jobs since as they have come off the press."

As Virginia settled into the print shop work God sent new equipment in various ways: folder, cutter, presses, platemaking machine and camera.

"Several people asked how I could manage such heavy work but all the praise and glory goes to the Lord. I have found over and over again that He never gives us anything to do beyond what He enables, in strength as well as wisdom. One glimpse of His guiding hand in my early training was that at Westmont, 'for fun,' I took instruction in weight lifting. I learned how to lift heavy weights with the least amount of effort and thus avoid muscle strain. I have found this invaluable."

— Leap of Faith

"I want to know Christ and the power of his resurrection and the fellowship of sharing in his sufferings" — Philippians 3:10.

There is a background to the manifestation of the mighty works of God through a human channel. Underlying resurrection is death. Paul to possess all things had nothing; to make many rich was poor; to be powerful and wise had become foolish and weak; to be remade had been broken. To share the intimate fellowship of a Savior he went the way of saviorhood, "suffered the loss of all things," "became conformable to death."

We know and can employ through the Spirit the powers of the world to come in the measure that we have died to enslavement to the possessions, glories, ways of this world. It is a real death, as prelude to a real new life. The Lord Christ made some strange statements, such as that it costs some an eye or limb to enter the Kingdom, that a disciple must forsake all, must "hate" loved ones, possessions, life.

By this He meant that such a one must pass through fires in which the selfish claims of natural loves and the selfish hold on the "good things" of life, not to speak of the bad, must be burnt out to make room for the influx of supernatural grace, vision and resources. Holy and hidden mystery —that through the cross is power, through the cross glory, through the cross joy, through the cross fruitfulness.

— *After C. T. Studd*

"He died for all, that those who live should no longer live for themselves . . ." — 2 Corinthians 5:15.

We can never get beyond the cross. But there certainly is a sense in which even the cross can be given a wrongful prominence. It is not meant to be in the foreground but in the background of the scene; it is not the superstructure but the foundation of the building. To parade the cross, whether in its outward form — as do the Roman Catholics with their crucifixes — or in its inward dynamic, by over-display of or overemphasis on the cost of discipleship, is to draw wrongful attention to it. It is life, not death, that is our message; a living and returning, not a crucified Christ. C. T. Studd put it rightly when he wrote on a postcard, when leaving for the heart of Africa:

Take my life and let it be
A hidden cross revealing Thee.

But, at the same time, just because the world lies in darkness and error and because we Christians ourselves can so easily be turned out of the narrow way, there has to be constant attention called to our foundations, and constant emphasis laid upon the fact there is no other foundation to the kingdom of God than the cross of Christ.

We know this very well as our entry into life. We have learned it as our way of deliverance from inner bondage. We see it now and finally as the law of harvest. We never get beyond the cross, neither in time nor eternity, for we have learned that release of life and power on the spiritual level can only come about through death on the natural level.

— *The Law of Faith*

"We have this treasure in jars of clay to show that this all-surpassing power is from God and not from us" — 2 Corinthians 4:7.

The daily cross, therefore, is not, as so often presented, a grim and unwilling endurance of adversities. It is the sole principle of fruitfulness, the law of the harvest. It is not the cross for sanctification, nor the efficacy of the blood for daily cleansing. It is the continual transmuting of weak human flesh and shrinking human reactions into cooperating channels of the Spirit. We *must* die all the time, *"always bearing about the dying of the Lord Jesus."*

By no other means can weak, separated selves, confronted by all kinds of overwhelming situations, be the soil for the spiritual harvest. The supernatural life only manifests itself through the yielded natural life, and the yielding is identification with Christ in His daily dying in us. Then, Paul says, we are "perplexed, but not in despair," knocked down but not knocked out: for in our inner man rises the spirit of faith (2 Corinthians 4:13). the recognition of our identification also with an ascended Christ, seated with Him on His royal throne, victors with Him far above all opposition, and dispensers of His gifts to men.

It means action, for no life is so dynamic, so vitalized as a Spirit-filled life. He who created, upholds and consummates all the activities of the universe, the unmoved Mover, has made us His body — and a body is to use, and to use at full stretch. Is it not obvious that He who is love and who gave His only Son for the world, will likewise give us, His sons by grace? He that spared not His own Son, will He spare us?

— *The Deep Things of God*

"I am obligated both to Greeks and non-Greeks. . . . I am eager to preach the gospel . . ."— Romans 1:14-15.

Nobody works like a Spirit-filled disciple. Every fiber of his being cries out, "To me to live is Christ," therefore "I am debtor" to all the world. The zeal of God's house consumes him. The world can only go a certain distance, for it works from a center of unrest and insufficiency. The servant of God has no limits, for his center is the rest of faith, the endless resources of God.

Nor is there an ounce of passivity in him. "My Father still works, and I work," said Jesus; and we are "workers together with God." God does His work by *our* minds, *our* hearts, *our* words and deeds. He sets us in action. Certainly it is dying and rising action, as we have seen. It starts by saying no to independent self-reactions, self-activities, self-inhibitions. It dies with Christ to them. But in the risen life we are altogether active. It is *our* travail, *our* sacrifice, *our* obedience of faith, *our* labors, *our* witness; yet it is really His. The paradox is true. "It all depends on God — it all depends on me." We *go* in the strength of the Lord God. It is never easy, and never will be, in the sense that there are always the steps of obedience we must take against feelings, against appearances, against natural reactions, against the tide. To that extent there is a preliminary step *we* take: at least it appears so, though actually even that is the constraint of the Spirit. That is the daily death which leads to resurrection. "Launch out into the deep. . . . At Thy word I will."

— *The Deep Things of God*

> *"Death is at work in us, but life is at work in you"*
> — 2 Corinthians 4:12.

This is the way of the intercessor. Jesus "poured out His soul unto death," and so, it says, "made intercession for the transgressors" (Isaiah 53:12). Because of that act of death-intercession, God poured His resurrection life both into the Savior's dead body and through Him into all who receive Him. The fruit of His intercession was the life-giving Spirit sent into the world, saving to the uttermost them that come unto God by Him. And every life of fruitful service has this at its roots: the corn of wheat must die, if the world is to feed on its fruit. We say, "That person must change; that situation must alter." God says, "You change first, the other will follow." As one has said, "I don't like you; what's the matter with *me*?" The first death in a human situation in which I am involved is in me, in my natural reactions of resentment, condemnation, unbelief.

Only when I am consciously "through" to resurrection ground, experienced in my heart by peace and praise and love, can divine life through me touch the situation. As this is true in every daily detail of life, in every domestic business or church trial, so is it true in the mainstream of our life's ministry. All the great intercessors of the Bible were living sacrifices for the people for whom they interceded; they lived and died vicariously. Not that there is merit or power in the outpoured life of a human intercessor, but it is the Interceding Spirit in him which takes him this death way.

— *The Deep Things of God*

"Everything is permissible . . . but not everything is beneficial" — 1 Corinthians 6:12.

To us the inescapable pressure of the Spirit comes, if we are really His to the limit, which will not allow us to live our lives on the comfortable level of such a word as "God has given us richly all things to enjoy," but rather on those others which say: "All things are lawful, but all things are not expedient." "Though I be free from all, yet have I made myself servant to all, that I might gain the more." "I endure all things for the elect's sake." Enjoyments there will be, many and continual, for all life has joy and zest in it when it is mediated through Christ; but a conscious binding sense of dedication will be upon us, a voluntarily accepted yoke of holy servitude. We are prisoners of the Lord, bound in spirit, even as Paul deliberately renounced certain of life's normal privileges that he might better preach the gospel, a kind of voluntary extremism. So will we, in this way or that, according to the measure of our faith and light, gladly give up some of the lesser good to gain the greater. We shall be a people with a purpose, even as for temporal ends the athlete denies himself, the scientist devotes himself, the soldier risks himself.

— *The Law of Faith*

"Because of the man's persistence he will get up and give him as much as he needs" — Luke 11:8.

A fine example of what prayer and endless persistence can accomplish may be seen from the story about Chiquinquira, the center of Virgin worship in Colombia, where the cathedral dedicated to her is visited by 250,000 pilgrims in one week. John Harbeson* began to work there in 1934. He had the usual experience of insults, threats with knives, and a period when persecution took the form of obtaining blood from the slaughterhouse, smearing it on the door and pouring buckets of it into the house. No one dared come to the meeting room, but John knows how to attack the Devil, both on his knees and on his feet. With his powerful voice he stood at the door of his empty meeting room and preached his sermons to the street.

Many would have sought an easier district as years passed and hearts seemed like stone, but the word of the Lord is the hammer that breaks the rock in pieces. Hungry hearts were drinking in the message behind curtains and open windows. The attitude of many local residents became increasingly friendly. On one or two occasions he passed by houses where he could see the occupants sitting and reading the Bible. A work of the Spirit came in 1938, when, through weekly visits to the jail, the jailor, his two elderly sisters and two other members of their family, which had influential connections in the city, publicly confessed Christ.

— *After C. T. Studd*

*A WEC missionary.

" 'Whoever believes in me, . . . streams of living water
will flow from within him.' By this he meant the Spirit. . . ."
— John 7:38-39.

We now consider power for service, and the principle is
exactly the same [as for victory over sin]. We must first
discover our need. The commonest way in which that
happens is by many experiences of our hopeless inability to
win others to Christ or to fulfill any spiritual ministry, and
at the same time to be challenged by the way God uses
others. What is the secret of power? we ask. The answer is as
before: "Christ the power of God." Christ "mighty in me
toward the Gentiles," wrote Paul. Not without wrestlings
was our faith brought to the simple receiving point for
sanctification, and then to "the full assurance of faith." And
not without heart-longings to the point of desperation will
the revelation dawn on us: He *has* come; He *is* in us: "Go in
this thy might"; "He that believeth on Me, out of his inmost
part *shall* flow rivers of living water. This spake He of the
Spirit."

Make no mistake, it has to be the word of God to
oneself, not merely a general word of Scripture; it must be
the engrafted word. We must come away from this dealing
of God with us with the solid knowledge that the Spirit of
enduement for service is in us, as surely as the Spirit of
regeneration and sanctification. Then only do we *know*
Him within in this threefold manner. He may thus come as a
rushing mighty wind with signs following; He may come, as
He did to me, by a revelation of His own self as the Executor
of the Trinity. The point is that it is He Himself, and we
know it is He.

— *The Deep Things of God*

"God cannot be tempted, . . . nor does he tempt anyone"
— James 1:13.

Temptation is enticement, and the channels by which temptation reaches us are always within ourselves. We may blame the thing that entices us. We would be wiser if we frankly recognized that temptation gets its grip through stimulated natural desires. Lusts, as James calls them: "Every man is tempted when he is drawn away of his own lust and enticed." As we become less susceptible to stimulation in various areas, so temptation in those areas will have less appeal to us. Instead, therefore, of blaming the stimuli to temptation about us, we would do well to seek and find an ever deeper integration in the Spirit, resulting in an ever greater occupation with God and quicker rejection of the first stirrings of false desire.

It is equally true, however, that the closer we draw to Him, the more deeply we find ourselves to be sinners in other areas in which we had not formerly recognized any sin, for we find sin to be anything even one per cent short of His perfection, any coming "short of the glory of God." So in that sense too we move from sin to sin, and, praise God, from cleansing to cleansing. But the track is always leading upwards, to that glorious conformity to the image of His Son, and to the day when it will be as true of us as of God Himself that we cannot be tempted with evil.

— *The Liberating Secret*

"Consider it pure joy . . . whenever you face trials of many kinds" — James 1:2.

If life is response to environment, and I live in two rival environments, those of the flesh and Spirit, then each must keep appealing to me, keep drawing me, in every part of my being which still responds to its appeals. I must be tempted, and should be tempted, wherever I am still temptable. Only by this means can I learn and relearn the areas of my life in which I need an ever more complete deliverance, and can I be stimulated to refuse the evil and choose the good and practice the way of faith by which alone that can be done.

It is plain that this life is probationary and progressive. It is from grace to grace, from faith to faith, from glory to glory; and temptation is the continual proof that God uses even Satan for these sanctifying purposes. God tempts no man, but from the beginning of time it has been by the devil's temptations that He has proved us, humbled us, taught us of ourselves and Himself; that He stimulates us to seek for victory, and finally perfects us. Even His own Son suffered, being tempted, and was only made perfect through "learning obedience by the things which He suffered." Let us then brace ourselves to this unalterable fact. We shall be tempted at all points by all means to the last day of our pilgrimage on earth. These temptations are our great blessings in disguise. Woe betide us if we were to be without them; rather let us obey the command of James and count them *all* joy.

— *The Liberating Secret*

"Each one is tempted when, by his own evil desire, he is dragged away and enticed" — James 1:14.

A closer examination of the mechanics of temptation, as given us by James (1:14-15), emphasizes, as we have already said, that its power is in its incitement of our desires in some illicit direction. Temptation makes us want to do a thing. It "entices" us. It makes us like it, and that like soon turns to love, and we are gone, for life is governed by love. What we love we inevitably do, unless we get that love redirected to a worthier end. We lust because we like to lust. We are angry because we want to be angry. We hate because we think we have good reason to hate.

None of these appetites or faculties are wrong in themselves. They were all in Adam, and all in Jesus, who "was tempted in all points like as we are." To be tempted does not affect the purity of our hearts or the reality of our relationship of union with Christ. Being wholly alive in spirit, soul and body, we are wholly susceptible to all forms of appeal; and the world sees to it that they are plentiful and blatant.

Temptation is not yet sin. "Every man is tempted when he is drawn away of his own lust and enticed." Young Christians must recognize the fact that the tempter is also the father of lies, and with all the various forms of temptation will constantly whisper the lie that because this or that continually pulls at us we are therefore slaves to it, or that we are not truly delivered.

— *The Liberating Secret*

> *"Watch and pray so that you will not fall into tempta-*
> *tion"* —Matthew 26:41.

We are clearly warned that many assaults of temptation
are our own fault. If we maintained a close walk with God,
our hearts would remain so filled and thrilled with His
presence that there would be immunity in the moment of
assault. "Watch and pray lest ye enter into temptation."
Christ wrestled while the disciples slept, and, when the
awful moment came, Christ was in calm mastery over His
very captors, while the disciples fled.

It is right to fear temptation and not meet it, still less
welcome it, in a spirit of bravado — lest it overwhelm us
with the suddenness of a cloudburst. Daily we are to pray:
"Lead us not into temptation," but at the same time we can
learn and see that temptation is our battleground and
opportunity. Such an understanding will give us a healthy,
hopeful, not repressed, defeatist or resentful, attitude to
life's conflicts.

One other point is of great importance. It is to have a
clear insight into the fact that temptation must by no means
be confused with sin. In no case is the actual temptation sin,
even though at times we have come within its influence
through neglect.

— *The Law of Faith*

"After desire has conceived, it gives birth to sin" —
James 1:15.

Temptation, James says, comes from an evil source; it is
the legacy of the Fall. Man is in the environment and
atmosphere of this evil thing, proceeding from an evil being,
the devil, through his evilly-infected agent, the world. The
way temptation works upon us, then, is this, says James: An
instinct, a natural desire (called in the KJV a "lust," which
can give a wrong impression, for the word "lust" is in the
original just a neutral "strong desire," not necessarily evil or
good) is stimulated by some object. It "draws" the man and
entices him. No wrong in this, except it be the general wrong
of a fallen condition which has corrupted man's instincts
and made them all too prone to "inordinate affections."
But, continues James, the crisis is in the choice; not in the
instinct which draws and entices, but in the will. It is here, he
says, that sin enters. "When lust hath conceived" — in other
words, when man's free will, his power of choice, has been
married to the enticing instinct — then the child of that
marriage is sin.

Many endure much inner condemnation and bondage
through constantly feeling that they have guilty desires, and
that as a consequence their Christian profession is hypocrisy because their inner condition is a secret contradiction to
it. Not so. It is natural for instincts to be the instrument for
temptation. The tempter is the evil one. The sin is in the
response, not in the instincts.

— *The Law of Faith*

"Blessed is the man who perseveres under trial" —
James 1:12.

Temptations met and mastered are the only high road to
stabilization of character and spiritual progress. Temptations always touch the vulnerable point. That is their chief
use, as well as their great danger. In a two-way world every
instinct of body, soul and spirit has to go through the
crucible of temptation, and go there again and again, until it
can come out purified and fixed in God. We may be sure
that every temptation that comes to us comes because it
exactly suits our condition, for we are only temptable at the
points where we are sensitive to that particular type of
appeal.

In fact, in one sense we draw our temptations to ourselves. Out of all life's innumerable stimuli which reach out
a beckoning hand to us, we respond to those with which we
have affinity. They draw us. But for every attraction in one
direction, in the nature of things there is a counterattraction
in the other. Thus a choice is forced upon us. We make it. If
we know the secret of the Spirit, we do not meet the pull of
the carnal with an ineffective "No" (the "thou shalt not" of
the law), which leaves the conflict unresolved, or at best
gives victory only by the skin of the teeth; but we meet it
with the positive, sublimating alternative of the gospel, the
"Christ hath delivered us from the curse of the law," the
ringing declaration that the "I" who might respond to the
temptation is "crucified with Christ."

— *The Law of Faith*

"He forgave us all our sins, having canceled the written code, with its regulations, that was against us . . ." — Colossians 2:13-14.

Law is always with us, as is the flesh, the devil, the world. They are not dead, but we dead to them. Therefore, law is always round the corner to catch us out, and we need catching out until we learn our lesson. Every sort of enticement can be law to an earnest soul. We read a stirring biography. Why aren't we like that? Down we go under false condemnation, because we have allowed an external "You ought" to slip in instead of "Christ is whatever He pleases to be in me." These constant exhortations to be better Christians, even the commands of Scripture, become external law to us, instead of, "Lord, You are all those things in me. Please live them out through me." For the hidden secret of the Bible is that its commands are to the new man, which is Christ in me, not just lonely me.

In temptation it is the same. Enticement comes, followed by the warning frown of the law, "You must not." If we follow that and try not to, we are back in the bondage of helpless self, and sin in the flesh. The answer is to remember Christ living in us. He is God's "way of escape" when temptations "take" us.

— *God Unlimited*

"Now that faith has come, we are no longer under the supervision of the law" — Galatians 3:25.

All normal human responses are listed in the Bible in different places as normal, not sinful. What matters is the use we make of them. Hate, anger, jealousy, fear, boasting, pride (glorying in a thing), envy, ambition (aiming for the highest), covetousness, and of course physical appetites, are all mentioned in different places as rightful attributes, and many of them of God Himself. What we have to understand is that our human responses are the negative to God's positive. Our own reactions, therefore, are bound to be and meant to be negative. We don't like this, we are not willing for that, we fear the other; we are disturbed, impatient, and the rest.

Now the point is, in which direction do we go from there? There are two possibilities. The old or new husband of Romans 7. We can listen to the law, know what we ought to do, act as if we can do it, and find ourselves doing the opposite, continuing bound to our negative human reaction or stimulated appetite, and now passing over from temptation to sin, by continuing as an attitude or action what had up till then only been a temptation. Alternatively, the temptations, these first negative feelings, become the stimulus to faith. They stir us to the action of "looking off unto Jesus." We affirm Him, as He thinks His thoughts in us. We do not necessarily at once lose the *feelings* of disturbance: that is a soul condition. But we have moved back by faith to where we truly are and what we truly are — Christ in us.

— *God Unlimited*

"He was chosen before the creation of the world, but was revealed in these last times for your sake" — 1 Peter 1:20.

The devil did not create us; he stole us. Yet God knew what He was doing from the beginning. He foreknew what would happen, we are told, and had made His preparations. He knew that man was going to fall before He created him (1 Peter 1:20). We may therefore be equally sure that He who foreknew all things knew that those heavenly beings who lost their first estate and first opened the kingdom of darkness would do this very thing.

There would be no means of demonstrating the true character of love which lays down its life for its enemies, which overcomes evil with good, which blesses those who curse it, if there were no enemies, no evil, no curses. And in our own lives we know, by Scripture and by experience, that it is our temptations which drive us into the cleft of our Rock; it is our sufferings which divorce us from the world and stabilize us in Christ. It is our frustrations and oppositions which give Him the opportunity to manifest His patience and love through us. If we were not harassed by temptation, we should not learn the lessons of abiding; if we were not faced with difficult situations, we should not practice the faith that overcomes them. So of this we are certain — that Satan never has had power or opportunity to take God by surprise, and to interfere in the smooth running of His creative plan and compel Him to change it.

— *The Deep Things of God*

> *"Because he himself suffered when he was tempted, he is able to help those who are being tempted"* — Hebrews 2:18.

We shall always start by feeling human hurts, fears, dislikes, unwillingness, coldness, powerlessness, lusts, angers, jealousies, and all the list of them. Start, we say, because the start of such reactions is not sin. A human must be human, and Jesus himself had to feel temptation to be tempted in all points. Sin is not in the start but in the continuance. Negative reactions are not sin. They are the negative stirrings which are the jumping-off point for faith.

Sins are when, instead of taking those jumps of faith, we continue in the reaction. "When lust hath conceived, it bringeth forth sin." When we "marry" the self-reaction, accept and continue in it, then the child is sin. We have already quoted how Paul went as far as to "take pleasure" in those experiences which hurt us humans: what he named as feeling his weakness, being hurt or insulted by others, having personal needs, being persecuted, having insoluble problems. "For," he said, "when I am weak, then am I strong." Note, not "then I shall be made strong or become strong or seek for strength." No, "then am I strong," because all he had to do was to recognize who he really was, Christ in him. So to have negative human reactions is not sin, but our opportunities for faith. Sin is when we continue in the reaction, as we all do at times, and then act out some form of "the works of the flesh."

— Who Am I?

The Second Crisis

"We know that our old self was crucified with him"
— Romans 6:6.

There is for most of us a second work of grace, if we like to call it that. There is a day, a season, usually prefaced by many agonizing days, when at last our straining self, stretched and taut like an elastic, gives way. We were crucified with Christ all along, but now faith enters into this intelligently as fact. If we were crucified with Him, we also rose with Him, and now at last we can see that that means the New One within is living His life in us. He was doing so since redemption, but He had to spend those months and often years working us out of ourselves by walking us into all sorts of frustrating situations, which we handled wrongly every time by our self-reactions to them. I reckon the Indwelling Christ has many a laugh as He sees us bumbling and stumbling along, and knows the good though painful lessons we are learning by stubbing our toes on this and then that; but knowing also that we shall see, because He has already started looking out on things His way through our eyes, and will go on until we learn and accept the difference between our looking through our own eyes and His looking through them.

This is a crisis in many lives. It was in mine; and with the example of most of the men and women of the Bible, we are surely justified in saying that it is a necessary crisis in most of our lives.

— God Unlimited

"We were buried with him through baptism into death in order that . . . we too may live a new life" — Romans 6:4.

Very often from our pulpits no nearer presentation of Christ is given to the believer than that He is a Friend close at hand, and so forth. The veil of a false separation is left over the eyes. Here, of course, as we have been showing in these pages, lies the great error. It leaves man to do the very thing he was never created nor redeemed to do — to carry on as best he can by self-effort — helped, he hopes, by the presence and blessing of God.

For most of us this deeper revelation of union has to come as a second experience. We can seldom see our outward sins and inner selves in one single exposure. The plainest proof of this is that the profound exposition of Romans 6-8 is given us separately and subsequently to chapters 1-5. It is not that there are two separate salvations, as it were. There is only one Savior, one glorious process of restoration through His death, resurrection and ascension, and one Holy Spirit. The twofoldness is not on His side. But for most of us there has to be a twofold appropriation of the two great deliverances that stream from the one Calvary: the deliverance from sin and wrath (1-5) and the deliverance from sin and independent self (6-8). They could conceivably be experienced together, for both are there for the taking; but an appropriation which produces a real experience of both at the same time, and not merely a mental apprehension, is rare.

— *The Liberating Secret*

The Second Crisis

"After beginning with the Spirit, are you now trying to attain your goal by human effort?" — Galatians 3:3.

In speaking of the self-exposure God has to give us — as He did to Moses, Jacob, Job, Peter, and the rest — to condition us for the revelation of Christ as the Other Self in us, I do not mean that it must always precede faith. When there is sufficient understanding to take the stand of faith that He is Himself in us, we take it. Much will depend on the level of teaching we have. To refrain from such a faith until we feel that something has happened to fit us for it would be moving right back from faith to works. "Received ye the Spirit by the works of the law or by the hearing of faith?" (only hearing, not experiencing anything). "Are ye so foolish? Having begun in the Spirit, are ye now made perfect by the flesh?"

Many seem stumbled, as we have already pointed out, by a sense that they believe mentally but not yet in the depths of their heart. We must not be stumbled by that. To hear intelligently is itself an evidence of an opened ear, which means an opened heart behind the ear. No, let us be thankful if it is given us to apprehend by any of our faculties that this wonderful Christ-in-you relationship is a fact. While we go on believing up to the measure of faith given us, God will go on working the consciousness of the fact in us, until we can cry with the Psalmist, "O God, my heart is fixed, my heart is fixed." Making Himself real to us in experience is God's business. Believing Him, quite apart from experience, is our business.

— *God Unlimited*

"Christ, who is our life" — Colossians 3:4.

What of the many (of whom I was one) who, though Christ's, know their need of this conscious union and the fruits of it but do not have it in experience? We have not made our Christian living work; there is a missing spot somewhere. We have neither the power for service, nor for consistent living, nor for the inner rest from strains, nor ability to handle our problems. We have neither love for God, nor love for our neighbor, nor love for the Bible and prayer as we should have. What can we do about it?

We are told in simple Bible terms that the answer is Christ, not just as our Savior and Lord, but our life. We may have varied explanations of what this means, or maybe no explanation. We may or may not know of such terms as full salvation, victorious living, the fullness of the Spirit, the baptism in the Spirit, entire sanctification, power for service, the second blessing, or union with God, as I have put it in these pages. Anyhow, by one means or another we are prepared to make this second leap of faith and settle it by this second word of faith: we say He is our all in all; He and we are joined in one spirit; He lives in me now, not I; He is the fullness, the power, the rest, the all I need — and that this is a fact now. Amen! We speak again that word of faith in our own terms. And it is now a fact in me, as much as His becoming my Savior by my word of faith was a fact.

— *Who Am I?*

"Now you are light in the Lord" — Ephesians 5:8.

It is one thing to know truth by being taught it, by seeing it in the Bible, or by grasping it mentally. That is a right start and we do not despise it; but the reason we stress the second crisis (call it by whatever name we like) is that being inner people, life is lived spontaneously and naturally only by a fixed inner consciousness. We are in outer life what we inwardly know we are. In our former life, before we were Christ's, we had a consciousness, though maybe a vague one, just of being ourselves, and so we lived on our self-level. Then after we had knowingly become children of God by the witness of the Spirit, we had a new fixed inner consciousness: we were now forgiven, loved, accepted, inheritors of eternal life; we were in living relationship with Jesus and the Father. And without any special effort this had its radical effects on our daily attitudes and actions.

But this was still a gap-consciousness. Here we were, and here was Christ with us or even known as in us.

But that is something different from a full and final union-consciousness that we are He in our human forms: not *we* living, but *He* living our lives, as Paul said. And Jesus even said that we are the light of the world, not *having* the light, but *being* the light. How could this be on any other basis than an inner unity? — for He is the light, we the negative non-light. Yet here He is saying *we* are the light!

— Who Am I?

"I am not ashamed, because I know whom I have believed, and am convinced that he is able to guard" — 2 Timothy 1:12.

We are saying there is a breakthrough in our consciousness to a union with God, call it by whatever name — baptism of the Spirit, fullness of the Spirit, entire sanctification, full salvation, the victorious life, entering into His rest, enduement with power, rivers of living water, the second blessing, the second work of grace. And we specifically mean by that, not an in-and-out relationship by which we have to find Him, call on Him, regard it as though in the events of our lives He is looking on, or has to be asked to take over and deliver us, as if there is always a gap between us which has to be bridged; and this, mind you, is the normal way we believers talk about our relationship with Him. We ask the Lord to bless. We ask Him to take something over. We ask Him to be present as if He were absent. That is not the relationship we are talking about.

We mean a consciously imparted recognition of unity, such as we have just seen exemplified by these men of the Bible in their whole change of understanding of how things are between them and God, and their consequent simplicity and boldness of authority in functioning as God's men. This is different.

— *Who Am I?*

> *"I no longer live, but Christ lives in me"* —
> Galatians 2:20.

Most of us do not settle into a given consciousness and new power in life until by some specific means, and usually a dated moment, we know that this is so. We see the same in what we call our "conversion experience." The Bible never says you must be able to point to a given date. But you must be able to say it is a given fact! Paul had a dramatic Damascus road conversion. When we do not know inner truth we may think such an outer experience is necessary. I thought so in early years. "If Jesus would appear to me like that, then I could believe Him," I would say. But of course it was not the shining of an outward light which blinded Paul; those with him saw no light and lost no sight; it was the inner illumination in his spirit which was his conversion. And I talk with those who cannot give a date or dramatic account of meeting with Jesus, and they get disturbed and begin to question about themselves when they hear the stories of these sudden conversions. Such disturbance is good; for we must know either by a reaffirmation of a former saving faith or by a new act of believing. All that matters is my ability to say with Paul, "I know whom I have believed." The fact is essential, the date a detail.

As in the new birth, so in the union relationship there is a meeting with God by the Spirit (for most of us in a crisis experience) which permanently affects our inner consciousness; and we move out into a spontaneous life of liberty, authority and fruitfulness.

— *Who Am I?*

"Moses reached out and took hold of the snake and it turned back into a staff in his hand" — Exodus 4:4.

The key to those forty years which Moses spent in the desert was the statement that he "was content to dwell with the man (Jethro)." So God could work in that yielded, puzzled heart, and every shred of the flesh could be cauterized in those lonely years of heart-searching. True, faith did not die — the faith that God could and would deliver His people — but faith in himself had its thorough funeral.

Then came the moment, the revelation of the permanent presence of the I AM, in the fire that never went out, the commission to a shrinking Moses (how changed from forty years before), the provision of the rod of faith. In one day the pygmy within had become a giant without, whereas forty years ago the seeming giant within was proved to be a pygmy without. God had joined Himself to that humbled, finite self. There was now room for Him.

What a man came back from Midian to Egypt! A child within in simple and humble dependence upon God, but a "god" without; the fugitive became a pursuer; a leader, rejected in the tinsel display of his own superiority, now revered and followed in the anointing of the Holy Spirit; a man who could not find enough power in his God to save him from the first threat of danger, now wielding all heaven's resources to rescue a nation, paralyze an opposing empire, feed two million for forty years, and give them moral laws which have been the foundation of a world civilization.

— The Law of Faith

"By faith . . . he persevered because he saw him who is invisible" — Hebrews 11:27.

In Moses, more than in any other life, is the necessity of self-exposure clearly seen. How complete was his consecration: rank, wealth, pleasure, coolly and deliberately rejected for the greater honor of suffering affliction with the people of God, and the greater riches of the reproach of Christ. Yet that same man was a helpless fugitive a few weeks later, his plans for leading Israel out of their bondage shattered to a thousand bits.

Not even God Himself can be the strength of a man, not even God Himself can lead him forward in triumph, until that false usurper, who has planted himself in every man's heart since the Fall, is cast out. Moses had left his sin and left the world, but he hadn't left himself. "Learned in all the wisdom of the Egyptians, mighty in words and in deeds, he supposed his brethren would have understood how that God by his hand would deliver them." Exactly. Moses had one enemy left — Moses. And so he had to tread the long, long trail of self-exposure, out in his case to the desert, to do the one job which an Egyptian execrated — shepherding. Truly the way to God is down, not up. It lies through the valley of humiliation. Blessed valley. It leads to the heights, but is the only trail to them.

But, as with others, Moses could take it. For these are not lessons for the rebellious. They are the secret things to be learned only by the wholehearted.

— *The Law of Faith*

*"Count yourselves dead to sin but alive to God in Christ
Jesus"* — Romans 6:11.

Faith may have to take a fresh stride forward in appreciation of the fuller meaning of that [verse], and it may be
reasonable and right to call that the "second work of grace"
when it refers specifically to the truth of our dying and rising
with Christ; whereas up till then His dying *for* us had been
all we had really appropriated. As we have pointed out, that
has to come as reality to most of us subsequent to the new
birth, and I do not believe such a profound crisis of faith can
be simply palmed off ironically by saying, "Second blessing?
Yes, and then the third and fourth and fifth."

So, second work of grace? Second blessing? Yes, if we
safeguard the statement by explaining that we do not mean
something further that has to be done to and in us as saved
sinners which was not done at regeneration. We affirm that
in receiving Christ we received the All in all, for the gospel is
not a change in the container but a change of the Person
whom we contain, and the only change in us is the quality of
life manifested by us as a consequence (a mighty change!).
But because we are usually too blind at our new birth to
grasp inwardly what has happened to us, we stumble about
in confusion and frustration; and that is God's way of
educating us until we can see more clearly the illusion of
self-sufficiency which we have carried over from our old life,
and are ready for the profounder affirmation of faith that
Galatians 2:20 and Romans 6:1-13 are also facts in us. If we
call that the "second work of grace," alright.

— *God Unlimited*

"Let us, therefore, make every effort to enter that rest"
— Hebrews 4:11.

Faith is not looking for a future revelation; it is realizing a present fact. Faith slips from its moorings when it listens to another's experiences and then says to itself: "I suppose God must come to me like that." Usually God comes in the way and at the time that we least expect, so that we know that it is God and not something worked up by our own efforts or imagination. To some, it may be just a gradual settling realization that these things are so; to another, a great and sudden inward assurance; to yet another there may be the accompaniment of an outward manifestation by dream, by vision, by some sign of the Spirit, as in Bible days.

So, in the spiritual fight of faith, the moment or period comes when we *know*. Every vestige of strain and labor has gone. Indeed, faith, as such, is not felt or recognized any more. The channel is lost sight of in the abundance of the supply. As we came to know that we were children of God by an inner certainty, a witness of the Spirit in our spirits, so now we come to know that the old "I" is crucified with Christ, the new "I" has Christ as its permanent life; spirit with Spirit have been fused into one, the branch grafted into the vine, the member joined to the body — and the problem of abiding becomes as natural as breathing.

— The Law of Faith

"You are in Christ Jesus, who has become for us wisdom from God — that is, our righteousness, holiness and redemption" — 1 Corinthians 1:30.

If a seeker is not sure that he is accepted of God, then we take every means of showing him from the Scripture that he may be sure, and we are not at ease until the light breaks upon him and he is able to say, "Whereas I was blind, now I see."

So it is, also, on the deeper level of Christian experience. I think this is often slurred over by Christian teachers. Emphasis is rightly put on knowing we are saved, then on a full surrender, a wholehearted acknowledgment of Christ as Lord as well as Savior; and then the seeking Christian is left to understand that the Holy Spirit automatically fills the emptied vessel.

But that is nothing like a profound or Scriptural enough presentation of the full way of life in Christ. It most certainly is not the gospel according to St. Paul. He takes a far more serious view of the indwelling enemy that has to be conquered, and gives a far more thorough account of how the victory is won. He makes it plain that the power of the flesh, the problem of sin in the believer's life, has to be as thoroughly faced, and the way of deliverance as completely found, as the earlier questions of sin and salvation have their full settlement. He could give as ringing a testimony to crucifixion with Christ, to his freedom from the old inner enemy, to Christ now living within, as he could to new birth, forgiveness, and justification.

— *The Law of Faith*

". . . that you may be filled to the measure of all the fullness of God" — Ephesians 3:19.

We have not a right to preach and stress the necessity of a "second work of grace" on the grounds that there is an old nature still left in the believer which was not removed at regeneration and has to be removed by this additional work of the Holy Spirit. If it is put like that, then the implication is that for some unexplained reason the fullness of salvation through grace is not available to any simple believer by the one act of saving faith. There is something mysteriously held back in the application of the full effects of Christ's completed work which was consummated at Pentecost. And if this is so, then of course a "second blessing" is a *sine qua non* for all. But it is plain to me that the New Testament presents us with all in Christ, with no arbitrary subdivisions in stages of experience.

But when it comes down to the pragmatic question "Have I experienced Christ's full salvation?", that is a different matter. I may come short through ignorance or through not yet being conditioned to understand the depths of my need and therefore the fullness of His supply. I may need and have a second crisis of faith, as most of us do, not because I have only received a partial salvation, but because the fullness of Christ in me and the fullness of what He has delivered me from have not been recognized and utilized by me.

— *God Unlimited*

"For to me, to live is Christ" — Philippians 1:21.

It is wholly right and wholly Biblical to say that, in the finished work of the Savior by His death, resurrection and ascension, and the coming of the Spirit, all was completed forever and there is not a thing to add to it, and it is all ours the moment we have entered by faith into the saving relationship with Him. I believe that wholly. The moment I am justified by faith, that same moment I am unified with the Father and the Son by the Spirit. I am there and then eternally a branch in the Vine, a member of the body joined to the Head, a vessel of mercy, the temple of the living God. I am sealed by the Spirit until the redemption of the purchased possession. I am sanctified by the offering of His body and perfected forever. I am endued with power from on high and filled with the Spirit, and baptized by Him into the one body.

My need, therefore, is not to have more but to possess my possessions. To know who I am, not who I ought to become. Not to acquire, but to recognize. Therefore I am saying that it is possible, and may be actual in some, that there is no second crisis: they entered into all at once.

All I can say is that I certainly did not know this fullness when I first came to Jesus and gave Him my life. And I am sure thousands are like me.

— *Who Am I?*

"Christ, who is your life" — Colossians 3:4.

We have seen plainly, from Paul's detailed explanation in his Roman letter, that Christ, our last Adam, completed a total redemption for us, the first Adam's family, in His death, resurrection, and ascension. But it can only become a living fact in our lives by us having a personal inner experience of Him. First there has to be a new birth of the Spirit, and then the Spirit bears witness to our human spirits that we are now the children of God. This witness is vital because we become operative persons in our spirit-selves only by an inner recognition of fact as fact. This is also why Christ's resurrection and ascension had to be confirmed inwardly to His disciples by the coming of the Spirit at Pentecost: it gave them an unshakeable inward confirmation regarding the One whom they'd outwardly seen and touched, but who had now disappeared from their sight. From then on no questions arose, even to the point of their dying for Him whom they knew. For faith was now knowledge. They knew what they knew! Outer facts had inner confirmation, and only by the inner was the outer established.

So now, by our new birth experience, we know what we know of our salvation and Savior. But we have gone on to recognize that knowing Christ as Savior from past sins must be accompanied by an equally certain knowing of Him as our personal sufficiency for our daily living, and for our sharing of such knowledge with others. Here is a *second stage* of knowing.

— Yes, I Am

The Second Crisis

"The law of the Spirit of life in Christ Jesus has set me free" ~ Romans 8:2 (RSV).

Bible biographies give plenty of evidence that we move on from a relationship-knowing at our new birth to a total *inner knowing*. Paul gives us the transforming details in Romans 7 and 8, as we follow him on from his penetrating understanding of the true facts about himself to his agonized cry, "O wretched man that I am! who shall deliver me from the body of this death?" and to his glorious liberated shout of inner recognition in 8:1-2, "Now I see! There is no more self-condemnation, no more beating my head against the brick wall of failure and defeat! I am set free! I *know* I am, and am free forever!" In his own written words, "The law of the Spirit of life in Christ Jesus has set me free from the law of sin and death" (RSV) — *has,* not might, may or will.

The Spirit was inwardly confirming what Paul had believed as a fact of history — that by Christ's body-death on Calvary, indwelling Satan was out and indwelling Christ was in; and Paul was underlining for us in this shout of victory that he was a liberated person, not only because Jesus had died and risen in history, but also because the Spirit inwardly confirmed it to him. It was the inner confirmation of the Spirit that set him free. No hearing of given facts, not even a reckoning on them, could do this for him; only the actual confirmation within him had finally "fixed him" in who he really was. I am free! I am free! Yes, *I am! I am! I am!*

— *Yes. I Am*

"You died, and your life is now hidden with Christ in God" — Colossians 3:3.

Don't deceive yourself; don't mistake your first believing of outer given facts for the spontaneous inner knowing. Get it clear. Faith starts off by my attaching myself to something. We have instanced food, a chair, going to a home. But that's not what makes it real to me. It is the response back, like an echo, from the thing to which I am attaching myself that makes the inner knowing. I take the food; I am conscious of it inside me. I sit in a chair: the chair makes me know it is holding me. *That* is the knowing. So the knowing does not come from my putting my faith into something, it comes from the something in which I put my faith. I must never mistake my faith in its first form — my attaching myself to something — for the completion of faith by which it has attached itself to me. Do you see this? So the final knowing of my eternal union — that it actually is *He* inwardly joined to me: that it is now *He* living in me, and *not* I — comes from Him the Spirit, and not from me the believer. *He* turns the faith into substance: absolute certainty.

So don't try any imaginings on this level, or try to make yourself *think* you have it. Don't *try* anything, for once again that is this old "sclf-effort stuff" we have died to. No, I keep doing my part, which is constantly affirming that *what the Scriptures have said about my union with Christ is fact.* I have been and am crucified with Him. I am dead to sin. I am crucified to the world. I now live in His resurrection. No, it is not I, it is He living in me. I *have* said it and *still* say it.
— *Yes, I Am*

"I have been crucified with Christ" — Galatians 2:20.

When and how will you know? Neither I nor an angel from heaven could tell you, because it is the prerogative of God Himself, God the Spirit, to speak that inner word. All we humans can say is "You'll know when you know!" Sometimes at once, sometimes after a time-gap.

I did not lightly move into my part of the believing. After five night-hours of battling around with it (so little did I understand the ease of faith in those days), I did finally put my finger on Galatians 2:20, or at least on the first phrase of it, and said right out, "I am crucified with Christ." Then I added a little bit of confessing with my mouth, which Paul said confirms the inner believing: I took a postcard, drew a tombstone, and wrote, "Here lies N.P.G., crucified with Christ." I had not reached far out into my resurrection by then!

But did I feel different or know anything different? No. My precious wife, Pauline, was with me and did the same. We had those five hours sitting in our little camp chairs in the forest, in the banana plantation of a precious African brother we had gone to visit. But the Spirit responded more quickly to Pauline. Within two weeks she felt what she took to be a touch on her shoulder, beneath the mosquito net on her camp bed. It was the Spirit confirming her word of faith, and she knew and has known ever since. Next morning, as we sat outside the little native hut in which we had been staying, breakfasting at our camp table, she began to say to me that she had something to tell me; but I said, "No need, your face shows it" — and her life has showed it all these years since.
                                                            — *Yes, I Am*

"We always carry around in our body the death of Jesus" — 2 Corinthians 4:10.

My first emphasis has to be on knowing that I really died with Him, because of my years of false condemnation of myself while being apparently alive in the flesh. But it is important to have it clear that when I say "I am crucified with Christ" I do not mean that I as a self have died to being a self — which is an absurdity. Yet preachers often mistakenly use the phrase "death to self." I cannot die to self, for I am eternally a self! I only die in the sense that my self has changed masters. I have "died" to having a job in a steel firm if I've crossed over and joined a cotton firm. That is the sense in which I have died in Christ.

There are also teachers who put such a strong emphasis on this death reality of the Romans 6 "death to sin" that they leave folks tossing about in a death-mindedness. It is necessary for a time, but then out we come from the tomb!

So Paul continues, in his famous Galatians 2:20 statement, with ". . . nevertheless I live; yet not I, but Christ liveth in me," and we continue in our faith affirmation along with him. We say categorically, and with no ifs or buts, "I am crucified with Christ" — cut off, dead to sin, dead as the old self which was Satan's dwelling place, dead to the world system in which I outwardly live. Dead, dead, dead, in His death. That I have to say before I can move on. But then I say, ". . . nevertheless I live" — meaning, of course, by His resurrection.

— *Yes, I Am*

"I know whom I have believed" — 2 Timothy 1:12.

But let me again and again make this abundantly clear: faith is *substantial*. Faith is the substance of the things hoped for, the *evidence* of the unseen. Therefore faith does not merely mean I have done *my part* by just believing and outwardly confessing. *That* is merely *my* faith attachment to something I desire to experience. I take food — no, food *takes me*; *then* faith is substance. I sit on a chair, yes, but the chair *upholds me,* not I it! Faith is *substance*: it produces *certainty.* "I *know* whom I have believed," says Paul. I believe first and *then* know, and in my new birth that inner knowing of the Spirit-reality became so much everything to me that outer things are no longer the real substance I mistakenly thought they were. Now *inner knowing, Spirit knowing,* has become the substance that neither world nor flesh nor devil can take from me.

So now in this *second* crisis of faith. Faith is substance. That substance does not come from us who do the believing and committing, but comes from that to which we have committed ourselves. The substance is the food, not the faith that takes it. The substance is the chair, not my faith that commits myself to it. And now the substance, the certainty, is that by some means, at some time — often immediately but not always — the witnessing Spirit *inwardly confirms to me* that it is He, no longer I, living my life. *I know.* I knew fifty-one years ago, fourteen years after my first knowing of salvation, and, of course, I know the same reality today.

— Yes, I Am

The Second Crisis

"He that is joined unto the Lord is one spirit" —
1 Corinthians 6:17 (KJV).

I now know that not only do I have Christ as my Savior from sin, but that I have passed through an inner experience of death to my former striving, sin-dominated, and self-condemning self. I now know that I am dead to sin, the world, flesh-dominion, and law; and now I equally know that I am no longer a lonely, independent "I," or still worse, have sin and Satan living in me. I know that in place of "I" it is now *Christ* living His life in me. And this I now *know* — actually *know* — without ever again having to reckon on it, or trying to reassure myself about it, or refreshing my recognition of it.

This does not mean that we are like two people separate within myself. No, we are one. I am "joined to the Lord — one spirit" (1 Corinthians 6:17); we are *two,* yet we are *one.* He is the One living in me, yet not as separate from me, but reproducing Himself by me — as vine through branch, head through body, husband through wife.

In that union relationship I can say that it is *Christ* who is manifested in my human form — just as it is when He says that both He and I are "the light of the world" (John 8:12, Matthew 5:14). In actual fact, we are two — light and lamp, and He is the light shining through the lamp. Yet we so forget the existence of the lamp that when we come into a room we don't say "Turn on the lamp" but "Turn on the light!" So in our conscious union relationship: though each Christian really is the two united in one, we don't see *ourselves* as thinking, speaking, acting, but it is *He expressed through our forms* doing the thinking, speaking and acting.
— *Yes, I Am*

"Woe to me if I do not preach the gospel!" —
1 Corinthians 9:16.

When we come consciously into the third level, the Spirit all the more consumes us with the desire to bring others to the liberation which is now ours — not only in the new birth, but in the fullness of the Spirit-filled life, with Christ in us as us. We become a fiddle with one string. Christ is our main topic of conversation. In place of sharing the scandals of life, we are thrilled to share what we see of Christ leading captivity captive. We are scandal-mongers of a different type!

But just as in our inner faith-activities — in the outflowing of the Spirit through our *spirit* — we move on from the normal faith-level of all God's redeemed people to the total use of faith in the management of all life, so now in the Spirit's use of our *body*.

This body use we speak of by the Bible word "intercessor." Nothing can be tied down to a word, but "intercessor" does conveniently explain what the Bible tells us of the Spirit's action through our body. It is really the Spirit making full use of His body temples, precisely as He did of the human body temple of God's own Son, who "through the eternal Spirit offered Himself without spot unto God." We see that the final glory of being a person is the saving of others at the price of ourself. It is as it was with Jesus: "He saved others; Himself He cannot save"; this was how they mocked Him as He hung on the cross.

— Yes, I Am

"Suppose one of you wants to build a tower. Will he not first sit down and estimate the cost?" — Luke 14:28.

There must be a serious weighing-up of our position on the third level, just as there has been on the first and second. We "count the cost," as Jesus said. We need to face the fact that it means that we don't assess life any more on the grounds of What do I get out of it? What happens to me? or Will I achieve what I'm meant to be? And when things "happen" to us in life, we no longer may say "Why this?", as if implying we have been hardly done by. No! We see it all in terms of His fulfilling some love and saving purpose *for others* through it, even though at the moment we cannot see that in it.

While that is the negative side of this third-level life, the positive is tremendous — so tremendous that it appears fantastic to our human sight. The positive is what Jesus taught about the Spirit's filling. It is not simply that we thirsting ones may fully drink of Him and remain filled, but Jesus says, "Stretch your believing further. The Holy Spirit didn't come merely to fill *you;* but from *your* fullness *others* will be filled." In other words, He is in you now as rivers of living water *flowing out from you.* This is Jesus' fantastic statement in John 7:38: "He that believeth on Me, . . . out of His inmost center shall flow rivers of living water." John, in verse 39, points out that because Jesus spoke this before the Spirit was poured out on all believers at Pentecost, the "shall" has been fulfilled and now *is!*

— Yes, I Am

"Whoever believes in me, . . . streams of living water will flow from within him" — John 7:38.

Out of us will never flow these rivers if we forget our union reality and look at ourselves in our humanity. It then becomes a joke. "Rivers — through me?" But once again, there is only the one way — faith. "He that believeth on Me." So we are right back where we started. Of course, again that "takes the heat" off *us*. "Jesus can save me, a sinner?" Yes! Just transfer your believing to Him and you are saved. "He can deliver me from the efforts of my striving self?" Yes! Just reckon yourself as dead to sin and risen in Him, and now He replaces that spirit of error in you. "There can be rivers of living waters flowing through me?" Yes! Drop your negative believing in your weak little self, stuck away in your small, local situation . . . and look to Him who said that rivers *are* flowing through those who are believing.

I took my first step into that third level (of John 7:38) as a young man, when starting out on my call to the Congo. I was so hesitant, and it seemed so absurd that rivers of the Spirit could flow out of me, that, though I did believe, I said, "Lord, I believe this word, at least for a muddy trickle to flow out!" But I did believe! And He has surely done more than I asked or thought! So BELIEVE — which is not one whit different from the believing in John 3:16 for salvation and in Galatians 2:20 for oneness. Stand there, laughing maybe — as I did — at the absurdity of its ever being fulfilled. But remember: faith is substance! The full entry by faith into this apostleship level is definitely a crisis experience involving a fixed inner knowing, as with the other two levels.

— Yes, I Am

> *"I write to you, dear children. . . . I write to you, fathers
> . . . . I write to you, young men"* — 1 John 2:12-13.

The simplest description of the three levels (because he uses a down-to-earth analogy) is John's, when he writes to his readers as "little children," "young men," and "fathers" (1 John 2:12-14).

When John says that we "fathers" know Him that is from the beginning, he means that, as fathers, we are in inner union with that Eternal One — not in His beginning, but as the One who now, as from the beginning, is in the process of completing what He has begun; and we are involved with Him in that completing process. Amazing grace! The point, then, is that we now are no longer dependent children but cooperating sons — Father and Sons, Inc.!

What John has given us on its three levels in such understandable terms is seen all through Scripture in those same three forms. We are united with Christ in His crucifixion, resurrection, and ascension — and Paul wrote letters which concentrate on each of these: Galatians on our identification with Him in His death; Colossians on our being risen with Him; Ephesians on our ascended life, seated with Him in the heavenlies, and its outcome.

Paul's Roman letter we all recognize as his fully developed, detailed, and authoritative statement of what he calls "my gospel." In this letter the three states are plain enough: chapters 3 to 5 — justification (little children); 6 to 8 — unification (young men); 9 to 15 — cooperation, cosaviorhood (fathers).

— *Yes, I Am*

"I urge you, brothers, . . . to offer your bodies as living sacrifices" — Romans 12:1.

The key scripture summoning us from the second level to the third is Romans 12:1: "I beseech you therefore, brethren, . . . that ye present your bodies a living sacrifice."

The second stage had been thoroughly established with its final triumphant shout of "no separation" — no separation possible from our eternal union. Paul's "Who shall separate us from the love of Christ? . . . I am persuaded that [nothing] can separate us . . ." (Romans 8:35-39). But now a shock! There is a new and glorious reversal from "no separation" to a voluntary separation from God, if necessary — even going to hell that our brother humans may be saved. For Paul immediately thereafter writes about his "great heaviness" for his own people: "I could wish myself accursed [i.e., separated] from Christ for my brethren." This was Paul the intercessor, and it is as such that he calls on us all — all who are redeemed — to present our bodies now as living sacrifices on the altar of *self-giving for others.* While death works in *us,* life will come to *them.* And from this point in his Roman letter, nothing is spoken about except how the light and life of Christ reaches out *by us* to the world.

What this means is a total move over, by the compulsion of the Spirit, to a life of unceasing love-activities in spirit and body — from the discipleship to the apostleship level, from the apprenticeship to the proficiency level, from the school of faith to the life of faith.

— *Yes, I Am*

"In bringing many sons to glory, it was fitting that God . . . should make the author of their salvation perfect through suffering" — Hebrews 2:10.

"That I may know Him, and the power of His resurrection, and the fellowship of His sufferings, being made conformable unto His death. . . ." To thus "know Him" means an inner understanding of His ways as the Savior: living by the power of His resurrection as a heavenly man in every earthly condition or daily demand, as Jesus did; fellowshiping with Him also in His sufferings, not now the joys of union but in Jesus' costly identification with the world in its needs, as well as meeting its antagonism.

Finally, it means pouring out one's life, not in some quiet retirement, but in God's appointed way — spiritually or physically dying that others may live. This Paul now embraced and lived out in his co-saviorhood, right to its last limit and into its final glory. As he wrote, ". . . if by any means I might attain unto the resurrection from among the dead" (literal Greek). In this he did not refer, of course, to his share in the bodily resurrection (which is a gift of God to all believers) but to a death like that of Jesus which brings resurrection to others — that "bringing many sons to glory" for which the Captain of our salvation tasted death (Hebrews 2:10).

To gain *this* — that by his dying many should live — Paul, now in his old age, pressed toward the mark in that high calling.

— Yes, I Am

"I fill up in my flesh what is still lacking in regard to Christ's afflictions" — Colossians 1:24.

[There] is as much a total entry into a fully meaningful relationship with Christ on this *third level* as with the entry into the "replaced life." It is entering into the final and total meaning of our portion of suffering in this life. From the suffering in our sin condition, to the suffering in our striving condition, to the suffering in our self-giving condition. It is revolutionary — and to those not settled and at home with the Trinity in our union relationship, it will again appear blasphemous — because we are really now saying that we are co-gods with God, just as the man Jesus said this to the Pharisees opposing Him (John 10:34-35).

So we see how we have now been permitted to share in the true purpose of sonship: no longer just the privilege of fallen sinners being sons and brothers with the Son, but joining with the Father in His eternal love-purposes for the "final reconciliation of all things," when He will be known as "God all in all." But if that is glorious for us, it is also most serious; for it means that as sons in this present moment of history, we are co-saviors, co-intercessors in completing the number of His elect, co-laborers with Him in the harvesting. That also means co-sufferers with Him in "filling up that which is behind [i.e., still lacking] of the afflictions of Christ . . . for His body's sake" (Colossians 1:24). We're on the saving level with Him, boldly accepting ourselves as such, carrying out the details of His plans, pressing toward the mark, paying the price, and "knowing that our labor is not in vain in the Lord."

— *Yes, I Am*

"If anyone does not hate his father and mother, his wife and children, . . . he cannot be my disciple" — Luke 14:26.

[After the third crisis] we recognize that we never again have any other meaning to our lives except *His loving others by us.* For as He is the God of love and thus the total self-giver for His universe, so are we. We no longer regard our lives from the aspect of our own convenience, or pleasant or unpleasant situations or relationships, not even our physical well-being. This is the outcome of what was settled within us on our discipleship (learning) level. Jesus had to speak of that in drastic terms to awaken us from any comfortable tendencies to drift along with the tide. He had to say it shockingly: "If any man . . . hate not his father, mother, wife, children, brethren, sisters, yea, and his own life also, he cannot be My disciple" (Luke 14:26).

What can that mean? How could Jesus say that? He said it like that to shock us into thinking it through. It seems so wrong, and even ridiculous, that we are forced to ask, What did He mean? It can't mean that! But when we do think it through, we see that all that ever motivated us in our unsaved days was self-love. Our love of others was really only to satisfy our self-love. *My* father, *my* mother, *my* wife, *my* children. The "my" was the real thing to us, not the "them." The *me, my, mine* is all I had. And it is "me" — not the loved ones — that I hate when I come to Christ. Then when I have come, and He to me, the miracle is that the *me, my, mine* is changed to *you* and *yours.* I am now a you-lover, not a me-lover. And now I have the kinsmen all back — to love them, rather than to be loved by them.

— *Yes, I Am*

"Seek first his kingdom and his righteousness, and all these things will be given to you as well" — Matthew 6:33.

[With the third crisis] an inner cutoff has taken place in which we really love *only One* and are joined to One, and our loves for others are secondary expressions of our one love. It is no longer God first and others second. No, it is God only, and all others we love as forms of Him. There is a detaching here which will certainly bring opposition, and maybe persecution, from some loved ones who feel — and rightly so — that they are replaced in the center of our hearts by our Eternal Lover.

It's not that we "try" to cut ourselves off from anything or anybody. No! *He* does the cutting off. It does not result in less concern for our loved ones but in more total concern for them to become the total people they really will be in Christ once they come to know Him, though meanwhile our attitude may appear to them as hate or neglect. Neither do we cut ourselves off from the normal way in which God provides our material security — by our jobs or investments. But in His own way *He* does an inner cutting off, by which we know *Him* as our true source of supply. Even if our employment or financial securities are taken from us, we only *praise* Him because He is giving us our chance of proving His faithfulness according to His Matthew 6:31-33 word about taking no anxious thought about food or clothing, but rather, "seek ye first the kingdom of God and His righteousness, and all these things shall be added unto you." But again, remember, it is *He* who lovingly loosens us from all earthly ties.

— Yes, I Am

"You will know that I am the Lord your God" —
Exodus 6:7.

I had never heard of Wayne Allen and the East Park Baptist Church in the city of Memphis, Tennessee, when in 1972 I received an invitation from him to come to his church for a three-day series of meetings. The Sunday congregation was about three hundred.

I was especially intrigued by my daily sessions with those he called his "Preacher Boys," about ten young fellows, all alive as witnesses for Christ and digging into every point I raised to find its Scriptural basis. I had no idea why Brother Wayne had invited me down until right at the end he asked me a question: "Brother Grubb, you've been talking to us a lot about speaking the word of faith. If I know it is God's will for me, cannot I speak the word of faith that we shall be the biggest church in Memphis?" (Memphis, a city of more than 600,000, has a great number of churches.) Recovering from the shock of such a statement from the pastor of this small city church, I said, "Well, brother, I know your motive. I know you are not just out for personal aggrandizement. Yes, you surely can speak that word of faith; only I would perhaps say 'one of the largest churches'!" And I added one more thing: "When God calls a man to do a thing, He says 'I will do it through you,' and that means you put your life at His disposal for it, will lay it down to see the completion of it, and will never look back until it is completed."

— *Nothing Is Impossible*

"Everyone who trusts in him will never be put to shame"
— Romans 10:11.

Later I heard from Alan Parker, then a lawyer with the Tennessee Valley Authority, about what happened a few days after I had that talk with Wayne.

"After you left, Wayne Allen told us that he had asked you, if God was leading him to believe that God would build a great church through him, did you think that God would really do it? And you said, 'Yes, if you are willing to dedicate your life to it.' Then the following Wednesday night at Prayer Meeting Wayne started speaking and I realized what he was doing. He was making a declaration of faith, and it was just marvelous. He said that God was going to build a great church through him here in Memphis and that he was giving his life to that."

But I heard no more after my conversation with Wayne until about a year later he called me and said he was visiting Philadelphia with a business friend, and would I have dinner with them. They first told me the remarkable story of the way the inner circle of the men of that church had obtained a 14-acre property on a piece of land in the residential area of the city, and then added, "And this coming Sunday is to be our special gift day, and God will give us a million dollars." Knowing the size of their membership, I would not have believed it. A few days later I heard the outcome — $1,384,000 in faith promises.

— *Nothing Is Impossible*

"Faith is being sure of what we hope for" —
Hebrews 11:1.

It was obvious that though Wayne seemed to be continuing in an average church ministry, the Spirit was fermenting within him, with a still undefined pressure to launch into greater things. Yet one flash point was needed — that faith does operate in practical facts so that nothing is impossible. That was what Wayne wanted to know: how to believe God. Some members of the church, Sandy, Doris, and Bill Brown, knew me and had read some of my books; and as they told Wayne about me and gave him one of the books, he sensed that I might be able to talk on how to believe God, especially as I had written the life of that great man of faith, Rees Howells. So that was why Wayne invited me. This is also why he was in such readiness of spirit to catch on to the secret made so plain in the biographies of the men of the Bible and in the lives of many whose names could be added to the "by faith" list in Hebrews 11, where we find the key to speaking the word of faith.

"After I had learned about the word of faith," says Wayne, "and how through faith God would come and make of us a great church and use us greatly, it was then that God let me see that He wanted to use us as an example of what He can do by a church. Then all could see that He can take a small, discouraged, weak church and really do something impossible through it."

— Nothing Is Impossible

"He rewards those who earnestly seek him" —
Hebrews 11:6.

There had been prepared ground for this giant leap of faith, for when Wayne first came to the church he had told them he definitely felt God would lead them into having a school. "We started looking over our grounds to see if we had enough room there, and we got an architect to show us the most we could build. But then we realized there was a state law that a high school has to be on at least eight acres of property, and we had only three; so we went to see if we could buy the land next door, but the man wouldn't sell it to us.

"We wanted at least ten acres of land," added Wayne, "and within two miles of our present location, because if we moved too far away the people who now come to church couldn't come.

"On Friday, December 29, I was at the hospital with a member who was having surgery, and a real estate agent called me and said, 'Brother Wayne, I've found the ideal land for you. It meets all your qualifications, but you just can't buy it.' When I asked why not, he explained that it was going to be sold on Tuesday on a sealed bid basis. Now Monday was January 1st, a holiday, and this was a holiday weekend. So I told him I wanted to see the land anyway, and I went with him to see it — 14.2 acres and ideally situated. It was just perfect. I told him, 'This is the land.' It was beautiful. A very wealthy lady had lived there and left it to be sold on a sealed bid basis. So I told him we were going to buy it."
— *Nothing Is Impossible*

"Faith is being . . . certain of what we do not see" —
Hebrews 11:1.

"We called 34 men together and I asked them to meet me
on Saturday morning and go see it. We all agreed that that
land was perfect. So we talked about what the price would
be. The real estate man had been checking, and one of the
men said, 'Well, I don't think $400,000 would buy it. I think
$425,000.' We discussed that a while and one of the men
said, 'If you pay $30,000 an acre for this, it will be about
$426,000 — I think we ought to bid $426,500.' We bowed
our heads and had prayer and I said, 'Now I want you to
keep your eyes closed and your heads bowed. The highest
figure was $426,500 and the lowest was $395,000. Now I am
going to start with the highest and go to the lowest. If you
feel God wants us to give $426,500, raise your hand.' And
they all raised their hands — all of them. So I called every
member of the church to be there Sunday.

"After the worship service, I asked our members to stay. I
explained about the land and asked them to commit themselves to the same commitment I had made. I was going to
give my life for this church, and I was asking my people,
'Are you going to give your life?' The vote was unanimous,
except for one [who later changed his mind].

"We put in our sealed bid. On Tuesday morning I had
some people who called me and said, 'Preacher, have you
heard yet?' 'Why, I don't have to hear; no need to hear, I
already know what is going to happen.' When they found
out that we had bought the property by just a $400 margin,
that really let them know how God had worked."

— *Nothing Is Impossible*

"Praise be to the Lord your God, who has delighted in you" — 2 Chronicles 9:8.

It was not until 1975 when I was in Memphis for a conference weekend and saw the size and beautiful construction and equipment of the church-school building, with the auditorium to seat 2,400 just nearing completion, that the magnitude of the project really registered with me. I was like the Queen of Sheba who said, "I believed not thy words until I came, and mine eyes had seen it, and behold the half was not told me!"

Wayne Allen told me in much more detail of the background of the Lord's inner urgings which led up to the completion of this building. I tramped through the endless corridors of what seemed like a modern airport, and was shown the spacious offices, the sixty "learning centers" with their magnificent equipment which *The New York Times* correspondent said is "the envy of public school administrators." I also saw the cafetorium seating 1,000 with its shining modern kitchen and service facilities, and took part in the opening dedication of the sanctuary.

Of much more importance, I entered into the purposes for which the Lord had led Wayne and his collaborators to take such a seven-league stride of faith, which had brought into being this largest church-school enterprise in the South. Then a word from the Lord came to me that it would be good to put some of this in print.

— *Nothing Is Impossible*

"It is with your heart that you believe" —
Romans 10:10.

It may be good to explain in more detail what has become so real to me in practicing the achieving faith which the Scriptures say in Hebrews 11 was the working principle of those great men of faith. This faith had become a working reality to me through my years of close fellowship with that modern man of faith, my friend Rees Howells. Its reality proved so immensely true in my own missionary circles where I was International Secretary of the Worldwide Evangelization Crusade for thirty-five years. We saw our numbers and world expansion develop from thirty-five workers in one field to 950* in thirty-five fields in the WEC, and 400* workers in thirty-eight fields in our brother Christian Literature Crusade. Each stage of advance was by this same working principle of faith. That is what I was now sharing with Wayne and his co-workers.

On this subject of speaking the word of faith, I had been pointing out to Wayne that faith is given a major priority in the Bible, not only in Hebrews 11, but in Jesus' constant references to "Thy faith hath saved thee. . . . If thou canst believe, all things are possible to him that believeth." It is called the law or principle of faith in Romans 3:27.

To bring it down to practical application, we see that faith is not merely a mental belief in a given fact, but the inner response of the will to something that confronts us in life, whether large or small. ("With the heart man believeth," not with the mind.)

— *Nothing Is Impossible*

*Now 1050 and 620 respectively.

"We have the mind of Christ" — 1 Corinthians 2:16.

Not only do we see with new eyes what we would *like* to happen, but we know the resources are already ours in the invisible. So by the word of faith we say that this is what we are now taking and are seeing happen. Our word of faith is declaring that, as in Jesus' life, what we see or need is in already existing supply, and thus is ours. We "say" that need is supplied, that thing has happened. In earthly affairs we go and fetch it or do it; but in the Spirit-dimension we say that God has already done it, and our faith is the agency for its manifestation. The very need itself is His signal to us to move over from the negative *seeing of needs* and problems and apparently unattainable projects, to the positive *seeing of Him* as both the instigator of the need and the provider of the already existing supply.

Thus, moving over to the positive seeing, we clinch it by the word of faith. We say it. We act on it as fact. We have a new boldness in taking for granted that our desires are God-implanted, instead of bringing up such childish hesitations as "Can it be His will?" We *are* His will in the union. We *have* the mind of Christ. We do not permit our inner-spirit center — where He and we dwell together — to be contaminated by the negative soul feelings of the apparent foolishness of it, or by our human thought patterns of earthly limitations. This is what I was sharing with Wayne; and this is what we now watch in action in this modern *Nothing Is Impossible* obedience of faith."

— *Nothing Is Impossible*

"He who did not spare his own Son, . . . will he not also . . . graciously give us all things?" — Romans 8:32.

The word of faith affirms His total sufficiency as present fact, and says that the need is already supplied. It then acts on that declared fact, and what is affirmed in faith becomes manifest in substance.

The news came back to me a week later of "the glorious day in the history of East Park Baptist Church when nearly a thousand people gathered for the first time on the property of 842 Sweetbriar, and it was announced that $1,384,000 had been committed to be given over a three to five year period."

But Wayne also tells how the joke was on him a short time later. "We had a picnic on Labor Day to let our people see the building. We were going to have the picnic in the parking lot. It had rained and rained. The men met me there to set up tables and do all the work, and then it started to sprinkle again. I asked my Building Committee chairman, 'Where are we going to have this picnic?' I was looking inside the building for some place. I had lost faith, and one of my deacons came up and said, 'Preacher, why aren't you putting the chairs out?' 'Otis, it looks like it is going to rain.' 'Preacher,' he said, 'where is your faith? I thought God planned this picnic. If you planned it, then we'd better just call it off. If God planned it, then it's not going to rain.' 'That's right, Otis.' So we got out and put the chairs out. We had the picnic and then the service, and from the parking lot we could look all around us and see it raining. It was just as if God had put an umbrella over us."

— *Nothing Is Impossible*

"Throw yourself into the sea" — Mark 11:23.

Jesus said, if I desire a thing, that is all the basis I need for praying the believing prayer. Note His promise: "When you pray, believe that you receive and you shall have" (Mark 11:24). Jesus did not say, what *He* desires, but whatever *we* desire.

The word of faith, then, has its confident basis. I speak it boldly. I *say* unto the mountain, "Be thou removed." I *say* God has done such and such in the invisible, and I act on the certainty that it will appear. The only inner enemies I have are my feelings (the soul part of me in contrast to the spirit where God and I are in union). These overwhelm me with the absurdity of saying such a thing. My reason (also part of my soul equipment) gives every proof of its impossibility, which is why Jesus was constantly saying, "Take no *thought*." I bypass these inner enemies by recognizing that I am I in my fixed inner spirit-union with God, where all is stillness and rest (for all power issues from rest). I do not let myself be controlled by the outer voices of my soul-disturbances.

If it is some larger issue which is challenging me, as this Briarcrest "miracle," or if it involves others besides myself in some new stride of faith, then we give time enough to weigh up all the circumstances. We examine the pressures which constrain us to consider such a launch of faith. We take note of every indication that God is in it, expect a general unity of conviction (though there may always be a doubter or two), and only then speak that combined word of faith and act on it.

— Nothing Is Impossible

"*If the Son sets you free, you will be free indeed*" —
John 8:36.

My overriding impression of Brother Wayne on my
various visits and in long personal talks with him has been
of a brother who was not carrying the many heavy burdens
that have to be carried in such an enterprise. Here was not a
busy, strained, preoccupied man, still less an official-type
pastor or director, but a man at rest, a man who was his
natural self, a man at ease. Of course I knew his secret, but I
like to hear him tell about it himself. He makes comments
that are often revolutionary and quite disturbing on some
subjects — but how I find my own spirit at one with his!

He opened the door to the secret of his ease among such
responsibilities in the simplest way. "In my life I was trying
too hard, wanting to achieve and wanting to serve God and
do something for God. I worked real hard, but so much of it
was just energy in the flesh, just self-effort. I went through a
very long process of being very legalistic and pharisaical,
and of course, this just robs you of your joy and freedom. I
was very judgmental, and most of my preaching centered on
pet sins and trying to convict people of them. My spiritual
life was not really enjoyable. I tried to say I was happy and
convince everyone I was. But it was phony, it was not real,
because I didn't have any freedom. Now I tell people I've
become childish, because I am as free as my five-year-old
boy is. Most of us have got the concept of salvation by faith
through grace without works, but we've never got the concept that we are His workmanship and He is the worker."

— *Nothing Is Impossible*

"Take my yoke upon you and learn from me ... and you will find rest for your souls" — Matthew 11:29.

[Wayne Allen's testimony continues:]

"You relax, and God is God, and you are the instrument He's using, and you just are real free and at ease. And it gives you an openness. I tell a lot of people things about myself I used not to speak of, because I was afraid of what they might think about me. Like about praying. I told one of the pastors here in town I just don't pray as I used to. My prayer life is just a natural flowing thing. When you come to the concept that Christ is one, and I am not I, but Christ, it's in the concept of talking to yourself. It's kind of strange to think of people talking to themselves. There's a freedom that you just don't have to worry about. It's a release. I've heard so many sermons and read so much about the Spirit setting you free and of the liberty in the Spirit, yet so few people really realize what it is all about. It's so clear when you see the concept and understand it and it becomes experiential knowledge; then you see so much of it in the Bible. It's a constant process, like being clay in the potter's hand.

"The problem so many times is that we can't enter into the real, relaxed, restful, and what I call *natural* Christian life, which means there is no real effort involved in it. The only way that people can see Christ is to see us! We are the demonstrations of what God is, and I think this is why it is so important that we always give a witness, a clear witness, that it is Christ operating in us."

— Nothing Is Impossible

"God, who is rich in mercy, made us alive with Christ"
— Ephesians 2:4-5.

"The world says you are an egotist just because you say 'I know I am saved and going to heaven' — we acknowledge that. But then when you start saying 'God is operating in me,' that of course you can't tell the world! In fact, you can't tell most Christians that 'I am a manifestation of Christ in the flesh.' They think you are crazy, yet it is the truth. I and Christ are one. We say it, but most times we don't come into realization of this unity in Christ. We get the old man crucified, but we never get the new man resurrected. We spend all our time and energy in reckoning ourselves dead. But Paul said in Ephesians 2:5, 'you hath He quickened,' and we know that; but then we forget that he went on in verse 10 to say that 'we are His workmanship, created in Christ Jesus unto good works.' The good works, of course, is just Christ living in us and working by us, and we being one like the vine and the branch. You can't separate them, they are one, and it is not a works thing.

"Christ has joined us to Himself and the Christ-life is just like breathing. It's an unconscious condition. Every time I start thinking about breathing, something is wrong. When you are always watching everything you are thinking, saying, or doing, and making sure you are doing everything by some set of rules, you can't be used, because all your attention is focused on yourself. But the union life is just a relaxed freedom, unbelievable freedom."

— *Nothing Is Impossible*

"By the grace of God I am what I am" —
1 Corinthians 15:10.

"You accept that physically God has a purpose in your personality and everything about you, and you accept yourself as God's perfect manifestation, just what He means you to be. Instead of 'trying' to reckon ourselves dead, we already are in Christ, and there is therefore no condemnation. I don't think then we need to be afraid of being an egotist or of what the world thinks of us.

"I think this positive attitude also builds people's confidence in a person, because accepting self is what most people can't do. It's the reality of Christ manifesting Himself in us, and when a person does have this self-confidence — which is not confidence in self, but in the Christ that is joined to self — this brings about leadership. We no longer stifle our imaginations of how big our God is. People are looking for someone who knows where he is going, who knows who he is and what he is. But some pastors give no clear leadership.

"Moses gave very clear leadership, as did Joshua and Caleb, whether people listened or not. When the spies said 'We cannot go up into the land, the giants will eat us up,' Caleb answered, in effect, 'Let us go up at once, and possess it; for we are well able to overcome it, and the giants will be bread for us'!

"Your people will know whether or not you do know the will of God, and if you are happy, because they will see it. As pastors we have to demonstrate this and be able to say, 'Yes, you can *know* the will of God, and *this* is what God is going to do.'"

— *Nothing Is Impossible*

"We proclaim him, admonishing and teaching . . . , so that we may present everyone perfect in Christ" — Colossians 1:28.

"All that you gain and do, grow and build, that's the Lord's. It's the Lord's thing. I don't have criticism from lost people; most of the criticism is from religious people. They feel a person like me is an egotist. Of course, that is the same problem that Jesus had, and I guess I'm supposed to have it too.

"When we begin to declare the unity we have with Christ — that I am in Christ and Christ is in me, and we are one — people don't believe that, and think we are crazy, or something is wrong. When I first came to East Park, a nurse in the church thought I was taking drugs. She came to me privately one day and said, 'Preacher, I want to ask you something in confidence and I pledge to you that I will never tell anybody, but I've got to know. How is it that you are happy all the time? Every time I see you, you are happy. So I want to ask, Are you taking something?' 'Yes, Polly,' I said, 'I do take something. I take a gos-*pill* every day. *That* is where I get it.' Christ in you and you in Christ, and you are one. That is the freedom, and people can't understand it when you are not burdened down by legalism. The more you come over to being totally free of what people think of you, the more you are just natural and are yourself. I don't have to be somber to be a preacher. I'm far from it. If I am a little crazy, then I am a little crazy, and if I like to cut up, I cut up. I am free to be myself, without putting on any airs, and that's Christ totally expressing Himself." [Wayne Allen]   — *Nothing Is Impossible*

"Our light and momentary troubles are achieving for us an eternal glory that far outweighs them all" — 2 Corinthians 4:17.

The cross has the glory in it. It is Paul's "light affliction which is but for a moment, which worketh for us a far more exceeding and eternal weight of glory." It is C. T. Studd's little rhyme, "Take my life and let it be a hidden cross revealing Thee." It is the voluntary taking up of my cross for others, in contradistinction to my coming to His cross for reconciliation, and being united in His cross for inner union. Its highest glory is seen in Isaiah 53:10: "It pleased the Lord to bruise Him," not bless, but bruise, that death might work in Him, but life in others.

Don't be afraid of being an intercessor. He is the Priest within and by us, and the way He takes us is always beautiful, good, perfect, and acceptable. So bring your human fears to the Lord, and tell Him to bring you through and not let you miss "the prize of the high calling of God in Christ Jesus." Intercession again is not works effort, but the inescapable compulsion of grace.

And resurrection of the interceded-for in place of the death of the intercessor is a law. Once accepted and entered into, the harvest must follow. John 12:24 is the key statement on that. Take that for granted. A prayer *may* be answered, an intercession *must*. That is why, as Wayne saw, you give yourself for life with no looking back.

Let us make it plain. There may be specific commissions to sacrifice our ambitions or even lay down our lives for a calling from God.

— *Nothing Is Impossible*

"Your faith has healed you" — Luke 8:48.

The one word which has stood out preeminently before us these years has been "faith." We found full authority in the Scriptures for a strong emphasis upon it. Outstandingly is this so in in Hebrews 11, where every life of notable achievement in the Bible is labeled with a single incisive phrase as its keynote, "by faith." Christ, too, put remarkable emphasis on faith. To practically every miracle of healing He added a comment such as, "Thy faith hath saved thee"; "According to your faith be it unto you"; "If thou canst believe, all things are possible to him that believeth."

All believers say in a general way "God is almighty," "God can do this or that." Only one in a thousand says, "God is almighty in *me*" and "God will do so and so through *me*." Here lay the essence of Moses' controversy with God at the burning bush. God was saying, "Come now, I will send *thee,* and *thou* wilt deliver My people." Moses was replying, "I believe You can and will do it, but not through *me*." God's almightiness was not the point in question. It was Moses' appropriation and obedience of faith that hung in the balance. Thus when Moses did set forth to carry out the commission, the Holy Spirit rightly says it was done "by faith." The same difference in the quality of believing makes the dividing line between Elijah and the 7,000 other true believers who had not bowed the knee to Baal and yet who had so little influence on the lives of their generation that Elijah did not know of their existence.

— *Touching the Invisible*

"Shout! For the Lord has given you the city!" —
Joshua 6:16.

Faith is always an involvement, not a sitting on the
fence. Faith is always a conquest of uncertainty. But the
point is that we come to a conclusion, and do not leave
things in the air. Faith can only be as strong as its object: if
the chair we seat ourselves on is strong, the faith is strong; if
the chair wobbles, the faith wobbles. But to come to a
conclusion that such-and-such is the will of God involves
our reputation, and that is where we stop short. That is why
we do not easily believe; it is the committal of ourselves to
something, and a taking of the consequences. That is why
the prayer of request is easy. We then only ask, "If it be Thy
will." If it does not happen, well, it was not His will; we are
not involved. But if I have said something is His will, and
then it fails to materialize, I appear to be the fool or false
prophet.

When the decision is settled in my mind, then the final
step of faith, of my human involvement, is taken. Faith
declares a thing done before it is done. It "calls the things
that be not as though they were." This is the crossing of the
Rubicon. Prayer puts its toes in the water; faith dives in. The
Bible is filled with such incidents in the lives of all the men of
faith, as well as in the Savior's life.

"Shout, for the Lord hath given you the city," said
Joshua to his army before Jericho.

— *The Spontaneous You*

"The Spirit himself testifies with our spirit that we are God's children" — Romans 8:16.

In the new birth we exchange faith. We were disillusioned with our former faith in our own righteousness, and we took the leap of faith from the matter to the spirit dimension by transferring our inner choosing from some material and visible earth-reliance to Him who died in history for our sins but is risen beyond history in the fourth dimension of Spirit. We then experienced the substance of our new believing. Our word of faith which confessed Him as Savior and Lord is replaced by our first consciousness of spiritual substance — the inner witness of His Spirit to our spirits that we are children of God. Faith has dissolved and become inner knowledge of Spirit-fact.

We now operate this same law of faith to experience, and become established in, the fullness of the endued and liberated life in Christ. According to Romans 6-8, we pass on from the ineffective struggles and constant failures of being the "wretched" man of Romans 7:24 — who cries out because he cannot get free from the slavery of the flesh. We now discover who we truly are — one cut off in Christ's death, according to Romans 6:1-14, from the claims and control of sin and flesh, and now by grace eternally united to Christ in His resurrection and ascension; the human *redeemed* self in eternal union with the *Divine Self,* according to such scriptures as Romans 8:1-9, Galatians 2:20, 1 Corinthians 6:17, John 15, etc. We are branches in The Vine; we are joined to the Lord, one spirit.

— *Nothing Is Impossible*

"I know whom I have believed" — 2 Timothy 1:12.

On Sunday morning you say your duty is to go to church. But you get a blustery day, wind and snow, and you don't feel like going. But you go anyway.

Why? Because down inside you purpose to go. You say, "Oh, I don't feel like going, but I'm going."

There you've got the point. Now you have moved from soul to spirit.

Reason is exactly the same. Reason is the faculty by which we explain things and argue about them and talk about them. I claim to know Jesus Christ; I try to explain myself to you — that's my reason.

I've always been one to dig into things. I took up philosophy just as a hobby and got my reason thoroughly shaken. I said to myself, "I'm really not so sure that there is a God at all. Yet," I said, "I know Him and love Him and have done so for years — yet He may not be a living Person at all!"

My reason conveyed doubts to me.

My spirit said, "But I *know* Him!"

So do you know what I came to? I said, "Well, if God is the big illusion, I'll be a little illusion alongside Him. I love the 'Illusion,' that's all."

You see, I would not be governed by my reason — my soul — because I had something deeper — more real.

Of course, in due time, I came out more strongly confirmed in soul, or reason, as well as spirit-knowledge. Doubts are the raw material of faith.

— *The Key to Everything*

"Tell the Israelites to move on" — Exodus 14:15.

It is always our speaking our word of faith which puts a person into action.

We named ten new workers as the first token of a world-wide advance to begin in the Congo. They would come in a year, by the first anniversary of C.T.'s glorification. We said it, named the number, and the day — July 16, 1932 — and used that scripture we have already quoted in Mark 11:24. We believed we had received it, as it says.

So for the rest of the year — no man knowing what was happening — we thanked, watched, and often laughed, as the ten came.

The next year we moved on to fifteen, the next twenty-five, the next fifty, the next seventy-five — and they came. There would be no point in giving further details, for we are looking at principles. But I thank God that the Worldwide Evangelization Crusade, coupled with the Christian Literature Crusade (which was born out of it), together have some 1500 workers, establishing the gospel in over forty fields. Thank God, today thousands around the world have confessed Christ and are themselves now forming national churches, spreading the gospel witness.

The whole company of Crusaders are still living with enthusiasm on the promises of God, applying these same principles of faith to all kinds of advances. Millions of dollars now come in annually . . . when it was but five thousand that first year. I do not mean to disregard the fact that there have been failures en route. And trials. For some there has even been the glory of martyrdom, as they have laid down their lives for Christ.   — *Yes, I Am*

*"What are you, O mighty mountain? Before Zerubbabel
you will become level ground"* — Zechariah 4:7.

Jesus commanded the fig tree to bear no more fruit
(Mark 11:14). The next morning, when they passed the
withered tree, Peter commented on it: "Master, look, the fig
tree you cursed is withered away." Jesus simply replied,
"Now *you* have this same 'faith of God'" (which is the literal
rendering, rather than "faith in God"). And what does that
mean? Obviously, *seeing as God see the situation,* and thus
believing with His believing. And how does God do this?
Through my eyes and inner comprehension. So if something appears like a mountain of difficulty to me, that is how
He is first causing me to see it.

Jesus then tells His disciples to *say* to any such mountain, "Be thou removed, and be thou cast into the sea," and
in doing so, to believe it is a completed fact. The result: "You
will have whatever you have said." It couldn't be simpler.
Don't beg. Don't beseech. Just *say it!* But there is the added
proviso that we don't doubt in our hearts — don't allow
mental soul-doubts, which we surely have, to disturb our
fixed, inner word of faith: "Whosoever . . . shall not doubt in
his heart, but shall believe that those things which he saith
shall come to pass, he shall have whatsoever he saith" (verse
23).

But how can I say "Be removed" to a mountain? Because
it is only a mountain to my human seeing. Read what God
said to Zerubbabel in Zechariah 4:7: "Who art thou, O great
mountain? Before Zerubbabel . . . a plain."

— *Yes, I Am*

"Go, throw yourself into the sea" — Mark 11:23.

Speaking the word of faith (having once settled what the desire is) could not be more simple. It is the "obedience of faith" (Romans 16:26). That is all the "works" involved. It is a *work* of faith to this extent: all that the outer appearances can pour on us at such a "speaking" moment, they will pour. That is to say, we shall likely feel the full impact of the foolishness of faith. It looks absurd. It *is* absurd, because the agony of faith is that *nothing* can ever be experienced until after we've committed ourselves to it, not before. As we've seen, that is actually true in a minor way of even the least act of everyday faith, like sitting on a chair. *How much more* when it is these leaps into what is invisible and impossible and unattainable by human methods!

So there is a travail of faith because of the new assaults on us by every emotional reaction to the absurdity and impossibility of it. And equally, by every rational objection to what spirit-faith has always been — the irrational. So in that sense, we say speaking this word is *not simple.* Yet it is, because it is just *speaking the word!* And that is why something equivalent to "confessing it with our mouth" is a seal on it — a means by which, once we have said a thing, it's a settled matter — and the affirmation to ourself or to others helps to settle us into it. But that's all. These are our *supreme moments* when the rivers of the Spirit are flowing out of us on our spirit level. This is the faith that gives substance to things hoped for.

— Yes, I Am

"Whatever you ask for in prayer, believe that you have received it, and it will be yours" — Mark 11:24.

The word of faith is the heartbeat of our prayer life. We have seen that we first need to know the mind of Christ, in each given situation, *expressed through our own minds* —relating to the challenge, the mountain that confronts us. Knowing that His mind and ours are in union, we come to a plain settlement (even if it takes time to sort things out) of what it is that *we* desire in the situation. We then boldly take it for granted that that means *His* desire *by us,* knowing that He freely said in Mark 11:24, "What things soever *ye* desire, when ye pray, believe that ye receive them, and ye shall have them."

And now we are moving into the heart of the matter. Jesus had just said, "*Say* unto this mountain, Be thou removed . . ." and you will have whatsoever you say. Now, speaking of naming our desires in prayer, He said, "*Believe* that you have received them, and they shall be granted you" — "*have received,*" not "receive" — and I quote the *New American Standard* version here, because it best brings out the meaning of the Greek aorist tense.

This is where the difference lies between my former request-type praying and what Jesus was saying to His disciples and now us. I see God marvelously privileging me and you to be *His agents of production* in lives and conditions. Just as we produce in the material realm by specifically deciding what we shall make and then making it, so now in the realm of the Spirit. For me, I ask no longer, unless I also believe and receive.

— Yes, I Am

"Continue in him, so that . . . we may be confident"
— 1 John 2:28.

It is only the "graveclothes" of suspicion of our old
self-seeking selves which make us hesitate about saying that
the thing we desire is His mind. But He has said, "What
things soever ye desire when ye pray, believe . . ." (verse 24).
You desire. Then let's be that simple. If He in us trusts our
desires to be His desires, let us trust ourselves. We have
discarded and rejected those doubtings and questionings of
our motives by accepting our vital Galatians 2:20 relationship, so let us now practice holy boldness, just as John keeps
saying in His union epistle: "We have confidence toward
God. . . . This is the confidence that we have in Him. . . . We
may have boldness [even] in the day of judgment."

Then, being bold in defining exactly what are the things
we are presently desiring in place of the mountain confronting us, and naming them, we speak the key word of the
countdown — we press the button marked "SAY." We do
that from our inner spirit-center, simply by our authority as
sons of God. Jesus has plainly told us to act *as God* by "the
faith of God" — by His inner believing imparted to us, by
our inner union of mind and understanding. This means
that in acting as He, all of His mighty resources are at *our*
disposal. It is not now a matter of us being at *His* disposal,
but of Him being at *our* disposal. He is operating in this
present world-system *by us*. We say with Caleb, "Let us go
up at once and possess it, for we are well able to overcome
it." And in so doing, we laugh the laugh of faith.

— *Yes, I Am*

"Pray continually" — 1 Thessalonians 5:17.

Speaking the word of faith makes a big difference to our prayer life. In explaining this new understanding of prayer I have sometimes said that "I don't pray any more." I should not say that, chiefly because the Bible is full of exhortations to prayer and illustrations of prayer. What I'm meaning is that at the heart of my praying, the prayer of request has been replaced by the prayer of acceptance of what I've asked for. Certainly, prayer cannot mean what we often interpret it to mean — having special times of prayer, etc. — because Paul has told us to pray without ceasing, and *that* we *cannot do* unless we see prayer to be a condition in which communion with God is always continuous, on our subconscious (and, as needful, conscious) level.

I am not now referring to those periods of corporate prayer expressing fellowship, worship and praise. Some enjoy them in the quietness of an Episcopal-type worship service, or of the Lord's Supper. Others, including myself, though being most at home in home fellowships, also enjoy the Spirit-led outpourings in more charismatic-type meetings when all are unitedly and vocally pouring out their hearts in praise; and this may often include both songs and singing in the Spirit, in one great volume of sound, sometimes interspersed with messages in tongues and interpretations. This was obviously part and parcel of the normal worship times in the early church (1 Corinthians 14:26-33). It shows how far we have cooled off from the flow and freedom of those days.

— *Yes, I Am*

> *"God . . . calls things that are not as though they were"*
> — Romans 4:17.

Folks say, "But doesn't God tell us to ask?" Yes, but asking is not to inform God of what I need. "Your heavenly Father knoweth that ye have need of these things," said Jesus. What *is* required is God getting me in my childish ignorance to the point of deciding what He is meaning me to ask for. Just as you get a child to choose which cookie he will take and then ask for just that one. So asking is just a stepping stone to receiving. As Jesus said, "Ask . . . seek . . . knock, and it shall be opened unto you." So to my asking I add taking and receiving. Indeed, as I get used to taking by the word of faith, I hardly notice I'm asking — one is almost dissolved into the other.

So I move right in and speak the desire into reality. How? By that word of faith which "calls the things that be not as though they were," which is said to be God's form of faith (Romans 4:17), and therefore mine. I speak that word. When it is on the mundane human level that I speak any such word, *I* then go on to fulfill it. This time I am recognizing that it is *God* speaking that word by me, and so *He* goes on to fulfill it — and it is precisely the same as when He brought the visible creation into being by the word of His Son.

— *Yes, I Am*

"Get your supplies ready. Three days from now you will cross the Jordan" — Joshua 1:11.

God spoke to Joshua and told him to go forward into the promised land, crossing the Jordan River. But by what authority did Joshua name "three days" and then say with total confidence that they would *then* cross the flooded river? God had not said that to him.

Then we [who were gathered together] saw the truth. We saw how Joshua and all such men spoke their words of faith. They named their needs. *They*, not God. "What things soever *ye* desire." This was the secret. The hidden key. This life is not to be we men pathetically depending on God, calling on God as though at a distance and not too willing to help. It is God's marvelous plan of entrusting Himself to man, joining Himself to man as man. It is man speaking as God. It is union in action, just like with Moses, Elijah and the rest. It was Joshua who, as a military commander, calculated the days needed for preparation and then fixed a timetable by the word of faith. He had got it! He understood that God had entrusted His own plans and the power for their fulfillment to His appointed agents — which we all are. *You define what you need and how much you need. Then you say so.* That's all. You say it is coming. That it is there already in your sight. "Within three days ye shall pass over."

It is always our speaking our word of faith which puts a person into action. But this is not human action. It is God-action, Spirit-action, and the river will dry up and the people cross. So we see that all hangs on this spoken word of faith, and that's all, because it really is God the Father speaking His word by His son or daughter, through whom the Spirit then moves into manifestation. *— Yes, I Am*

"Where your treasure is, there your heart will be also"
— Matthew 6:21.

When someone asks me to pray with them for a loved
one, maybe a husband or wife, I say briefly to her (supposing it's a wife), "It isn't your husband who is the problem.
You are the problem. You as a daughter of God have the
right to speak the word of faith that God *has* your loved one
saved or delivered." I give her the scriptures and the promises. Then I say, "I won't pray for you more than this one
time. But if you like — and you see that you have this right
to believe — I will join you now in your word of faith." That
is much more help to her than my just praying a prayer with
her. It is helping her to be the wife of faith.

And if someone says, "But how can you say by faith that
God has your loved one saved? Hasn't he a will of his own?",
my answer is that *his will is not what controls him*. It is his
wants, and *his will will follow his wants*. And God has His
own clever way of changing our wants. He can make us sick
of what we used to want from this world, and can make us
want *Him*. Then our will will follow our want.

— *Yes, I Am*

"Whatever you ask for in prayer, believe that you have received it, and it will be yours" — Mark 11:24.

I was preparing the January issue of the magazine and said to the Lord that I could not again publish the statement that fifteen [new workers and needed finance] would be with us by July unless I had a seal (confirmation) from Him. The final proof had to go to the printer the next day, so I said, "If You will send me £100 before 11 A.M. tomorrow, I will take that as a seal. But if You do not, I will not put in the article." 11 A.M. came. I had the proof on the desk in front of me, but no £100. So I said to the Lord that I was very sorry, but in these circumstances I must drop the fifteen and publish nothing further about it. As I said that, I saw Colonel Munro coming across from the office. He entered the room waving something in his hand. It was a check from Scotland for £100. The article went in.

The fallacy and weakness of my action, and the mercy of God, are obvious. If the exercise of faith means that first we find the will of God, then we receive our request when we pray (Mark 11:24), how can we be foolish enough to go about asking for seals on a thing which we have said that we already have?

— *After C. T. Studd*

> *"The Son can do nothing by himself; he can do only what he sees his Father doing"* — John 5:19.

We don't "work up" the knowing. Should you be reading this and say, "Well, I've said that 'word of faith'; I have *believed,* but I can't say *I know,* then don't, don't try to know. Knowing does not come from self-effort; that would be back under the law of "you ought" again. The knowing comes from the Spirit. So what you do is to keep firmly affirming that *you are* what you have now said you are by faith. Your job is to maintain the affirmation. The confirmation comes from Him, and any trying or searching of your own will only insert a fog of unbelief which hinders the Spirit from giving the confirmation. But there *is* the confirmation.

What more perfect pattern are we given of what a normal person is than Jesus Himself? And nothing about this ideal man is more striking than His constant disclaimer of doing anything or being anything *of Himself.* "I do nothing of Myself," John quoted Him several times as saying. When questioned about His work, He said, "The Son can do nothing of Himself, but what He seeth the Father do"; and about His statements, "As I hear, I judge"; and finally, when asked by Philip to show them the Father, to whom He said He was soon going, He gave them this startling answer: "He that hath seen Me hath seen the Father."

— *Yes, I Am*

> *"You will be for me a kingdom of priests"* —
> Exodus 19:6.

The highest vocation for which God has destined man has not changed through the centuries. When He was preparing a peculiar people to be His agent of world redemption, He told Moses that the true sign that He had sent him to rescue them from Egypt would be what He would say to them when they reached Mount Horeb. Evidently, therefore, the important point would be His commission to them. That would be the way they were to serve Him in the future. And what did He say to them? He reminded them of the way He had delivered them from their oppressors and brought them to Himself "on eagles' wings," to be His peculiar treasure (although His eye and heart were really on all peoples, for "all the earth is Mine"), and that His purpose was for them to be a "kingdom of priests" (Exodus 19:4-6).

Priests are not priests for their own benefit, but for others. Thus if the whole of Israel was to be a kingdom of priests, it could only have been as intercessors for a lost world. It was for that reason, doubtless, that when God gave them this calling He added the words, "for all the earth is Mine." Not a specially selected number to be priests among them, but all to be priests. That is of great significance. And not only priests, but "a kingdom of priests," called by Peter, when applying this statement to the church, "a royal priesthood."

— *The Liberating Secret*

"It was fitting that God . . . should make the author of their salvation perfect through suffering" — Hebrews 2:10.

In Hebrews 1 the incomparable glory of the Son of God is set before us in mounting phrase upon phrase: Lord of all things; by whom He made the worlds; outshining of His glory; express image of His person; sat down on the right hand of the Majesty on high. Our hearts are awed and melted in worship. Highest of the high, "Let all the angels of God worship Him." At His name shall every knee bow, and ours among them.

In the middle of these sparkling gems of glory there is one blood-red stone. It seems out of place. It takes us by surprise: "When He had by Himself purged our sins." The next chapter explains. "We see Jesus," called here by that human name for the first time, "made a little lower than the angels for the suffering of death . . . that He by the grace of God should taste death for every man" (taste it, not here referring to its beneficial effects for us, but to the experience it gave Him of drinking to the last drop the cup of humanity), and fall even under the dominion of "him who had the power of death, that is, the devil." Here is the great High Priest, the Intercessor, descending from the highest heights to lowest depths, to share and bear humanity's sufferings, frailty and sin. The priest identifies himself with those for whom he intercedes. He sits where they sit. He bears what they bear.

— *The Liberating Secret*

"Christ Jesus . . . is at the right hand of God and is also interceding for us" — Romans 8:34.

Our great High Priest has been the unique Intercessor. None but He could be a propitiation for our sins. But we also, as priests, have a law of intercession to fulfill, and this helps us to get a clear sight of it. To be kings and priests is our high calling, a royal priesthood. But first a *priest*, as He was first the High Priest. And that means identification, intercession, and finally authority.

Intercession has often been mistaken by many as a heightened form of prayer. But it is something different. An intercessor was sought for by God in the Old Testament times of desperate national backsliding, as someone whom He could rely on to turn the tide, a task of no mean order. In Isaiah's day God "wondered that there was no intercessor"; in Ezekiel's time He "sought for a man among them that should make up the hedge, and stand in the gap." In other words, all those dedicated men through Bible history, who knew their redemptive commission, who gave themselves without stint to the fulfillment of it — which involved them in all kinds of eccentric renunciations and strange activities for God's glory and man's salvation — were intercessors.

— *The Liberating Secret*

"Please forgive their sin — but if not, then blot me out of the book" — Exodus 32:32.

The true intercessor is ready to go to the limit in identification. It will take many forms of physical and material renunciation, as we see — of costly and often startling behavior, and unaccustomed ways of living; but they are mere symbols of the inner cross-bearing. Just once or twice in Scripture the final implications of intercession are seen. Moses, from the time of his first renunciation, when it came into his heart to visit his brethren, went to every outward length of identification. He accepted in willing submission the many early disciplines of the spirit, in changing his station from prince to menial.

But the depths were plumbed at the Mount. Previously he gave his body; now he gave his soul. As if to underline the total indifference of the intercessor to his own self-interest, when God's wrath was upon the people for their gross idolatry, He said to Moses, "Let Me alone that I may consume them; and I will make of thee a great nation." Moses totally ignored it. He wasn't even interested. He took the final step of identification, not now in his body but in his immortal soul. "If Thou wilt forgive their sin — and if not, blot me, I pray Thee, out of Thy book which Thou hast written." "Save them, or damn me with them!" If I cannot go to heaven with them, I'll go to hell with them. God can never refuse a holy desperation like that. It changed His mind. Of course it did, because it always was His mind to save them.

— *The Liberating Secret*

*"I could wish that I myself were cursed and cut off from
Christ for the sake of my brothers"* — Romans 9:3.

Paul was the Moses of the New Testament. There is no
more significant illustration of the true character of the
interceding Spirit than the change between the Paul who
wrote Romans 8 and the Paul through whose lips the agonized cry of Romans 9 breaks forth. In the former chapter
Paul is still bolstering up the faith of the fearful saints. Yes,
they have the quickening Spirit within them by whom they
are guided; yet the day of inheritance has not yet dawned,
and meanwhile they must face many forms of tribulation.
But they need not fear, for all things work together for good
to them that love God, and nothing in heaven, earth or hell
can separate them from the love of God in Christ Jesus our
Lord.

Can it be the same voice a few moments later in chapter 9
which pours out its soul agony with the most abrupt change
of subject, and having just said that nothing can separate us
from God, now asks for everlasting separation, and that
with a curse, unless his people Israel can be saved?

"I could wish that myself were accursed [separated] from
Christ for my brethren, my kinsmen according to the flesh."
Once again an immortal soul is presented as a living sacrifice for the salvation of his people. Once again it was the
last-resort prayer of the intercessor. "Save them, or damn
me!"

— *The Liberating Secret*

"You are a chosen people, a royal priesthood" —
1 Peter 2:9.

It is vital that we grasp the long-term aspect of our royal priesthood. "Ye are a chosen generation, a royal priesthood" — all of us, not just a few special ones. We all, by the royal High Priest within us, are to have that sense of a holy calling, a redemptive purpose, serving our own generation in the fear of God. We all are to feel the inner urgings of the groaning, interceding Spirit, constraining us in various ways to identify ourselves with the world's needs by prayer, by sacrifice, by action. And most of all, we are all to exercise the authority and patience of faith which keeps us in spirit on the winning side. "Confident of this very thing, that He which hath begun a good work" in the world "will perform it until the day of Jesus Christ."

But we are also to exercise a short-term present-tense authority, which produces visible and immediate results, as those who are now seated with Him in the heavenly places, sharing His ascended power with Him who leads captivity captive and gives gifts unto men.

All the men of faith and power through the centuries saw God at work by them in their daily lives. We have no business to see less. If they did not see all their hearts' desires, they saw enough to make it patently true that "the people who know their God shall be strong, and do exploits." We see no license in the Bible for a fruitless, powerless ministry.

— *The Liberating Secret*

"He is able to save completely those who come to God through him" — Hebrews 7:25.

An intercessor is not "working for God"; he is the human means by which God is doing His own work — and that's all. The fundamental difference is between the way we "tried" to be God's servants, when we were still under the delusion that the redeemed man does God's work for Him and with His help, and the revelation now given us that we are not really we at all, but He in us that He may be He by us. We, indeed, need to have this clear deep down to the center of our consciousness, so that our basic outlook on what we commonly call Christian service has been revolutionized; and we cannot, simply cannot, be caught up again in that frustrating, ulcer-causing, nervous-breakdown-producing rat race of "doing our best for Him."

Our calling is to activity, non-stop activity, probably more ceaseless and intense activity than in that former way; to a sacrifice that, as with C. T. Studd and so many thousands of others, may bring us the honor of empty pockets, worn-out bodies, lives laid down (and we reckon it the highest honor God could ever give a man when it was said of Jesus, "It pleased the Lord to bruise him"). All this is now God in saving action by us, God reaching man through man. The intercessor is commissioned (Isaiah 59:16). The intercessor is involved (Isaiah 53:12). But all this is meaningless unless the intercessor is also authoritative (Hebrews 7:25).

— *The Spontaneous You*

"Anyone who enters God's rest also rests from his own work. . . . Make every effort to enter that rest" — Hebrews 4:10-11.

An intercessor is a man of action. What God commissions him to do, he does with body, mind and soul, and does not stop doing. He is a man with a purpose, a man with a goal to be reached, and the word from heaven has come to him, as to Moses, Joshua, the prophets, and to Jesus Himself: "This I am going to do, and I'm going to do it by you."

Once again we say: Let no man think this refers to special activities by special people in special places. No, this word from heaven is being heard and heeded by thousands and tens of thousands of God's intercessors in all nations all the time, and being acted upon in thousands of different ways — and among them you and me. The church of Christ is this day "terrible as an army with banners." Let us never think that, because in former days we were active for God and exhausted ourselves in good works before we knew the secret of our inner resources in Christ, therefore there should be less activity now. No, the opposite. More activity than ever, more straight aiming than ever, because now our resources are endless. Then we only knew how to rest *from* our work; now we know how to rest *in* our work. No one can out-work, out-think, out-pray a man in whom the Spirit of God is.

— *The Spontaneous You*

"Every high priest is selected from among men and is appointed to represent them in matters related to God" — Hebrews 5:1.

The priest has been "taken from among men" (redeemed); "ordained for men" (commissioned) — "in things pertaining to God" (to bring men to Christ and build them up in Him).

Get that down to specifics in our daily lives, and we see it best if we understand what is meant by our being intercessors — the chief work of a priest.

In the Bible an intercessor is anyone, everyone, who sees a situation with God's eyes and moves in on it. That is to say, the whole of our life, all our lives, are full of frustrating yet challenging situations. God, it was said, "wondered that there was no intercessor" and "looked for a man to stand in the gap and make up the hedge."

Millions of gaps, millions of hedges. But the point is to have eyes to see them; and we are exactly positioned, every one of us, to be just where we are and what we are so as to fill some gap, make up some hedge.

So every life is nothing but a mass of opportunities, and we have been put there to seize them and grasp them. Intercessors, therefore, are not some peculiar people, any more than priests are, but are you and I, in the most ordinary business, workshop, or domestic situation; put there because there is something — it may be in our own household, in our church, district, city, country, world — which we are meant to have eyes to see as intercessors, and to stand in that gap.

— *The Spontaneous You*

"Paul, an apostle of Christ Jesus by the will of God"
— Colossians 1:1.

An intercessor is God's strategist. He sees what God is after and goes along with Him. The men of the Bible always understood their specific commission. So must we. Any one of us in any kind of circumstances can draw aside with God and examine before Him the whys and wherefores of what is happening. It will not take long before we begin to see clearly.

I well remember how clearly, soon after my conversion, just before World War I when I had received my commission to join the regiment as a Second Lieutenant, the Spirit of God was wrestling with me about my affection for an unsaved girl and telling me I could not have Christ and Antichrist in my heart at the same time. There was self blocking the vision all right! The battle was won the day I took the train to our training center, and clear as daylight in that railway compartment an inner word was then spoken to me, though I was the youngest of untaught Christians in those days. It said, "You are joining your regiment. You will train for a year and then get out in the trenches. Many of you will be dead in a year. You make sure that some of those fellows receive the gift of eternal life you now have." I couldn't "see" that great commission until the self-block was out and I had died; but then I knew with no uncertainty my real commission within my King's commission for the next five years of war.

— *The Spontaneous You*

"You have made them to be a kingdom and priests to serve our God" — Revelation 5:10.

We are royal priests because we have our authority from the Ascended Christ, and so function authoritatively in His name.

But to be a priest is to be an intercessor. That is the height of his calling; an intercessor takes the place of those he intercedes for, and is responsible to bring them to God. That is something different from the exercise of prayer and faith in general. It means that there are defined boundaries to this special commission. I am conscious that this person, this particular set of people, this class, this church fellowship, this mission field, this special group I am called to minister to, this has been set apart for me. Now that again I don't seek out. It seeks me out. I mean that as my heart and eyes are open to where the Lord has placed me, and I find myself caught up or involved with certain people or special interests, it will dawn on me that God has put me just there. Obviously I am involved with them, and I can sense a direct word from the Lord, "That is for you. I have put you there; I have stirred your heart with special interest in them. Now go to it. You are My intercessor for them." So there are special commissions. I have clearly seen and accepted this in each stage of my life.

Perhaps it has not occurred to you to look at yourself that way. However, you are a royal priest. You are to be an intercessor. For what particularly?

— Who Am I?

Intercession

"I looked for a man among them who would . . . stand before me in the gap" — Ezekiel 22:30.

Every member of Christ's body is a member of the royal priesthood. We are what Israel was meant to be, "a kingdom of priests." You and I are part of this "holy priesthood."

Then how does that work out in normal daily living? Like this. A priest is an intercessor. An intercessor is one who recognizes that he is set apart by God to stand in some gap against the enemy of souls (Ezekiel 22:30). How and where? Just exactly where you are. Open your eyes so that God is looking through them at your situation, and you will surely see your commission; for all life is a commission for those who can see it.

Then accept the commission. That will be bearing about in your body the dying of the Lord Jesus, because it may well go against your human grain to accept it. You may have a real battle to do so. The way to fight and win is to recognize that it is He and none else who is living just there in you, and has put you there and brought to you the pressure and burdens which form your present environment. Accept it, even though you feel the opposite and continue to feel it. You are now consciously in the privileged position of being an intercessor, a royal priest.

— God Unlimited

"Hezekiah received the letter . . . and spread it out before the Lord" — Isaiah 37:14.

Learn to *release* your burdens, not carry them. Prayer itself may often be unbelief, for instead of glorying in a God who has already done in the invisible what is not yet apparent in the visible, we are nagging at Him to do it! Many a time we are so burdened and occupied in hopelessly hoping for an answer to a prayer which we have not really believed that we have no freedom or largeness of heart to encompass the burdens of others or of a world.

A wife can set her husband's salvation back by her "burden" for him, often expressed in unwise preaching at him! Whereas, if she releases him to God by the act of deliberate faith, and keeps repeating that act, she will be more occupied in hopefully loving him than in unbelievingly tearing him down. A mother can be so obsessed with the need of her unsaved children, instead of releasing them to God in faith in the accomplished fact, that she has no heart or vision for the thousands of other unsaved mothers' sons.

Prayer meetings are dead affairs when they are merely asking sessions; there is adventure, hope and life when they are believing sessions, and the faith is corporately, practically and deliberately affirmed.

— *God Unlimited*

> *"I urge . . . that requests, prayers, intercession and thanksgiving be made for everyone"* — 1 Timothy 2:1.

Prayer is the product of our union with Christ. He in us is the Pray-er. So the first need in the prayer life is not to pray but to relax! Quietly, naturally, recognizing the Real One within us, we sort out what warms or stirs our heart with a sense of definite need or challenge. Now we are ready to pray.

What form is our prayer to take? Supplication? Importunity? One fact seems to me to stand out from the lives of the men of the Bible. However they might start their praying, it must end up in faith. It must be the prayer of faith. Indeed they are all called men of faith, rather than prayer, in the Hebrews 11 survey, though it is true that their exploits of faith, when studied in detail, have a background of travail in prayer. And what is significant about their contacts with God? Invariably, as they meet with Him, He tells them that He has something already in hand which He is now going to manifest through them. For Abraham there is God's fixed assurance that he would become a great nation. For Moses there is the sure word that God is going to bring the people out of Egypt and into Canaan, and that he can go before Pharaoh and through the trials in the wilderness in that certainty. For Joshua it is the same; the crossing of the Jordan and the capture of Jericho are declared to him as settled facts well before they took place. And so through all Biblical history.

— God Unlimited

"[He] who has faith in me will do . . . even greater things than these" — John 14:12.

Mr. Howells would often speak of "the gained position of intercession," and the truth of it is obvious on many occasions in his life. It is a fact of experience. The price is paid, the obedience is fulfilled, the inner wrestlings and groanings take their full course, and then "the word of the Lord comes." The weak channel is clothed with authority by the Holy Ghost and can speak the word of deliverance. "Greater works" are done.

Not only this, but a new position in grace is gained and maintained, although, even then, that grace can only be appropriated and applied in each instance under the direct guidance of the Spirit. Mr. Howells used to speak of it, in Mr. Muller's phrases, as entering "the grace of faith," in contrast to receiving "the gifts of faith." What he meant was that, when we pray in a normal way, we may hope that God of His goodness will give us the thing. If He does, we rejoice; it is His gift to us; but we have no power or authority to say that we can always get that same answer at any time. Such are the gifts of faith. But when an intercessor has gained the place of intercession in a certain realm, then he has entered into "the grace of faith"; along that special line the measureless sea of God's grace is open to him. That is the gained place of intercession.

— *Rees Howells, Intercessor*

"God raised us up with Christ and seated us with him in the heavenly realms in Christ Jesus" — Ephesians 2:6.

The literal translation of the phrase "in heavenly places" is merely "in the heavenlies," or "in heavenly things" — just one word in the Greek. We stress that, because we have to get away from the idea that in some mysterious manner we are whisked away in spirit to some distant heavenly realm which is not very realistic for us down here. The truth is that "the heavenlies" are everywhere, only hidden from the natural eye, for God is everywhere. Therefore this reigning Christ ("far above all principalities and powers" of evil) of whom we are a part, is the enthroned Christ just where we are, in ourselves, in our circumstances, in our situations of need and apparent satanic mastery.

And why does He thus reign and we with Him? Because He is wholly occupied, in the person of His Spirit, in making His saving grace now known to the world by the members of His body — ourselves — and in "adding to the church daily such as should be saved," and "always causing us to triumph" in Himself as He makes manifest by us "the savor of His knowledge in every place . . . in them that are saved and in them that perish." There is our praying ground. Not as suppliants in the sense of great distance from Him, of separation from Him, of uncertainty of His will and of a liberal answer; but prayer is seen to be a sharing of His mind on a situation, and our tongues are His mouthpiece in speaking the word of faith.

— *God Unlimited*

"We have not stopped praying for you" —
Colossians 1:9.

Intercession has often been mistaken by many as a heightened form of prayer. But it is something far different. Only those who know their redemptive commission, and give of themselves without stint to the fulfillment of it, are intercessors.

An intercessor takes the place of those he intercedes for and is responsible to bring them to God. That is far different from the exercise of prayer and faith in general. I am conscious that this person, this particular set of people, this class, this church fellowship, this mission field, this special group, has been set apart for me. I don't seek it out, it seeks me out. These are special commissions.

An intercessor is one who recognizes that he is set apart by God to stand in some gap against the enemies of our souls. Open your eyes so that God is looking through them at your situation and you will surely see your commission, for all life is a commission for those who can see it.

But an intercessor does more than accept a situation. He is a person with a purpose, because the purposing Christ is within him.

— *The Liberating Secret; Who Am I?; God Unlimited*

"Epaphras . . . is always wrestling in prayer for you" —
Colossians 4:12.

Intercession does not mean some passing prayer and
faith interest in which we can passingly take a share. It
means that this intercession is specifically mine to see
through, and there is no giving up on it. I will pay the price,
and the fruit must follow. There is no "may" about it, only a
"must."

We *may* get what we pray for; we *must* get what we
intercede for. We are responsible to do so, and we lay down
our lives to obtain it.

The character of our work is not the point, it is the spirit
in which we do it. An intercessor may be bringing up children, tapping a typewriter, turning a lathe, and yet be in the
full and conscious stream of God's redemptive purpose. But
it must be purposeful activity. It is not the drift of a piece of
straw in a stream; it is not killing time, but redeeming it.

— *Who Am I?; The Liberating Secret*

"I die every day" — 1 Corinthians 15:31.

In the Bible an intercessor is anyone, everyone, who sees a situation with God's eyes and moves in on it. The whole of our life, all our lives, are full of frustrating yet challenging situations — opportunities to seize and grasp.

Here is a principle of constant "dyings" — daily maybe — affecting every kind of normal situation in life, not by any means in what we might call our "religious activity." Anything which hurts or disturbs our *status quo*, be it in our personal lives or in some big public affair, is a place of dying when we change from self's resistance to acceptance as a step in God's saving plans. Instead of remaining in hurt self, we recognize them to be part of some redemptive purpose of God through us in others. This is adulthood.

We can now begin to be intercessors. We see what God is after, and the first effect is a joy, release, sense of adventure, praise where there seems nothing to praise for, for we now see the redemptive purpose.

— *The Spontaneous You*

"He was appalled that there was no one to intercede"
— Isaiah 59:16.

Intercession is the whole mountain of which prayer is
one peak. There are only one or two places in Scripture
where the word intercession is linked just to prayer. So let us
lift it out and put it in its full perspective, and see that we
ourselves accept our highest privilege as intercessors, who
are also saying, "A body hast Thou prepared me. . . . Lo, I
come to do Thy will, O God"; and each in his unique calling
into intercession.

Intercession is revealed in the Bible as God looking for
special men by whom He will give some special deliverance.
In Isaiah 59:16, God wonders that there is no man, no
intercessor, among Israel in its backslidden condition; and
then the prophet leaps on from Israel's failure to have
the-man-for-that-moment to speak of the-Man-for-the-
whole-of-history: "And the Redeemer shall come to Zion
. . . [for] My Spirit is upon thee" (Isaiah 59:20-21).

So we see the intercessor is the Spirit Himself through
His chosen bodies. And the way of intercession is "death" in
the soul and body of the human intercessor that others
might live. Of Jesus it was said: "He hath poured out His
soul unto death . . . and He bare the sin of many, and made
intercession for the transgressors" (Isaiah 53:12).

— *Yes, I Am*

"A body you prepared for me" — Hebrews 10:5.

The body is the localized individual means by which the Spirit reaches out through us. By our human spirits He can reach out universally and can encompass everything — by faith unlimited. By our bodies He can do only one specific thing, and a different one by each particular body. So this is His highest personalized activity for us, and the highest for each of us. It was said by Jesus, "A body hast Thou prepared for Me," and by this one special body-commitment the Son said to the Father, "Lo, I come to do Thy will, O God." In this world of body people it was only by His body that "we are sanctified by the offering of the body of Jesus once for all."

Therefore it is *only by our bodies* that God can fulfill His saving purpose in this body world. Let us have this plainly understood. Our service to Christ is only fulfilled by some body action of ours — by body dedication. Only by this means does redemption reach the multimillion bodies of our human brotherhood. There still is for us a body death and body involvement by which God's saving purposes are fulfilled, as by His own Son's body. This is intercession.

The first form intercession takes is *commission*. The Spirit causes me to know that there is something He will do, and do it by me, specifically. It is not something I sought, but it sought me. I'm simply caught by it and cannot escape. I just find myself immersed in it and obsessed by it. So get this clear: It is not a matter of my running around and trying to *find* my commission. No, *it finds me. It is from the Holy Spirit.*

— *Yes, I Am*

"He learned obedience from what he suffered" — Hebrews 5:8.

Christ the Intercessor, after His early years of personal training, went out to do His intercessory work at the command of the anointing Spirit, and gained His position of faith, the right to be Savior, after three years of obedience unto death. Again and again He referred to the pressure on His spirit during those years: "I have a baptism to be baptized with, and how am I straitened until it be accomplished." To His disciples, in His early ministry, He said: "My meat is to do the will of Him that sent Me, and to finish His work." To His Father, just before Calvary: "I have finished the work Thou gavest Me to do." To the world, with His last breath: "It is finished." It was said twice over by the writer to the Hebrews that it was through His sufferings that He was perfected as pioneer of our salvation and author of eternal life to all who obey Him. And now we see Him still the Intercessor, not in the heat of battle, but enthroned in triumph. Then He was pouring out His soul unto death, but now dispensing the fruits of His victory — "able to save to the uttermost them that come unto God by Him, seeing He ever liveth to make intercession for them." On the basis of that battle once fought, that life once poured out utterly for our transgressions, He can now lead captivity captive and give the constant gift of His Holy Spirit to men.

We also, in our lesser spheres, can gain positions of faith and do the full work of an intercessor.

— *The Law of Faith*

"I could wish that I myself were cursed and cut off from Christ for the sake of my brothers" — Romans 9:3.

At the roots of every golden harvest field of souls reaped by the Spirit of God there lies a life or lives which have been intercessors, lives lived under a deep and enduring sense of urgency, clear direction, absolute dedication to the task. They have *had* to carry this specific burden in prayer night and day. They have had to go and live long years amongst that strange tribe. They have had to give and give and give again out of their sometimes dwindling resources. They have had to stick to their tract distributing, open-air meetings, sick visitations, or whatever it may be, large or small; for the intensity of the devotion, not the size of the commission, is what matters to God.

And then comes a time in such a single-hearted ministry when the break occurs, sometimes in the lifetime of the intercessors, sometimes after, and it seems as if heaven's windows are open and God's storehouses unlocked, and the blessing just flows. It is the Pentecost after Calvary.

It is good to understand this spiritual law of the harvest. It helps us to fulfill our ministry strategically, intelligently. We are fulfilling certain unchangeable laws of the Spirit under the guidance and by the inspiration of the Spirit.

— *The Law of Faith*

> *"The prince of the Persian kingdom resisted me twenty-one days"* — Daniel 10:13.

To liberate souls by prayer or to move a company to repentance or revival is a far more difficult task than getting material things. There is an enemy to overcome. The one who spoke to Daniel in a vision after his three-week fast said he was prevented from coming for twenty-one days by satanic opposition. There is man's will to be moved. How a free will can be compelled by prayer to make a certain choice, and yet remain free, is a point more of philosophical than practical interest. We know no adequate explanation; but we know that the Bible presents us with the unsolved paradox of God's almightiness and man's free will, and tells us to believe both and act on either as the need arises — and both prove true!

Both these citadels need storming, and the history of the church is crammed with evidence that only by travail of soul, by prayer and fasting, by a faith that wrestles on towards heaven 'gainst storm and wind and tide, are brands plucked from the burning; by the mother who agonizes through nights and days for her boy, and, when he comes back at last to God, tells him that she always held him fast in her faith and love; by the minister or praying group who seek God's face till they find Him for an outpouring of the Spirit which will melt and fuse and revitalize the Christians, and start a saving work amongst the unconverted.

— *The Law of Faith*

"This is what the Lord says: Do not be afraid of what you have heard" — Isaiah 37:6.

Christ said, "Say unto this mountain." *Say* not *pray.* The word is most significant. The thought is not that prayer should be omitted — for the Word counsels us to pray. *Prayer* is the attitude of one who has not and needs. *Saying* the word of faith is the attitude of one who has and dispenses what he has. Such is the "throne life" as we commonly speak of it. A throne is occupied by a king. A king is a possessor and dispenser of gifts.

Examine the men of God through the Bible — prophets, apostles — and you will find this conscious attitude of authoritative faith to be theirs. The difference stands out clearly with Hezekiah and Isaiah. Hezekiah was a man of prayer. The threats of the enemy came upon him with overwhelming force. He prayed. He bemoaned weakness. "This day is a day of trouble, and of rebuke, and of blasphemy; for the children are come to the birth, and there is not strength to bring forth" (Isaiah 37:3). "Not strength" was his emphasis. Then he sent word of the situation to the man of faith. Hear Isaiah's answer, a declaration, a saying unto this mountain. "Thus saith the Lord, Be not afraid of the words that thou has heard, wherewith the servants of the king of Assyria have blasphemed Me. Behold, I will send a blast upon him, and he shall . . . return to his own land" (verses 6-7).

— *Throne Life*

"Outwardly we are wasting away, but inwardly we are being renewed day by day" — 2 Corinthians 4:16.

I would say that right up to today God gives us the privilege of being intercessors. As my years in our direct WEC activities ceased, the Lord gave me the plain calling — another definite commission — to get around the U.S.A. with the message of union and replacement in Christ which has been the mainstream of this book. I had to do it. I had to go round and repeat unendingly what God has made so real to me. There are always new facets of light, but the heart of the message is ever the same. The price of this intercession is to continue nonstop into my eighties, even though my old leg injury makes walking a difficulty — though in fact, you don't notice the dying when absorbed in the harvesting.

And now, after going round for about ten years, the Lord Himself has called in co-intercessors, all unknown to me. Bill and Marge Volkman had the call from God five years ago to start the *Union Life Magazine,* which is now spreading widely and being the voice of the Spirit to many. Dan and Barbara Stone and Jan Ord have also had the call of God to give themselves fulltime to the spread of the message — all looking to the Lord alone for their material supplies.

— Yes, I Am

"He . . . made intercession for the transgressors" —
Isaiah 53:12.

It is costly to be an intercessor, reaching far beyond the
ordinary prayer-life of request and supplication, for there is
expenditure of heart's blood and agony of soul in it. "He
poured out His soul unto death," we read, "and was num-
bered with the transgressors, and bare the sin of many"; and
so, it says, "He made intercession for the transgressors."

The reward of the intercessor is as great as his travail. He
fulfills the law of the harvest. He goes through the processes
of death, accepts them voluntarily, has them laid on him by
the travailing Spirit who groans within him with groanings
which cannot be uttered; and by so doing the upspringing of
the harvest, resurrection life for the world, is as sure as that
spring and summer follow winter.

And here he is no longer in the school of faith but the
life of faith; for this death and resurrection process is not
now for his own sanctification but for a world's need. God
has at last found His servant on whom He can lay the kind
of burdens the Savior carried, not for himself and for his
own growth in grace, but for others. It is a share in the
fellowship of Christ's sufferings. It is the third and final
meaning of the cross in the individual life; the cross first
borne by Christ alone for our sins, then shared by us with
Christ for our sanctification, and now borne in turn by us for
our neighbor's salvation. It is the outworking of the cross
referred to by Paul when he said, "So death worketh in us,
but life in you."

— *The Law of Faith*

"Who will rescue me ... ? Thanks be to God — through Jesus Christ our Lord!" — Romans 7:24-25.

[A certain woman's] husband holds a public position in his profession and is a man who loves the Lord. What a shock when she found out that he had a secret liaison, with visits to a motel, with one who was a close friend in whom she confided.

She first challenged her husband about this adultery over the phone. He is an honest man who knows the Lord, and he admitted his descent into the flesh, and his sin against God and wrong against her. But then he said, "If the woman's husband learns of this, he is a man of such influence that he could destroy me in my profession." My friend's answer straightaway to her unfaithful husband was, "I am your wife. If you have a crash professionally, then I crash along with you."

The result of that was that the husband — who, as I say, knows the Lord — took one big jump of faith right then and there, and he has told me how he moved from being the struggling and defeated man of Romans 7 to the liberated man in Romans 8. He saw "in a flash of the Spirit" that there was no more condemnation, and that he was released "by the law of the Spirit of life in Christ Jesus." The result in their marriage is that where there had been an unhappy relationship between them, it has so changed that she now tells me her husband is her best friend!

— *Yes, I Am*

"The Spirit himself intercedes for us with groans that words cannot express" — Romans 8:26.

The husband of a close friend was in a good professional position and a good home-provider, but he showed no outward response to Christianity. The time came when she discovered, as a great shock, that he was having an ongoing adulterous relationship with a married woman. She faced out with the Lord the shock, hurt and resentment. What should she do? Knowing that she was not herself but Christ in her, she knew the difference between her soul hates and resentments and the love she had for her husband in her spirit, for it was God loving him by her. So instead of a marital blowout and possible divorce, she informed her husband that she had found out what was going on, but that she loved him as ever. That shook him!

This brought a reply to her which was another shock — a good one. He said, "Well, if that is Christianity, I can listen to it!" After some weeks, while she knew the adulterous relationship continued, the moment came when she told her husband that she would like to meet with him and the woman. She said to them: "It can't go on like this. Make the choice. Either go with her and leave me and the children, or break off the relationship and return to me." The husband and the woman both agreed. The severance was made, and he returned home. But far more than that, God has done such a transforming work in him, with repentance and renewal, that he is now a strong witness for Christ and busy helping other men who get caught in that same trap. This is intercession.

— *Yes, I Am*

"Pressed on every side, but not crushed; perplexed, but not in despair; persecuted, but not abandoned; struck down, but not destroyed" — 2 Corinthians 4:8-9.

One who brought to light the principle of intercession to the church in our generation was Rees Howells, to whom I have several times referred. He always spoke concerning intercession as "the first fruits going to the altar," which referred in type to the meal offering of Leviticus 2. There the first handful of the flour is burned on the altar, and the rest feeds the priests. By that he meant that there would be this "death" in which the self-life, the body-soul life, has had its human setbacks, sacrifice, maybe failure in the eyes of the world or church, and out of that death came the life to others. It is the 2 Corinthians 4:7-12 principle, but this time in specific rather than general form — for this is where Paul is speaking about bearing in our body the dying of the Lord Jesus. He then writes, "So death worketh in us, but life in you."

The intercession is completed, first by being gained on the level of faith, as the intercessor becomes settled in his inner consciousness that the Lord has done it; and second, by his own continued involvement in it, by whatever action accompanies it, while the Spirit brings the thing to pass. And it continues until the intercessor knows that his part in it is *fulfilled*.

Commission. Cost. Completion.

— Yes, I Am

"You intended to harm me, but God intended it for good" — Genesis 50:20.

When the adventure of adversity is seen in its true perspective, it is found to be the doorway into God's most transcendent secret — that adversities and sufferings, which in their origin are the effects of sin and instruments of the devil, in the grasp of faith become *redemptive*. They are transfigured from the realm of merely something to be endured as an opposition of Satan to something to be used to conquer their author and redeem his victims. Faith in time of adversity makes the serpent swallow itself! Once again the supreme proof of this is that when Satan made his fiercest attack in history on the person of Christ, God used that attack, through the faith and endurance of the Sufferer, to bring about the world's salvation. *God uses evil to bring about good* — not causing it, but using it.

The consequence of a clear grasp of this fact, that Satan and all evil circumstances in our lives are God's most useful instruments for the fulfillment of His purposes, is obvious. All attacks of Satan are seen to be our blessings. We "count them all joy." We "rejoice in tribulation." We use them as special opportunities to see the manifestation of God's power, instead of merely enduring them with a struggle as "judgments" or "tests."

— Touching the Invisible

*"If you will only look upon your servant . . . and give her
a son, then I will give him to the Lord"* — 1 Samuel 1:11.

Being humans, and meant to be humans, we always start
by disliking uncomfortable situations and being hurt by
them, resenting them, or being bored by them, questioning
why such things should be in our lives; or maybe nominally
accepting them as what we miscall the cross, and putting up
with them; or if they disturb our routine and challenge us to
sacrificial action, finding some reason to leave others to
handle them. This is not wrong. It means that we are
humanly involved and thus livingly related to a situation,
and can, therefore, be a vital factor in it. But while we
remain hurt or resistant, we cannot see beyond our hurt
selves. The way is blocked.

Look at Hannah, the mother of Samuel, hurt because
God did not answer her prayer by giving her children. But
Hannah knew God, and the moment had come when He
could speak a hidden word to her, and she could take it. Did
she not realize how selfish all her praying had been? She
wanted sons just to prove that God was with her, and maybe
to have an answer for Peninnah. Why not change the thing
around and want a son for God's purposes, not hers? She
saw the point and struck a bargain of faith with Him. If He
would give her a son, He should have him.

— *The Spontaneous You*

"God has poured out his love into our hearts by the Holy Spirit" — Romans 5:5.

All our awkward situations and our normal negative reactions to them — dislike, fear, unwillingness, inadequacy, frustration — are the only way we can react as humans. If that is all we are — just humans — then we would be in bad shape, enchained in the prison of our own reactions. But to us who are at home in the fact of the Other Self — the not I, but Christ in me — pressures, trials, temptations are a springboard to faith. We dislike a person, so we take a leap of faith. We move over and say, "I don't like this person, but You are love in me. You love him, so with Your love, I love him."

Our negative human reactions are necessary to God. The positive must have its negative for its manifestation. We do not, therefore, blame or condemn ourselves because we are the have-nots, and guiltily feel we are wrong to react as we do. We are what we are, and what we are meant to be. We may well laugh at ourselves, but not throw ourselves out with disgust. We are not God's liabilities, we are God's assets.

The secret is always replacement. We don't work hard at pushing darkness out of a room. We turn our backs on the darkness and switch on the light – where is the darkness? We transfer our attention from the negative to the positive. That is the secret. Not resistance, but replacement.

The Spontaneous You

"It was not you who sent me here, but God" —
Genesis 45:8.

Everything that comes to us comes from God — what we call evil as well as the good. God, of course, is not the cause of evil, but deliberately directs everything for good ends. The Bible uses strong terms of "God sending" the unpleasant as well as the pleasant, and sending is a positive word, not just a passive permission (for many talk of the "permissive" will of God).

Peter in his first speech after Pentecost said that they had taken and crucified Jesus "through the determinate counsel and foreknowledge of God." No mistaking that. God determined that wicked men should do what they purposed to do and it would really fulfill His purpose — which was to save the people doing it! Such is God!

Joseph said that by his brethren selling him into slavery, God "sent me before you to preserve life. . . . You thought evil against me, but God meant it unto good."

Whatever happens, we say, "All right, God, You sent this. It may tear me apart to say so, but I say so." From there the next step is easier: "God, this has some purpose outside of me to meet the need of others. Just show me what."

The important fact to recognize is that God has only one aim in His present dealings with our world — to get all of us who will respond to Him off the wrong road on to the right. It was said of Jesus "that the world through him might be saved."

— *The Spontaneous You*

"We can certainly do it" — Numbers 13:30.

Every battle of life is fought and won *within* ourselves, not without. Gain the inner spiritual victory and the outer follows as sure as the day the night. How hard it is for us to learn that we control and conquer from within. We are used to dealing with the outward, with things and people, and we fly to the outward for supply; we wrestle against the outward in adversity, cry out against the outward when wronged. Poor blinded creatures, scratching about for the bits and pieces on the outside, when all the wealth and power of the universe streams into us through the Creator, and He is to be found where spirit meets with Spirit — within!

Who were the poised and powerful among the twelve spies whom Moses sent out? Were they the ten who were influenced by the outward, by the giants and walled cities of Canaan, and who cried out on their return, "We be not able to go up against the people, for they are stronger than we.... It is a land that eateth up the inhabitants thereof"? Or the two, Caleb and Joshua, from their standpoint of inner vision and victory, whose minds were stayed on God and who said, "Let us go up at once, and possess it; for we are well able to overcome it.... Neither fear ye the people of the land; for they are bread for us"? Who proved right?

— The Law of Faith

"Suffering produces perseverance; perseverance, character; and character, hope" — Romans 5:3-4.

Daily life is by no means just easy, smooth-running times. It is constantly disturbed by things small or big. Something lost, something gone wrong, responsibilities to fulfill, demanding children, finances, sickness, clashes of personalities, differences of viewpoint, decisions to be made. At these moments, self comes very much alive and we have our human reactions. It is at this spot that we find it hard to grasp that this is precisely God's purpose that His sons should be involved in disturbing human situations. The positive must have its negative to manifest through, so we must learn to the full what it is to be a negative. It was said of Jesus Himself that though He was a Son, yet He learned obedience through the things which He suffered, and clearly knew that the Son could do nothing of Himself.

We ask a useless question and mistake the meaning of life if we say, "Will there be no letup from continual pressures?" No. If I am to function in my proper place as a son and inheritor of God's universe in my eternal destiny, I need to learn first how a son functions in adverse circumstances. A swimmer grows strong against the tide, not with it. It is the trial of my faith which works maturity in me, says James. When we see that, we can expect and welcome what the world calls problems and frustrations.

— *Who Am I?*

"We always carry around in our body the death of Jesus" — 2 Corinthians 4:10.

Adversity is prosperity in disguise; and the assaults of Satan, or "the slings and arrows of outrageous fortune," or the contradiction of sinners, when our eyes are opened, are Christ walking to us on the waters.

Paul calls that "always bearing about in the body the dying of the Lord Jesus," and being "always delivered unto death for Jesus' sake." That means that we are accepting unpleasant situations or daily pressures rather than resisting them, even as Jesus accepted Calvary; indeed, that it is He Himself in us continuing His death-process — "the dying of the Lord Jesus" — in our daily lives. This has nothing to do with the death relationship we have with Him in His once-for-all death to sin, which is never to be repeated in Him or us. That death was for our deliverance. These daily deaths are for the deliverance of others through us. That was the death of the old man. These are the daily deaths of the new man. It is not wrong that we dislike difficult situations; it is merely human. But these are deaths to our human reactions. We deliberately accept these things as ways in which God, not Satan or man, is coming to us, and therefore all we can do is to give thanks. "I *take pleasure* in infirmities, in reproaches, in necessities, in persecutions, in distresses for Christ's sake: for when I am weak, then am I strong."

— *God Unlimited*

*"I have worked much harder, been in prison more
frequently, been flogged more severely, and been exposed
to death again and again"* — 2 Corinthians 11:23.

For what reason does God come to us in adverse circumstances or in contradictory people? The answer is that it is *not* for our personal benefit, for our testing or further sanctification or something. We are so used to relating everything to ourselves in the spiritual life as much as in the material that we tend to interpret everything in that light — what is God doing or saying to *me* through this? Not at all. God, who is pure outgoing love, has other ends in view.

We are now His body, and a person has a body not for feeding or clothing or coddling but for using. So Christ in His body. He lives over again in us in all sorts of circumstances to reach others by us. Now that turns adverse situations into adventure. They are not for the dreary purpose of some more self-improvement (an impossibility anyhow!), they are the outflowing of the rivers to others. It is pitiful to hear so often even elderly saints still regarding their trials, physical or material, as some further lessons from which they are to learn, instead of the freshness of the outlook: Here is God, even in my old age, opening further doors for sharing Him with others.

— *God Unlimited*

"All this is for your benefit" — 2 Corinthians 4:15.

If I am as He is, how does it work out in practical life? It means a revolution in my outlook. Normally, I interpret all happenings of life in terms of their effect on myself. My physical condition, my home affairs, my business affairs, my social life — how do they affect me? What difference does this situation, this crisis, this tragedy or problem, this success, make to me? If I am a Christian, I may seek a Christian interpretation — this is for the testing of my faith, for the maturing of my walk with God; but still it is in terms of its effect on me.

The new outlook is: This has happened to me as some way by which I am to meet the need of others. As Paul says in Second Corinthians, "All things are for your sakes."

The fact stands, and the change which has taken place in us is because it is no longer a question of my own life being for myself, or of God being for my convenience, or my salvation or sustenance.

So I practice a changed outlook. My normal human reaction will always be: Why has this happened to me? But now I say: This is for others. I move over from my outlook to God's. I may not in the least see how it is for others. It may be merely that my going through a tough experience with God fits me to share and show the way to others going through the same experience without God. But the difference between frustration and opportunity comes through my seeing life in its total dimension — that life's only meaning is God and others.

— *The Spontaneous You*

344

"I am the way and the truth and the life" — John 14:6.

We talk of love or hate, faith or unbelief, sin or holiness, and so on, as if they were things in themselves, things we either need to attain or avoid. But love is not a thing; it is a person loving. Faith is not a thing, but a person believing. Life is not a thing, but a person living. There could be no such "things" if it were not that people loved and hated, were holy or sinful. For convenience' sake we abstract these various characteristics of a living person, isolate them (as a research student would say), label them, and then so often get into the quicksands of a fruitless, despairing search for love, power, faith, holiness in our own lives. We are missing the vital mark.

It is quite plain that life is a Person, because God is life. "I am . . . life," said God the Son. "Christ our life," writes Paul. "This is the true God, and eternal life," writes John again. Therefore, "that which was from the beginning" is a Living Person, who is all — love, light, life, power, wisdom, holiness (wholeness). Is there love? God is love. Is there light? God is light. Is there wisdom? He is wisdom. Is there faith? He is the eternal believer in Himself, for *"I Am"* is His name. Life is never found by searching for or possessing things. Life is a Person, and is found only in living relationship with the Person.

— The Liberating Secret

*"You did not receive a spirit that makes you a slave, . . .
but you received the Spirit of sonship"* — Romans 8:15.

Before we know our exchanged life, while still in the
struggles and self-condemnation of Romans 7, we dislike
and downgrade ourselves — "O wretched man that I am!"
We are compulsively negative about ourselves and deeply
suspicious of what we think are our dangerous tendencies.
So now it is an altogether new thing, and may take a little
time to sink into us, that so far from downgrading ourselves,
because He now accepts us, we now accept ourselves as His
precious vessel, branch, body, member, bride. Every part of
us — our physical appetites, our soulish emotions and
reasoning powers — are beautiful and wholly valuable as
His outer means of manifestation. It usually takes a little
time to realize this, just because we've been so used to
thinking the opposite about ourselves.

So now we're free to be ourselves, because we now know
we are wholly His human forms. We live with raised, not
lowered heads! Sure, we're not unaware of the subtle misuse
today by psychologists and many others of a false "self-
acceptance" and "self-liberation to be ourselves." Indeed,
this is universal, because the deceived natural man assumes
he has no self *except* himself, and his only remedy for his self
problems is the fraudulent build-up of himself as "inher-
ently good." But just because there is a wave of modern,
false emphasis on the build-up of self, that must not inhibit
us from boldly accepting and affirming ourselves — we who
truly know who we truly are!

— *Yes, I Am*

"As for me, I am filled with power, with the Spirit of the Lord" — Micah 3:8.

A person might think that this inner consciousness of Christ in me would give me an enlarged consciousness of Him and an increased glorying in Him. It does . . . even though He has already been, for years, my precious Christ in the love relationship of the Song of Songs.

But what becomes paradoxically new to me is a totally new *self-acceptance.* And here, at once, we move onto "dangerous ground" — not dangerous to us, but to onlookers like the daughters of Jerusalem in the Song! Because it seems to produce a newly inflated ego. It does. But of course, we who have entered in and are now in on the secret know the *whole* key — that it is a Satan-expressing ego which has first disappeared forever in His cross, reappearing as our new Christ-expressing ego. But it is a total *re*appearing of the "I!" Why? Because it has been God's fixed plan of grace from before the foundation of the world that He was going to have a vast company of fully liberated sons by whom He would fully be *Himself* embodied in human forms. Yet in that paradoxical relationship, unintelligible to those not initiated into it, the human "I" is its full spontaneous self, and acting as such. That is why I often say there is no egoist in history equal to our Lord Jesus Christ! He was always I, I, I — "I am the door," "I am the living bread," "I am the light," "I am the way." *Emphatic self.* Yet we who know Him are also aware that He was always saying "I do nothing by Myself, but only what I see My Father do."

— *Yes, I Am*

"Whatever the Father does the Son also does" —
John 5:19.

Christ "learned obedience." He worked out as a Man the perfect submission and interaction of the self-life with its true Indweller. He went the way of probation and self-abnegation that Adam failed to go, which was to have had its consummation at the Tree of Life. By Him, that was realized in the descent of the Holy Spirit like a dove upon Him. It was the full sunlight of realized union. "This is my beloved Son." "I and My Father are One." "The Spirit of the Lord is upon Me."

And, in the glorious ministry which followed, no emphasis of His was stronger than upon the fact that "the Son can do nothing of Himself"; "I came not to do My own will"; "The words that I speak, I speak not of Myself"; "I came not of Myself." Always it was "The Father that sent Me," "He that sent Me," "I do always those things that please Him." Total self-emptying, total God-filling; and, in that holy and perfect relationship, the greatest life was lived in three years that ever has been or can be lived, the greatest words spoken, the greatest death died. How plainly the lesson comes home: Self-realization begins, continues and ends with self-emptying.

— *The Law of Faith*

"When I am weak, then I am strong" — 2 Corinthians 12:10.

"Abide in me, and I in you" — John 15:4 (KJV).

"Abiding" in that John 15 chapter is, in the Greek, just "remaining"; and we remain by simple faith-recognition. This is the negative to God the Positive, and necessary as a negative — for only when we are consciously weak, as Paul said, then is His strength perfectly manifested. When we are fearing, He is courage. When we dislike, He is the love. And Paul goes as far as to say that he personally takes pleasure in negative situations of weakness, hurts, needs, problems — for when he is weak, then he is strong.

There is no doubt that this is the biggest tie-up in thousands of God's people; in fact, all of us have to start "tangled" to get the knots untied. We are just so bogged down in taking ourselves for granted as normal functioning people, and are so used to preserving an image, that it is a second spiritual breakthrough for us to grasp the fact of helplessness. We had come to acknowledge that we had not kept God's law and were guilty sinners. But it is another thing, when we are the Lord's, to discover and admit that we are also helpless saints. We can't do it, and not only can't but are not meant to. We call that "the second collapse."

— *Who Am I?*

"For you died, and your life is now hidden with Christ in God" — Colossians 3:3.

The root of our release is found in the substitutionary death of Christ and our realization of our identification with Him in the cross. This does not mean that some part of us is to die, but that we are to see ourselves in Christ as those who have passed through an experience of death so far as any further acknowledgment of the lordship of Satan and union with sin are concerned. Nothing in us ourselves has died. There is no such thing as the death of self or death to self. Rather, God now reunites us to Himself for the purpose of expressing His own glory *through* our "selves." We have passed on beyond the cross — out of the tomb and into the *resurrection*. The emotions now express love for God and man, hatred of evil, jealousy for God's glory, pride (glory) in the cross. The imagination and intuition are vibrant with a constant sight and sense of Him whom having not seen we love, and with a vision of His love for the world. The will makes choices and declarations of faith. The body uses its capacities both in sounding forth His praise and sharing in the preaching of the gospel to every creature. The same self, the same "I," but now the willing servant and son of the Spirit.

— *Touching the Invisible*

"How much more will those who receive God's abundant provision of grace ... reign in life through the one man, Jesus Christ" — Romans 5:17.

There *is* a joy unspeakable and full of glory, a peace that passeth understanding, and an all-sufficiency in all things by which we are able to abound unto every good work. Though we are always only the earthen vessels in which "the excellency of the power is of God, and not of us," there *is* a reigning in life by Christ, a bearing of the good fruit of the Spirit, an overcoming in all things. There *is* a self-release from bondage into liberty, an overflowing of the rivers of the Spirit, and a counting and experiencing of temptations and trials as "all joy" instead of miseries to be avoided or endured. Because all is centered in the one Reality, our Lord Jesus Christ — crucified, risen, ascended, who now lives His life in His body members — we experience life as adventure, zest, thrill, and gaiety at the heart of a desperate seriousness. Immersed in meeting the needs of others, travailing in birth until Christ is formed in them as in us, we are privileged to bear about in our bodies the dying of the Lord Jesus, so that "death works in us, but life in you."

The endless problems and frustrations in life, including personality clashes, are seen to be the necessary negatives by which He, the Positive, can reveal Himself; and we enjoy the process with Him. We move right on to the simplicity and constant use of the "word of faith" in our prayer life, and to the highest of all, the life of intercession, in which we are given a privileged and effective place in meeting the world's needs.

— *Yes, I Am*

"We have this treasure in jars of clay to show that this all-surpassing power is from God and not from us" — 2 Corinthians 4:7.

The illustration that settled me into seeing my proper place as a human was the discovery that several times in the Scriptures we are called "vessels." A vessel is there only to contain. It does not *become* what it contains. The cup does not become the coffee, nor the coffee the cup. That ray of light shot into me. In other words, God was saying, "Stop fussing about your human self, where you fail and where you need improvement. Drop that whole false idea. Vessels don't improve, they just contain. Now turn your attention away from what you are as a vessel — or think you should be. With a single eye, turn your full attention on *Me,* the One the vessel contains." That was enough to move me on to my crisis leap — into the reality of Galatians 2:20, which is now my favorite verse of Scripture: "I am crucified with Christ, nevertheless I live; yet not I, but Christ liveth in me; and the life which I now live in the flesh I live by the faith of the Son of God, who loved me and gave Himself for me."

This was the first revelation of the Spirit (and it *has* to be revealed by the Spirit) that I am just the container. It was the beginning of what has never left me since and has so greatly expanded.

— *Yes, I Am*

"Let him who boasts, boast in the Lord" —
1 Corinthians 1:31.

I am to cease to look for improvements in myself, or to center my attention around what I feel or don't feel, whether I am this or have that, why I fail in this or am defeated by that — the whole outlook on life which fixes my attention on myself and my reactions or my adequacies or inadequacies.

The most illuminating illustration I found in the Bible was the several times we are called vessels, because a vessel, a cup, a vase, a can, is strictly limited to one function only. It only exists to be a container; it can be nothing else. And here was this simple though humbling illustration of my relation as a human to God. I only exist to contain Him.

This transferred my attention from worrying about myself as not being this, or being that. Leave myself alone. I am just the container. In place of this, I had it clearly that I was containing a totally exclusive Person who does not *give* me something but is all; and I don't contain Him in a relationship in which He imparts various gifts and graces to me, but I am just a means by which He can be Himself in a human container. This means that my main function in life changes from activity to receptivity.

— *The Spontaneous You*

"The thief comes only to steal and kill and destroy; I have come that they may have life" — John 10:10.

Conviction of sin does not come from the inward, but the upward look. Sin is not seen to be sin by self-examination, but by the light of God. Conviction and repentance are gifts of God as much as salvation is (Acts 5:31). There is a world of difference between the nagging, corroding condemnations of the devil and the clear convictions of the Spirit. The devil speaks in generalities, seeking to smear us by a general sense of failure, uncleanness, confusion, heaviness of spirit. The answer to that is there is now no condemnation to those who are in Christ Jesus. The Spirit speaks specifically, and His voice, although rebuking us, is sweet and clean and true and acceptable. He points out some exact and immediate action by which we have given temporary entrance to sin. Satan points downward to despair, but the Spirit points upwards to cleansing.

So the detection of sin in our daily lives is no difficulty. If the cups do not run over, the red light is on. There is sin somewhere. But the One with whom we walk is light. Look honestly and frankly to Him, and it won't take Him long to clarify for us the point where we have sinned.

Now comes the crucial moment. Having seen the light, will we walk in it? Walking is not standing still! It is progressing. Will we now walk forward, take the next step, and admit the truth about ourselves?

— *The Liberating Secret*

"It is God who works in you to will and to act according to his good purpose" — Philippians 2:13.

In affirming a God-implanted faith in this tremendous fact of Christ's full redemptive work in us, replacing the spirit of self-love in us by His Spirit of self-giving, implicit in such a faith is the recognition that He is going to live another quality of life in us, and that therefore He will make any necessary changes in us, even though humanly we are not even willing. He will impart His willingness to us, which will not only overcome our unwillingness but actually change us into willing His will with Him, according to Paul's statement that "it is God which worketh in us to will and to do of His good pleasure"; and note that it is His good pleasure, and if He enjoys what He does in us, we shall enjoy it too.

I know no better account of the reality of the struggle of a self confronted with the offer of God to live in that life, wanting it yet not wanting it, facing its implications pragmatically point by point, than the chapter in the life of *Rees Howells, Intercessor* on how he received the Holy Ghost; how ultimately he had to come to the crisis point, and cried out he was not willing, but the Voice came back to him, Are you willing to be *made* willing? And that ended the week-long conflict.

— *God Unlimited*

*"You were dead ... in sins ... when you followed ... the
spirit who is now at work in those who are disobedient"* —
Ephesians 2:1-2.

Few seem to have grasped that man is not just an independent self doing as he pleases and doing it in his own
strength. He never has been this. He has always been
indwelt by a god. He has always had an inner union — to
whom? "Greater is He that is in you (the believer) than *he*
that is in the world." Who is this second "he" in the world, if
not the Satanic spirit? And he is actually named a few verses
later (1 John 4:6): "Hereby know we the Spirit of truth and
the spirit of error." We have already quoted the great passage descriptive of the condition of fallen humanity —
Ephesians 2:1-3   which includes that statement, "the spirit
that now worketh *in* the children of disobedience"; or the
other, "*in* whom the god of this world hath blinded the
minds. . . ."

The fact that is hidden from many is that sin is essen-
tially a person, just as holiness is a Person. Holiness is the
"Spirit of holiness" (Romans 1:4), the Holy Spirit. We have
pointed out all along that since the human is the container
of the Divine Person, all goodness, love, righteousness,
wisdom, power, holiness and the rest are, not we, but *He* in
us, "Jesus Christ who has been made unto us wisdom,
righteousness, sanctification, redemption." But the opposite is equally and logically true. Sin is not a thing, but an
indwelling person, the spirit of fear, the spirit of bondage,
the evil spirit, the spirit of the world, the spirit of antichrist.

— *God Unlimited*

"According to your faith will it be done to you" —
Matthew 9:29.

All Christian experience is dependent upon the sole
condition "according to your faith be it unto you," and we
note that beyond this no single method of realizing the
Spirit-filled life is revealed. An outline of truth is given,
especially in the basic Epistle to the Romans, expounding
the full implications of the process of Christ in His incarnation, life, death, resurrection, ascension and return. Justification is there set forth (Romans 3), then Sanctification
(Romans 6), then the Triumphing Life, the Guided Life, the
Fruitful Life, the Empowered Life, the Sacrificial Life, and
so on (Romans 8).

It does not seem to us that the exact way of realization is
delineated in the form of special crises, but rather that the
table is spread and then we are told that faith helps itself.
But it does insist that the evidence of true life in God is that
we do help ourselves and go from grace to grace and from
strength to strength. We are justified; well, are we sanctified? Do we have a vital experience of Christ's death and
resurrection inwrought in us as outlined in Romans 6, as
well as merely appropriated by us in a vicarious and outward sense for sins forgiven? Are we only vaguely "reckoning" ourselves as dead and risen with Him, with an underlying unbelief that it really is so? Or is it an actual inwrought
experience?

— *Touching the Invisible*

"Christ in you, the hope of glory" — Colossians 1:27.

Christ in you. This is the heart of the mystery of God in His dealings with men. Here we reach the summit of His ways. And coupled with this, the other side of the same relationship, we in Christ, as Paul adds: "that we may present every man perfect in Christ Jesus" (Colossians 1:28). But this is exactly what we have seen eternal life to be: Three Persons dwelling in each other, in everlasting union and fellowship. Therefore when we are given the gift of participation in eternal life, we must of necessity share in this union, for there is no other life. Life is God in Three Persons dwelling in each other; the gift of life to us, therefore, is our introduction into this same mutual indwelling. It is the life of union, the one with The Other, distinct from each other yet one in each other, interpenetrating. Mystery indeed, and foolishness to the natural man.

The only life we know in our fallen condition, in this three-dimensional world, is one separate from the other, communing with each other over space that divides us — I here, you there; and, as we shall see more clearly later, that same sense of distance and separation is what we carry over into our faith relationships with the Lord, and is the prime cause of our spiritual frustrations and defeats.

— *The Liberating Secret*

"If we claim we have not sinned, we make him out to be a liar" — 1 John 1:10.

We face the raw fact that sudden sin, almost before we know where we are, does get an entry quite often in most of our lives. We suddenly realize that we are a bit hot in an argument, a bit hard towards or jealous of another, depressed through fear or unbelief, disturbed or strained instead of restful, self-pitying or self-conscious, stirred in mind or desire by lust, malicious or exaggerating in our words. Sin has got its lodgment. We may say to ourselves that perhaps it is only on the temptation level, and has not yet become accepted in our hearts. Maybe. The line between them is often very fine. But generally speaking, the thing which is not at once rejected and from which there is not the sense of immediate and complete deliverance has got some hold, and must be regarded as a motion of sin in our members, needing repentance and the cleansing of the blood.

When sin does enter, above all, let us not be hypocrites. Jesus had special warnings for such. If we have taken our place in union with Christ by faith and assurance, if we have testified to this full salvation, it is very tempting to us to seek some means to avoid calling sin by its proper name. [Let us not fall into this trap.]

— *The Liberating Secret*

"Love is made complete among us so that we will have confidence on the day of judgment, because in this world we are like him" — 1 John 4:17.

Jesus lived His human life, as the archetypal man, by the Father dwelling in Him (John 14:10) — which was a startling surprise to His disciples who, in their separated human outlook, expected an external revelation when they asked Him to show them the Father. And He went on to say that this was why He had come as redeemer, so that God the Spirit who was in Him would be God the Spirit in an inner unity with all who receive Him. And that was Pentecost —not the outward manifestations, which were but a means; but the end, an inner fixed consciousness of their union with Him.

Christ within. The Holy Spirit within. God dwelling in us — then in that realized union through free choice, in Christ's cross and resurrection, the human spirit of self-centeredness is united to the divine Spirit of self-giving. "Dead to sin and alive unto God," man becomes a human expression of God who is love — a perfectly normal man in his perfectly normal environment with his normal human reactions and human weaknesses, yet with God's strength made perfect in weakness.

But God as the Person can only be a person through persons, so that in this living union in Christ, as He is limitless love so we are love in endless variety of expression, for "as He is, so are we in this world."

— *Once Caught, No Escape*

"Those who wait for the Lord will gain new strength" —
Isaiah 40:31 (NASB).

We were praying together, four months after our return
to England, when Pauline turned to me on her knees and
said, "Father has gone home. I know it. We are to start anew
with God." I knew it too. We were dumb with shock for a
time. But it was God's voice. Shortly after, a cablegram was
handed to us at the breakfast table. We glanced at each
other before we opened it, for we guessed its contents.
"Bwana [C. T. Studd] glorified July 16th."

Prepared thus by the Spirit, we knew what lay before us.
We were to take up the sword C. T. Studd had laid down.
Something else had also happened in the blackness of that
night. Some of the "treasures of darkness," of which Isaiah
speaks, had been laid open to us, and one supremely great
secret of effective service had become vividly real to us. It
was the answer to that simple but fundamental problem,
how can I know God's will?

We made one change in the daily program at headquarters, but that change made all the difference. It was customary to start the day's work with a half-hour of Scripture
reading and prayer; then followed the real business, letters,
interviews, and committees. Now the emphasis was to be
changed. The reading and prayer was to be the real business
of the day and the rest fit in as best it might. In other words,
our first occupation became not to exercise our own minds
but to find His mind.

— *After C. T. Studd*

"The things that come from God . . . are spiritually discerned" — 1 Corinthians 2:14.

To find God's mind does not mean an emptied human mind or a desireless human heart, but that the mind and heart are exercised not to cling to their own ways but to yield them up, to die to them; then to substitute for them a search for God's way. Ponder over what indications there are of the way God is leading. Think and pray them over. Use the mind; it is given to reason, analyze, select. And the heart; it is given to have living desire, to quicken the will into action; but let it be set on delighting itself in the Lord and running the way of His commandments.

But, above all, let there be no confusion between our thinking and desiring and His unspoken word. The difference between them is the difference between light and darkness. One issues from the human soul; the other breaks forth in the spirit. Only the spiritual, the Spirit-born, can tell the difference, but they can tell it — infallibly. Paul said that, when he told the Corinthians that the "natural man receiveth not the things of the Spirit of God, neither can he know them, because they are spiritually discerned. But he that is spiritual discerneth all things."

It is here that patience is needed. God is light and His word in our spirit is light: "like a clear heat after rain, like a cloud of dew in the heat of harvest." The least obscurity, the least vestige of doubt, the faintest element of drive or pressure in the spirit, is clear evidence that God's word has not yet shone fully into our hearts.

— *The Law of Faith*

"Do not be like the horse or the mule, which have no understanding but must be controlled by bit and bridle" —Psalm 32:9.

We recognize and utilize the mind in its rightful position. It is at this point that there is the most confusion in the matter of guidance. Some put too much emphasis on the human reason, "common sense," confusing it with the Lord's voice; others too little, turning from it as from a carnal thing and attempting to find guidance with an emptied mind. The truth is that the human reason is a preeminently useful servant, but was never created to be the final arbiter of truth in the human personality. The exaltation of the human reason to the throne of authority in life is the sin of "the wise of this world."

The reason is the great sorting house, but not the sorter. Its function is to investigate, tabulate, theorize, memorize, but not to direct. That is the function of the Spirit in the regenerated life. Sanctified reason remains the noble endowment by which man can contemplate and expound the heights and depths of the divine mysteries; but direction leading to decision is to be found in the renewed spirit, the dwelling place and throne room of the Holy Spirit. Moses made the distinction clear when he said, "Hereby ye shall know that the Lord hath sent me to do all these works; for I have not done them of my own mind" (Numbers 16:28). Reason is to be the instrument of guidance, but not the guide.

— *Touching the Invisible*

> *"Those who are led by the Spirit of God are sons of God"* — Romans 8:14.

Visions and voices are extremely rare, indeed unknown in the experience of the writer, though we have no right to limit God in His manner of revelation; but communion with an indwelling Person is the privilege of all, and the unceasing experience of some.

Another point to be noted is that guidance is the direct communication of the Spirit with our spirits and is not to be confused with the Scriptures. God's written Word is the general guide to His people. The Bible is the inspired and infallible revelation of the principles of Christian living, and any individual guidance which does not conform to it is from a false source. Also, in some cases a sentence of Scripture may be the medium by which the Spirit speaks to us. Even then the point that makes it guidance to me is its application *by the Spirit* to a given situation; its leaping, as it were, out of the book into my heart. *The Spirit* gives the guidance. It is always in conformity with the Scriptures and may be in the words of Scripture, but it is the indwelling Spirit who guides.

Romans 8:16 gives us the primary instance of spiritual communion in every believer's life, the Spirit bearing witness with our spirit. Guidance as to the details of living is only an extension of the inner speaking and hearing then established through the blood of reconciliation and recognition of the indwelling Spirit.

— *Touching the Invisible*

Knowing God's Will

"There is no fear in love. But perfect love drives out fear" — 1 John 4:18.

One of the devil's favorite weapons with immature Christians is false accusation, producing self-torment. Before we are saved, he would keep God's voice away from us altogether, if he could. If he cannot and if we respond to the divine voice in conviction and conversion, then he uses another method. He transforms himself into an angel of light and pretends to speak to us with God's voice, knowing that we will quickly and sensitively respond. He constantly enlarges on our faults and failings, points out every vestige of self in us, and keeps us mourning over ourselves till we wonder whether God can have any more to do with us. Instead of the spirit of adoption, which makes us feel so at home with God that we call Him "Abba, Father" (the equivalent of the modern "Daddy"), we are kept in the spirit of bondage again to fear.

The way to distinguish between these two voices, that of God and that of Satan, is indicated by John in this passage. The voice of the enemy, bringing fear and condemnation, always torments. There is no fear, no torment, in love. Therefore when our inmost thoughts produce bondage and distress, pain and depression, we can always know they are from the pit. It is the voice of the stranger which the sheep are not to know. When God is speaking, there is light and peace, assurance and largeness in our hearts, even though the Voice may have in it a word of rebuke.

— The Law of Faith

"God did not give us a spirit of timidity, but a spirit of power, of love and of self-discipline" — 2 Timothy 1:7.

There is an underground river flowing in us. It is that the real I is not this human I at all! It is He, of whom my I is an outer form. There is a unity — fixed, eternal, inwardly realized — in which He, the Positive, is the Real One living; and I, the negative, am also real, but really the expression of Him. Now the curious effect is that it is very much I living a human life in all the hurly-burly of human living, yet that is no longer my primary consciousness. Here I am with my ups and downs, my ins and outs; I deal with them as they arise, yet they don't upset me or occupy my thinking or produce the usual self-condemning as they used to. I have moved over from having a self-consciousness in the center to a God-consciousness in and through my daily living self. I have begun to live positively, overflowing the fact of my negative human self.

This is the new *spontaneous living.* Not one iota new in my environment. I am precisely who I was and where I have been all these years. But I am *inwardly new* in my consciousness, and, as we have been continually saying, we *live* by our inner consciousness because we are spirits, inner people.

— Who Am I?

Index of Scriptures

368